Jesus the Riddler

Other Westminster John Knox Press books by Tom Thatcher

Why John Wrote a Gospel: Jesus—Memory—History
Jesus in Johannine Tradition (coedited with Robert T. Fortna)

JESUS THE RIDDLER

The Power of Ambiguity in the Gospels

Tom Thatcher

Westminster John Knox Press
LOUISVILLE • LONDON

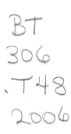
Except where noted, all Scripture translations are the author's.

Book design by Sharon Adams
Cover design by Lisa Buckley
Cover art: Christ with the Crown of Thorns, *from the mural in the Angels' Chapel, Seckau Monastery, Styria, Austria. 1959 Copyright Herbert Boeckl (1894–1966).*
Photo credit: Erich Lessing/Art Resource, NY.

First edition
Published by Westminster John Knox Press
Louisville, Kentucky

This book is printed on acid-free paper that meets the American National Standards Institute Z39.48 standard. ∞

PRINTED IN THE UNITED STATES OF AMERICA

06 07 08 09 10 11 12 13 14 15—10 9 8 7 6 5 4 3 2 1

Library of Congress Cataloging-in-Publication Data is on file at the Library of Congress, Washington, D.C.

ISBN-13: 978-0-664-22640-4
ISBN-10: 0-664-22640-X

Whoever discovers
the interpretation of these sayings
will not taste death.

Jesus said,
"The Kingdom of God is among you;
there is nothing hidden that will not be revealed.
But the sheep will not follow a stranger;
rather, they will flee from him,
because they do not know the voice of strangers."

Jesus told them this riddle
but they did not know what he was saying to them.
And no one was able to answer him a word,
and all his enemies were shamed
because they could make no reply.
After that day no one dared to ask him anything.

But everyone who heard him was marveling
at his understanding and his answers,
saying,
"Where did he get these things?
What is this wisdom given to him?"
And they were astonished at his teaching.
And the large crowd was listening to him gladly.

Then some of his disciples
were saying to one another,
"What is this thing that he is saying to us?
We do not know what he is saying.
This is a hard saying.
Who is able to listen to him?"

And immediately, Jesus said to them,
"Why are you thinking this way in your hearts?
Don't you understand yet?

"These things I have spoken to you in riddles,
so that those who cannot see would see
and so that those who can see
would become
blind."

Anyone who has ears to hear, let them hear.

(Matt. 22:46; Mark 1:22; 2:8; 6:2; 8:21; 12:37; Luke 2:47; 13:17; 14:6; 17:21;
John 6:60; 9:39; 10:5–6; 16:17–19, 25; *Thomas* 1:1; 5:2)

This book is dedicated . . .

to Carey Newman,
whose vision and enthusiasm
conceived it,
and Jon Berquist,
whose care and guidance
brought it into the world;

to Robert Fortna,
who showed me the value of thinking
that Jesus intended for his disciples
to actually follow his teachings,
and who has also shown me
what the Kingdom of God looks like,
although I never deserved his love;

to Becky, Aaron, and Julie,
who are in so many ways
and for so many reasons
the only reason
that I am alive today.

Contents

Preface

The Quest for Jesus the Riddler; or What This Book Will and Won't (Try to) Prove

This book will argue that Jesus used riddles both to establish his authority as a teacher and to communicate his message. The fact that Jesus was regularly asked riddles by other people and used this elusive form of speech himself holds significant implications for our understandings of the way that his contemporaries thought about him and of the way that Jesus himself thought about the Kingdom of God.

THE LOST FORM OF JESUS' TEACHING

My thesis, as stated above, may surprise readers from modern Western societies, who normally expect "riddles" to look something like this:

> What goes on four legs in the morning
> Two legs in the afternoon
> And three legs in the evening?[1]

> Out of the eater came something to eat
> Out of the strong came something sweet.[2]

> Into this world I came hanging,
> And when from the same I was ganging,
> I was cruelly battered and squeezed,
> And men, with my blood, they were pleased.[3]

Humpty Dumpty sat on a wall.
Humpty Dumpty had a great fall.
All the king's horses and all the king's men
Couldn't put Humpty together again.

This thing all things devours:
Birds, beasts, trees, flowers;
Gnaws iron, bites steel;
Grinds hard stones to meal;
Slays king, ruins town,
And beats high mountain down.[4]

   In modern Western cultures, verbal puzzles like these are usually confined
to fantasy novels, magazines in the dentist's office, and other social settings
oriented toward entertainment and relaxation. Thomas Burns calls them
"leisure-time" riddles, riddles and jokes that people tell to amuse themselves
when they have nothing better to do. Although riddles perform a wide variety
of social functions cross-culturally, Westerners tend to think that leisure-time
riddles are the norm for the genre. This assumption is not limited to popular
conceptions, as leisure-time riddles have been "the focus of the great majority
of the [academic] literature on the riddle and riddling."[5] For example, the
work of the most significant recent contributors to riddle research, W. J. Pepicello and Thomas A. Green, takes as its database a hodgepodge of published
riddles; oral riddles collected informally from "colleagues and students at the
University of Delaware, Temple University, and Texas A&M University"; several jokes "recorded at a brief riddle session between two seven-year-old children"; and various verbal puzzles "provided by audience members who
approached us after paper presentations at professional meetings."[6] Pepicello
and Green's scholarship is insightful, yet their shallow data pool illustrates the
Western tendency to confine riddles to children's rhymes and video quiz
games in bars, settings far removed from the discussion of such serious matters as the teachings of the historical Jesus.
   Many biblical scholars, following this popular conception, have failed to
seriously consider the possibility that Jesus may have used riddles in his teaching, or at least to explore and develop the implications of that possibility. For
example, the Jesus Seminar, perhaps the most concerted effort in history to
recover the authentic words and deeds of Jesus, has excluded many statements
that might be classified as riddles from its official database of Jesus' sayings.
This is sometimes the case because they judge the content of a saying to be
uncharacteristic of Jesus' teaching, but in other instances simply because they
do not feel that Jesus would have spoken in this manner. For example, Mark
12:35–37 bears many similarities to the verbal puzzles cited above:

Jesus said, "How can the scribes say,
'The Christ is the Son of David'?
David himself said by the Holy Spirit,
'The Lord said to my Lord,
"Sit at my right hand until I put your enemies under your feet." '
If David himself calls him [the Christ] 'Lord,'
How is he David's 'son'?"

In *The Five Gospels*, a summary of the Jesus Seminar's findings on the sayings of Jesus recorded in the canonical gospels and the *Gospel of Thomas*, the passage above is deemed inauthentic both on the basis of its content and because "it is difficult to think of a plausible context for this *piece of sophistry—a clever manipulation of the data and logic for the sake of the point*—during Jesus' life." The parallel at Matthew 22:41–46 is explained in a similar way: "Jesus is represented here as contesting that the messiah is the son of David *by a clever piece of sophistry*," an approach that seems "*unduly pedantic* for Jesus." "Is this way of handling issues," they ask, "consonant with his [teaching] style?"—a rhetorical question that begs the inquiring reader to say, "Why, of course not! Jesus was no sophist (whatever that is)."[7] The commentary in the Seminar's red-letter edition of Mark, which explains that 74 percent of Seminar members

> From *The Oxford English Dictionary* (2nd ed.):
>
> **pedantic** (pĭdæ·ntik), *a. (sb.)* Having the character of, or characteristic of, a pedant [one who lays excessive stress upon trifling details of knowledge]; . . . exaggeratedly, unseasonably, or absurdly learned.
>
> **sophistry** (sǫ·fistri?) *sb.* **1.** Specious but fallacious reasoning; employment of arguments which are intentionally deceptive. **2.** The use or practice of specious reasoning as an art or dialectic exercise. **3.** Cunning, trickery, craft.

voted that 12:35–37 should be printed in black (meaning that it has no direct connection to Jesus' actual teaching), is equally severe. After reiterating that this passage is a "piece of sophistry," the commentator asks, "What would be the point of demonstrating that the Messiah was not the son of David?"[8] And since they could find no place for this obtuse statement in the repertoire of the historical Jesus, the Seminar was forced to conclude that Mark and Matthew's respective narrative frameworks for the saying must also be considered suspect.[9] Against the backdrop of common Western assumptions about riddles and similar verbal puzzles, one can easily understand the Seminar's concern.

LEARNING TO THINK LESS CLEARLY

I did my PhD at Southern Baptist Theological Seminary in Louisville, Kentucky, a school that wisely required doctoral students to take at least a fourth of their course work outside their department and, preferably, outside the institution. In fulfillment of this obligation, and being very interested anyway in rhetoric and orality theory, I spent a semester at the University of Cincinnati. One of my courses was a directed private study in folkloristics with Prof. Edgar Slotkin, an expert on the epic traditions of Ireland and a generally fascinating individual on the subject of oral cultures. Dr. Slotkin gave me a list of about fifteen books and told me to meet with him each week to discuss my progress through their contents. This was a wonderfully enriching experience, both because my previous researches in this field had been unguided and, especially, because Dr. Slotkin's outlook was essentially untainted by the concerns of biblical scholarship. He had done some work with Susan Niditch on the Hebrew Bible, but otherwise easily maintained an objective distance from my topic, only occasionally referring to something that he thought was in the New Testament when it promised to help me understand a point he was trying to make.[10]

In the course of that course, one beautiful spring morning I was confined to my study reading *Oral Cultures Past and Present* by Viv Edwards and Thomas Sienkewicz, a good introductory text on traditional societies whose broad scope is indicated by its subtitle, *Rappin' and Homer*. Toward the end of that volume there is a brief discussion of the riddle as a cross-cultural performance genre.[11] This surprised me somewhat, because to that point in time I had never been particularly interested in riddles or jokes and certainly had never thought of them as a serious object of academic inquiry. Indeed, my prior exposure to the genre was pretty much limited to a pop-up book of riddles that I had lovingly preserved from childhood because it was one of the first books I could read on my own. Even this precious volume bears the scars of my early disrespect for the genre, as I tore out several of the 3-D images and threw them into the fireplace at my grandparents' house because they scared me. This childish act reveals my early indoctrination into the Western view that riddles are supposed to amuse us and aren't worth our time when they don't.

Now it so happened that at the time that Edwards and Sienkewicz were introducing me to the deeper things of riddling, I was also reading every day in the Greek text of the Gospel of John. My advisor at Southern, Professor Gerald Borchert, was writing a two-volume commentary on the Fourth Gospel, and since I was more interested in interpretive theory than in any particular section of the canon, I deemed it politically expedient to go with the flow, as it were, and do my own thesis in the Johannine literature as well. This plan was complicated only by the fact that I had entered the program knowing next to nothing about Johannine studies. I had never been that interested in John—it had always seemed to me that he was saying the same thing over and over again—and, besides, I come from a theological tradition that gives pride of place to Luke–Acts. To compensate for this deficiency, I was trying to read a little bit of the Fourth Gospel every day, looking for notable literary features or traces of oral composition or anything else that I could lay my hands on to write a dissertation.

Thus it was that, after reading Edwards and Sienkewicz's discussion of riddles in the morning and watching an episode of *The Andy Griffith Show* over lunch, I picked up my Greek New Testament to glance at a few pages from the Gospel of John before turning to the work of the afternoon. For some reason, my eye landed on John 1:15, where John the Baptist says this:

ὁ ὀπίσω μου ἐρχόμενος	ἔμπροσθέν μου γέγονεν	ὅτι πρῶτός μου ἦν
"the one behind me coming	ahead of me became	because before me he was"

Smoothing it out a bit to accommodate English idiom: "the one coming behind me became ahead of me because he was before me." I cannot say that I was even aware of the existence of this verse before that moment; doubtless I had read it many times before but passed by with indifference. But in the context of my thoughts at that particular moment, as if to illustrate Schleiermacher's "hermeneutical circle," I immediately noted that the Baptist's "witness" is, in fact, a riddle. If someone "has become *ahead*" (ἔμπροσθεν) of John, how can that person also be "coming *behind*" (ὀπίσω) him at the same time? And how did he get "*behind*" John in the first place, if he was, in fact, "*before*" (πρῶτος) him?

Of course, the answer to this puzzle is obvious to anyone who knows anything about the Fourth Evangelist's thinking about the relationship between the Baptizer and Jesus—by which I mean, obvious to anyone who would bother to read the remaining seventeen verses of the Prologue. Jesus "was before" John in the sense that he existed in the Father's bosom "in the beginning" (John 1:1); Jesus "came behind" John in the sense that Jesus' ministry began after the Baptist had completed his "witness," his work of revealing Jesus to the world as the "Lamb of God" (1:6–8, 19–34); Jesus therefore naturally "became ahead" of John in his status as the ultimate revelator of God, a fact that the Baptist himself readily recognizes (1:8; 3:27–36). So much seems obvious to the Christian reader of today. Yet even though the Fourth Evangelist gives away the answer, John 1:15 clearly and intentionally violates normal patterns of language and thought, making that verse a riddle in form and substance.

Riddles take different forms in different cultures, but all riddles are intentionally ambiguous statements that challenge the audience to identify which of several possible things the speaker is talking about. The riddler appears to be describing something the wrong way, or her words could potentially refer to so many different things that the audience can't tell which one is the true subject of the comment. Hence, all riddles must be "answered"—the audience is challenged to identify what or who the riddler is describing. At John 1:15, for example, the Baptist's unspecified audience (and John's reader) is challenged to identify a person who could be both "behind" John and "ahead" of him at the same time, an impossibility in the literal sense of those terms, and to explain how this person could achieve such a feat. In modern Western cultures, the challenge is usually not a serious one: there's nothing at stake if we can't figure out the puzzles on the back of the cereal box, or can't guess the punch line of a joke. Yet in traditional cultures, such as the cultures in which the Fourth Evangelist, John the Baptist, and Jesus lived, the ability to pose and answer difficult verbal puzzles often carries high stakes in the marketplace of ideas—in this case, stakes as high as "eternal life."

Pleased with my little discovery, I shared this passage—John 1:15—with Dr. Slotkin, who immediately confirmed my observation and advised me that Jesus most likely used riddles frequently, although he (not being, as I mentioned, expert in the biblical literature) could not think of any in particular at that moment. "Jesus," he said—and please note that I am paraphrasing Dr. Slotkin's words more than a decade after the conversation, and therefore assume full responsibility for any error or misrepresentation—"was a popular teacher in a traditional culture, a culture in which intelligence and authority would often be established through verbal contests, as is evident both from modern anthropological research and the fact that riddle performance has been widely documented throughout the ancient world. This being the case, I would imagine that your gospels"—not the *Gospel of Thomas*, but also and primarily the Synoptics and John—"are probably full of riddles, as others in your field have doubtless observed. The trick would be setting up the right criteria to find them."

Dr. Slotkin's words intrigued me, and encouraged by his confirmation, I began to study riddles, and to search for them in the accounts of Jesus' life, more urgently. My research, at that time still focused on the Fourth Gospel, led me to see that Dr. Slotkin's intuitions were completely correct on two counts, yet very wide of the mark on a third. First, Dr. Slotkin was correct to suspect that the Gospel of John is, in fact, rife with riddles: almost forty appear in that text, and they perform a wide variety of functions.[12] These observations led me to look, in my spare moments after lunch and the *Andy Griffith* show, into the other Gospels as well, where I also immediately noticed glaring specimens of the genre—they now stood out like diamonds in a box of Cracker Jack. But, second, Dr. Slotkin was mistaken to assume that Jesus scholars had already located these gems, and would perhaps be surprised to know that they had discarded much of what they found. As noted above, the Jesus Seminar and many other historical Jesus researchers have overlooked riddles—or, perhaps more accurately, have sometimes noted the effects of riddles but have not known what to do with them—and as a result they have not seriously considered that passages such as Mark 12:35–37 may reflect an important facet of Jesus' life and teaching. This neglect has been the case because, third, we—biblical scholars in general—have not been able to figure out the "trick" of the right criteria for finding riddles, either in the texts of the Gospels or in the career of the historical Jesus. As a result, Jesus' use of riddles and the implications of this usage have not been studied in a very systematic way.

This book will attempt to prove that Dr. Slotkin's suspicions were right—that riddles were a key element in Jesus' repertoire—and that this fact will become manifest once we overcome the methodological obstacles that have, to this point, blocked that conclusion. Before diving into that discussion, I will briefly preview the road before us and, more importantly, reveal some of my key presuppositions for the journey.

JESUS THE RIDDLER: TOOLS FOR THE DIG

If you are at all familiar with academic discussions of the Gospels over, say, the past two decades, the preceding paragraphs may seem misguided, or at least misinformed. Almost forty years ago, Herbert Leroy demonstrated that riddles are a key component of the Johannine theme of "misunderstanding"; almost twenty-five years ago, David Rhoads and Donald Michie included a discussion of riddles in their groundbreaking *Mark as Story*; more than ten years ago, Robert Fowler offered an excellent definition of "ambiguity" and discussed Mark's use of this literary device extensively; N. T. Wright's magisterial *Jesus and the Victory of God* includes sections entitled "Royal Riddles," "The Riddles of the Cross," and "Jesus' Riddles of Return and Exaltation"; in 2000, I myself released a book that analyzed each of the almost forty riddles in John in (too) great detail; even more recently, Narry Santos has published a monograph on Mark's use of paradox. So what's so new about the idea that Jesus was a riddler?[13] In one sense, nothing—a fact that I take to mean that I may be on the right track.

But while the topic is vaguely familiar, this book is different from other studies in at least two ways. It might be more accurate to say that it combines two dimensions of the issue that have generally been viewed in isolation. First, many of these earlier works were concerned with ambiguity and paradox as *literary motifs*, rhetorical devices that the Gospel authors used to impact their

readers in a particular way. This is not a weakness of these books, but rather
their strength. They are explicitly concerned with narrative-critical issues and
the reader's interaction with the text: "What were Mark and John saying to us
through ambiguity and paradox, and what do we hear?" As such, they do a
good job of locating riddles in the *sources* for the historical Jesus, but do not
even attempt to locate them in the *ministry* of the historical Jesus. Second,
some of these previous studies have located riddles in the teaching of the historical Jesus, but they have come to this conclusion more on the basis of the
content of certain things that he said than on the form of the sayings themselves. Wright, for example, intuitively recognizes many riddles in the Gospels
on the basis of the fact that their ambiguity seems inconsistent with the interests of the early church.[14] This conclusion is sufficient for his purposes, and as
a result he does not need to explore in detail how riddles work. Essentially,
then, a few scholars have recognized that riddles appear in the Gospels; a few
others have recognized that they possibly appeared in the ministry of Jesus;
but very few have explored *both* the literary/rhetorical and social/historical
dimensions of Jesus' riddling in any level of detail. Even my own previous
study, based as it was on folkloristics and orality theory, at best tried to suggest
that the Fourth Gospel's riddles were "traditional" in the sense that John didn't
just make all of them up, all the while avoiding the issue of whether those traditions, in turn, went back to Jesus.

Here and now, in this book, I seek to define the riddle as a genre, locate riddles in the ministry of the historical Jesus, and briefly explore the implications
of the possibility that he used them (and used them fairly often). Yet very early
in my quest for Jesus the Riddler, it became obvious that the conventional tools
of historical Jesus research, fashioned mainly from the soft elements Form
Criticism and Source Criticism, would be of little use for my purposes. There
are a variety of reasons for this, primary among them the fact that Form Criticism and its successors—even some of the more recent hi-tech composites,
fortified with Ong and Foley—depend largely on a certain continuity and sta-
bility in language and oral tradition. Specifically, most studies of Jesus traditions have depended on the notion that oral sayings and stories tend to stay
basically the same, and that when they change they evolve along predictable
trajectories. We should see evidence of these trajectories in the written
Gospels, and from this evidence we should be able to determine whether and
how specific statements developed over time. We should also be able to determine which of several parallel versions of a story or saying is more "primitive,"
meaning that it is more likely to go back to the historical Jesus. This approach
has its relative strengths and weaknesses, but in any case it is problematic in
the search for riddles in the Gospels for at least two reasons.

First, the key structural elements of the riddle as a speech genre—the formal features that make it possible to identify something that someone says as a "riddle"—are often not evident on the surface of the text. Let me stress this point at the outset: *the things that make a statement a "riddle" are not always things that you can see or hear in the statement itself.* This fact is well documented in the anthropological literature, and is evident from the many different types of riddles that appear cross-culturally and sometimes even within a single culture.[15] All riddles are, by definition, intentionally ambiguous, but ambiguity can be achieved in a variety of ways. As a result, any statement in any form—any form at all—can be used as a riddle, depending on the context and the speaker's intentions. While folklorists have ways around this problem (like field research and interviews with living sources), the arsenal of historical Jesus research does not include the silver bullets you need to do battle with shapeshifters. Form-critical methods love genres of speech that look pretty much the same everywhere they appear: dominical sayings, parables, pronouncement stories, and so forth. Since riddles do not meet the criterion of formal consistency—they don't always look or work the same from context to context—it is difficult for traditional methods of Jesus research to find them, or even to adequately describe them.

The second problem in the relationship between riddles and the methods of historical Jesus scholarship is related to the first. Jesus uses many riddles in the extant sources, both canonical and noncanonical, yet rarely does any single riddle appear in more than one context—offhand, I can't think of more than one or two that do. As a result, even when one can identify a riddle in the Gospels, it probably will not meet the "criterion of multiple attestation," the principle that a saying that appears in more than one independent source is more likely to go back to Jesus. For example, John 10:1–5 looks like a riddle and the author explicitly identifies it as such, but it appears only in the Gospel of John; Mark 12:35–37 appears also in Matthew and Luke, but that doesn't count because most scholars think that Matthew and Luke copied the saying from Mark, making Mark the sole source of this information. Hence, even if a specific riddle seems very much consistent with the overall tone of Jesus' teaching, most Jesus researchers will be hesitant to say that he said it.

To complicate matters further (and this is a problem that draws the limits of conventional form-critical methods in **bold underline**): even when there is multiple attestation for a particular riddle, sometimes one Gospel will treat that saying as a riddle while another does not. As a result, such sayings do not fit neatly into the "form-content-function" triad that has been so helpful in the analysis of biblical genres of literature and speech. For example, all four of the canonical Gospels record Jesus' feeding of the five thousand, and all four preface that event with Jesus telling the disciples that they need to find food for the huge crowd (Mark 6:37; Matt. 14:16; Luke 9:13 [with triple verbatim agreement]; John 6:5). In all four accounts, the disciples point out the obvious impossibility of this proposal—"six months' wages couldn't buy enough food"—but John, and John alone, makes Jesus' statement a "riddle" by informing the reader that "he [Jesus] was saying this to *test* them, for he already knew what he was about to do" (6:6). John's aside makes Jesus' statement both ironic and ambiguous: the disciples will, in fact, serve food to the five thousand; the challenge is for them to understand how this will take place. Yet this is a unique feature of John's presentation. Similarly, both Matthew and Luke include Jesus' remarkable claim that the person who is "least" in the Kingdom of God is greater than John the Baptist (Matt. 11:11; Luke 7:28). In Matthew's version, the saying is clearly a riddle (clear to me, at least), both because the larger dialogue in which it occurs is structured as a riddling session and because Jesus explicitly uses a riddling formula (all this will be discussed in a later chapter). Luke, on the other hand, does everything in his power to eliminate any ambiguity about the meaning of Jesus' comment—neither Jesus' original audience nor the reader of the Gospel should, in Luke's view, have any trouble understanding this saying at all (see 7:29–30). In both of these instances, different sources have Jesus saying the same thing, yet the same saying does not function as a riddle each time it occurs. Hence, while I can say with confidence, "The parable of the Sower appears in Mark, Matthew, Luke, and Thomas," I cannot exactly say, "The riddle of the Baptist appears in Matthew and Luke," because Luke doesn't seem to think that that statement is a riddle. Riddles thus illustrate the inherent limitations of the "criterion of multiple attestation" in evaluating sayings that do not work the same way from one Gospel to another.

Because of these two methodological problems, both of which reflect lingering limitations of the older generation of form criticism, this book will differ significantly from most studies of the historical Jesus at two key points, one relating to method and the other relating to scope and object.

First, in terms of *method*, this book will entirely depart from conventional form-critical and source-critical models of analysis. Instead, it will depend exclusively on contemporary folklore models for its understanding of speech genres in general and of riddles in particular. Of course, there are many points where the respective research methods of Jesus studies and folkloristics overlap, and these points of intersection will doubtless be obvious to informed readers. But from the perspective of my intentions, these points of intersection are entirely accidental, and as a result I will not take time to highlight them, nor even really to acknowledge them. My thinking about these issues, with all its strengths and weaknesses, is driven by folkloristics and contemporary orality theory, and there is no point for me to pretend that my conclusions were developed in dialogue with mainline historical Jesus scholarship. Chalk and cheese may look the same, yet a taste proves that they are of very different substances; similarly, this study will at many points look and feel like a book on the historical Jesus, but it will likely taste quite different from other tidbits on that plate.

Second, my variant methodology, reflecting problems unique to riddle analysis, will naturally impact the *scope and object* of my quest. Specifically, this book will not attempt to determine the "original form" of any riddles that appear in more than one of the sources, nor to figure out which ones "really go back to Jesus." So, for example, when Jesus asks his disciples, without giving any indication of what he is talking about or the point of his comment, why a person would light a lamp and put it under a basket, I will not be concerned to compare the versions in Mark, Q, and *Thomas* to determine which form of the saying came first and/or which is more likely to have come from the lips of Jesus (Mark 4:21; Luke 8:16; *Thomas* 33:2). Instead, my conclusions will depend on general verisimilitude between the extant sources and a type speech that Jesus is *likely* to have used on a variety of occasions. I assert that it is likely that Jesus asked and answered riddles on a regular basis; I am not concerned about particular riddles recorded in the Gospels but about whether he engaged in riddling *at all*. I claim that if Jesus engaged in riddling *at all*, this fact is significant to key aspects of our understanding of his social posture and message.

I need to stress this point, because it is critical to everything that follows in this book. As noted above, the Jesus Seminar, on the basis of a variety of criteria of historical authenticity, has concluded that Mark 12:35–37 likely did not emerge from the mouth of the historical Jesus. The Seminar similarly asserts that Matthew 17:25 and John 7:23, two other texts that I would identify as riddles, did not originate with Jesus. I think that all three statements probably did, but this book is not concerned with whether any of them did or did not. In other words, my argument does not depend on whether or not Jesus actually asked people how the Messiah could be both "David's son" and "David's lord" at the same time. My argument depends, instead, on the fact that Mark, Matthew, Luke, John, *Thomas*, and virtually every other extant ancient source for Jesus' teaching claims that *Jesus said things like this to people on a regular basis*.

Because my scope and object are general rather than specific, this study will be grounded on a single "criterion of authenticity." I conclude that the historical Jesus regularly engaged in riddling, both asking and answering verbal challenges. I conclude this on the basis of the facts that (a) the anthropological and sociological data suggest that he likely would have done so and (b) a wide range of extant sources for Jesus show him engaging in this activity. This criterion cannot, of course, prove definitively that Mark 3:33 goes back to Jesus, but it can, in my simple way of thinking, give us very good reasons to think that Mark 3:33 at least reflects something that Jesus really did. My conclusions will build on the social implications of the fact that Jesus "really did this," not on the content of any of his specific statements.

By way of analogy: I was not alive when Abraham Lincoln was president of the United States, and therefore have no firsthand knowledge of his beliefs and activities. For this reason, I cannot say with certainty that Lincoln delivered the Gettysburg Address in 1863. But I conclude that he must have delivered public speeches from time to time, on the basis of the facts that (a) historians insist that American politicians from that era regularly delivered public speeches and (b) a variety of extant sources suggest that Lincoln himself regularly engaged in that activity. I think it fair to say, then, that Lincoln was an orator, even though this fact alone could not prove that he said something at Gettysburg in 1863. But my inability to prove this point would become a problem only if my conclusions about Lincoln depended on the specific contents of the Gettysburg Address. If my point depended instead on the more general issue of whether or not Abraham Lincoln *ever* delivered public speeches, the specific contents of the Gettysburg Address would make no difference to my argument. Similarly, my conclusions here will not build on the contents of any particular riddle, or group of riddles, uttered by Jesus. They will build instead on the general portrait of Jesus the Riddler that emerges from the available sources.

While this approach will no doubt appear timid to many, I adopt it shamelessly because my subject and method make it both necessary and practical. "Necessary" because the theories of folklore, tradition, and memory to which I subscribe do not support the notion that written texts can be compared and dissected to reproduce oral originals that can then be evaluated to determine their precise historicity. "Practical" because my basic thesis will not depend on any one thing that Jesus said, but rather on the inherent implications of the fact that Jesus must have talked in this way. Early Christians from a variety of theological perspectives preserved memories of Jesus doing something that anthropologists suggest that he must have done—ask and answer riddles. It is this universal portrait of Jesus as a riddler, not hard and fast proof that he uttered specific statements, that is significant to my argument. Of course, my conclusions may impact how others address the question of whether specific riddles originated with the historical Jesus. For example, the riddle genre, as I will define it here, inherently satisfies many of the criteria typically utilized in historical Jesus research, such as the criterion of "distinctive discourse" (the doctrine that Jesus' authentic sayings "surprise and shock," often by frustrating "ordinary, everyday expectations"), that Jesus' genuine sayings are often characterized by exaggeration and paradox, that Jesus tended to offer questions and "unclear references," and that his remarks "cut against the social and religious grain."[16] Whether or not these criteria genuinely represent Jesus' message, all are completely characteristic of the riddle genre, and I would be interested to know how others think this fact might impact narrower questions of authenticity. But that type of discussion will not be the focus of my inquiry here.

Even though I will not utilize tight historical criteria for determining whether certain specific sayings originated with Jesus, I will discuss in detail criteria for identifying riddles and riddling sessions in the extant literary sources. These criteria could theoretically produce a definitive database of riddle texts, a database that could, in turn, be subjected to narrower historical criteria than those I have utilized in order to determine which individual units of tradition are authentic. In fact, early on I planned to include a Table of Jesus' Riddles in an appendix, but in the end chose not to do so because I felt it would violate the spirit of my argument. At the same time, however, I would stress that all the riddles discussed here were chosen for analysis because they do meet these literary criteria, and that in general I have attempted to apply these criteria as strictly as possible so as to ensure that the passages under consideration would arguably look like riddles to any folklorist (at least, to any folklorist who agrees with my basic definition of the genre).

JESUS THE RIDDLER: THE SCOPE OF THE DATABASE

Once I had developed literary criteria and identified riddles in the sources, I was left with the task of choosing which ambiguous sayings should be highlighted in this study. There are far too many to discuss all of them in detail, and again, because I am not seeking to prove that Jesus did or did not say specific things, I did not feel compelled to analyze every single riddle that appears in the sources. But if I were to do so, and if I were then to group all of these riddles on the basis of their apparent function in their present literary contexts (which are really the only contexts in which we can be absolutely certain that they ever appeared), three major categories would emerge: "dramatic riddles," "mission riddles," and "sage riddles." A brief definition of each type will reveal the reasons why I have decided to focus exclusively on the "sage riddles."

A *dramatic riddle* functions in the sources to enhance the tension of a scene. The inherently agonistic tone of riddling sessions is very compatible with the sort of oral storytelling that lies behind our written Gospels, and dramatic riddles add interest to an episode by introducing a touch of ambiguity and/or irony. To return to an example noted above: at John 6:5–7, Jesus looks over the crowd of five thousand and asks Philip, "Where will we buy bread so that these people can eat?" Philip, unaware of Jesus' purposes, can only point out the obvious: six months' wages couldn't buy enough food to feed such a mob. But the narrator reveals that Jesus' words are ambiguous and—not very surprising for the Fourth Gospel—also ironic. Jesus had already decided how to deal with the situation and was only "testing" his disciple to see what he would say. This brief exchange doesn't really tell us much about Jesus, and the story could work just as well without it. It does, however, add an element of irony and suspense that slightly magnifies the significance of the feeding miracle to follow, and for this reason Jesus' ambiguous question at John 6:5 may be called a "dramatic riddle."

A *mission riddle* functions in the sources to explore some aspect of Jesus' unique identity. While they may also add drama to a scene, mission riddles betray an explicitly christological interest. To take another example from the Fourth Gospel, which majors in mission riddles: at John 6:35–38, shortly after the feeding miracle mentioned above, Jesus informs the Jews that he is, in fact, "the bread of life" that has "come down from heaven," similar, but very far superior, to the manna that Moses provided in the wilderness. The Jews point out the inherent ambiguity of this statement by noting that Jesus is actually "the son of Joseph"; this being the case, "How does he now say, 'I have come down from heaven?'" (6:41–42). At first glance, we might call the "I Am" saying about the "bread of life" a "dramatic riddle" because it adds interest and tension to the scene through a heavy play on Johannine irony—as the reader well knows by now, the Jews are quite wrong to think that Jesus is "Joseph's son." Yet it appears that this irony actually serves the deeper purpose of highlighting an aspect of Jesus' identity: because he did "come down from heaven," the Jews must consume his flesh and blood in order to obtain "life" (6:48–58). This riddle depends, in other words, on a very particular understanding of who Jesus was and what he was all about. The "bread from heaven" saying develops a major theological theme related to Jesus' identity and purpose, and as such it is best classified as a mission riddle, one that seeks to explicitly promote an aspect of John's Christology.

A *sage riddle*, like a mission riddle, develops some aspect of Jesus' identity, but does not make claims that would be overtly christological. Rather, the sage riddles showcase Jesus' remarkable wit and wisdom and generally function in the sources to establish his credentials as a rabbi and/or to promote key aspects of his message. To take yet a third example from the Gospel of John (although probably not from the Fourth Evangelist): at John 8:4–5, the scribes and Pharisees attempt to trap Jesus by asking him whether an adulterous woman should be executed in accordance with Leviticus 20:10 and Deuteronomy 22:22. I will discuss this episode in much more detail in a later chapter, but for now it is relevant to note that this question places Jesus in a very awkward situation: if he rules in favor of the woman's life, he will thereby appear to take a lax stance on adultery and, further, to question Moses; if he rules against her, his reputation as a champion of the oppressed will be ruined, and the Romans may even come after him for inciting a riot. Jesus escapes by offering a famous counter-riddle that his inquisitors cannot answer: "The sinless one among you, let him cast a stone at her first" (John 8:7). This statement turns the dilemma back onto the scribes, who cannot respond at all (8:9), and in the process it both establishes Jesus' superior wit and makes a significant teaching point about the evils of a judgmental spirit. Yet it really does nothing more than this—Jesus does not have to be "the Christ, the Son of God" (John 20:31) in order to come up with this riddle; we could easily imagine an ancient rabbi of Jesus' day, such as Hillel or Shammai, saying something along these lines in a similar situation. The sage riddles showcase Jesus' incredible wit and/or are used by Jesus as a teaching tool, and as such they make no explicit claims about his deity or messianic status.

For sake of convenience, and to engage the broadest number of similar studies, I have chosen to discuss only those riddles that demonstrate Jesus' wisdom as a sage and to focus on the implications of that smaller group of ambiguous sayings. The dramatic riddles are not particularly helpful here because they don't really reveal anything specific about Jesus' message (although they might tell us something about his general teaching style). The mission riddles could say a great deal about that message, and also about Jesus' identity and social posture, but most of their claims would be rejected by the majority of historical Jesus scholars. I will therefore take the path of least resistance and focus on the thirty-some sage riddles that appear in Mark, Matthew, Luke, John, and *Thomas*. This is a very significant limitation, in view of the fact that the sources very often use riddles to discuss Jesus' identity and mission. Most of the riddles in the Gospel of John, for example, relate in some way to Jesus' self-image and the soteriological implications of his ministry, as do a great many in *Thomas* and even the Synoptics.[17] My exclusion of these sayings does not reflect an opinion that the mission riddles are necessarily less "historical" than the others; it reflects, instead, the fact that many of my readers would doubt that these sayings are historical, so that a discussion of them here would distract from the main thrust of my argument. I am ultimately interested in what Jesus' riddling says about core issues in his teaching, and the less disputable sage riddles are sufficient by themselves to make that point. In my view, a further inquiry into other types of riddles that appear in the sources, such as my own prior study of riddles in the Fourth Gospel, would only deepen and complement my conclusions here. I cannot see how it would contradict these conclusions, although of course I can only ever see what lies within my own field of vision.

As a final note on method and database, my analysis will be limited to Jesus' teaching and will not discuss his deeds, even though the sources often connect his riddles to specific actions. At many points, of course, the conclusions of this study may complement research on Jesus' deeds, and some of the things that

Jesus did would support the interpretation of his teaching offered here. For example, one might argue that Jesus' ability to pose and answer riddles would lead his contemporaries to believe that God had given him a special gift of spiritual insight, one that we might call "prophetic." Such a claim would perhaps be affirmed if Jesus was, as the Synoptics suggest, an exorcist, or, as all the canonical Gospels suggest, a healer. But the specific theoretical basis of this book—folkloristic research into riddles and related speech genres—lends itself more logically to an exclusive emphasis on Jesus' teaching. You may take this *caveat* as my admission that the book is unbalanced; I hope it remains steady enough to make its primary point.

A FINAL NOTE ON THE PRESENTATION

Finally, before we dive into the topic at hand, I wish to offer an explanatory note about the tone of this book that will perhaps waylay certain criticisms. Careful readers may feel that my argument lacks two things: extensive proof that people in Jesus' world used riddles, and more copious footnotes to support the theoretical discussion. My argument does, in fact, lack these things, but not accidentally—I simply felt that such information would not be of interest to most readers. But for those of you who demand further proof, or who are just interested in the deeper things of riddling, let me note the following.

First, all the available data indicate that a person like Jesus in a culture like Jesus' culture would have used riddles. I could argue this point solely on the basis of the modern anthropological literature, even if there were no literary evidence from Jesus' time to support such a claim, and essentially that's the approach I've taken in this book. But in fact, riddles and riddling sessions have been widely documented in the ancient world. The riddle was recognized as a distinct genre of speech in the Greco-Roman world at least as early as Aristotle (*Poetics* 22.1–7), and Archer Taylor has demonstrated that riddles have been well known to the Jewish community from the composition of the Hebrew Bible through the Middle Ages to the modern era.[18] The riddle is a universal speech genre, appearing in every culture that can be documented in every time and place. For purposes of this book, I have taken this premise as common knowledge, and as a result have not rehearsed the literature that would prove it. Instead, I will refer all interested parties to the bibliography in note 19 and stress that riddles are historically and ideologically compatible both with late Second Temple Judaism and with early Christianity.[19]

Second, on the relative paucity of footnotes here: in the late 1990s, I took my doctoral dissertation on riddles in John, cut about 100 pages, added about 150 pages, and published it in the Society of Biblical Literature Monograph

Series under the title *The Riddles of Jesus in John: A Study in Tradition and Folk-lore*. That book includes a very lengthy, detailed, and quite boring discussion of my personal theories of speech genres in general and the riddle in particular, with extension interaction with various theorists and a depressing number of footnotes (even some that take up three-quarters of a page). The book that you are holding now, however, is intended to be accessible and even a little bit interesting, and in pursuit of these ambitious goals I have avoided the type of tedious discussion that characterized that earlier monograph. As a result, this book does not include numerous notes, nor discussions of the key differences between the structural and the ethnographic approaches to folk texts, nor detailed reviews of Archer Taylor and Donn Hart and Elli Köngäs Maranda—no doubt much to the relief of those readers who could not care less about the finer points of folkloristics. But if your interest is piqued, and if you wish to pursue research into riddles further, I would refer you to my earlier book and its bibliography as an inroad to this fascinating topic.

PART I

The Art of Ambiguity:
What Riddles Are
and How to Find Them

1

So What Is a "Riddle"?
The Art of Ambiguity

A "riddle" is an interrogative statement that intentionally obscures its referent (the thing or idea that it is talking about) and asks the audience to name it. Riddles obscure their referents through controlled ambiguity, the artful use of language that could reasonably refer to more than one thing. More simply, a "riddle" is a question that purposefully suggests several possible answers and leaves it to the audience to guess which answer is the right one, where "right" means the answer the riddler wants at that moment. The words "intentionally" and "purposefully" must be stressed here to distinguish riddles from statements that are confusing simply because they are poorly stated or just plain inept. Since language generally seeks clarity, most confusing statements are accidents; riddles are confusing on purpose. Riddles use language that is confusing in an intentional and artistic way.[1]

CLARITY, AMBIGUITY, VAGUENESS

All riddles ask a question and, like all questions, riddles seek an "answer," some type of response from the audience. This is true regardless of the actual sound and/or shape of the statement: riddles in books may not end with question marks (?), and spoken riddles may not evidence the vocal inflection typical of interrogative statements, as in the tendency of American English to raise the pitch of the voice at the end of a question ("Do you want some cóf-fee?"). The "riddler," the person telling the riddle, is always asking for something, and the "riddlee," the person listening to or reading the riddle, is supposed to provide it. All riddles are thus agonistic to some degree, meaning that they involve a sort of competition. The riddler wins if the riddlee can't answer; the riddlee wins if she can. The stakes in this question-and-answer contest depend on the value that a particular culture attributes to riddling.

But riddles differ from normal questions in at least two ways. First, the riddler always knows the answer before the question is asked—the riddlee will never provide information that the riddler does not already have. Hence, while the questions "What time is it?" and "What's the best day of the week to get a tan?" may look the same on the surface, they are delivered with a very different intention. This "different intention" is the second way that riddles differ from normal questions: normal questions seek information to bring clarity to a situation; riddles introduce ambiguity into a situation to generate confusion.[2] This aspect of riddle performance, the use of intentional ambiguity, is the key element of the genre, so we will need to define "ambiguous" language a bit more precisely.

Most of the time, we try to use language that is "clear." When we speak "clearly," we are attempting to avoid confusion by making the referent of our words—the thing or idea that we are talking about—as obvious as possible. Clear statements thus create a 1:1 correlation in the mind of the listener/reader between the words we are using and the thing under consideration. The context of a statement often helps us achieve this clarity by directing our audience's attention to what we are talking about. When, for example, my friend and I are looking at his computer and he refers to the "screen," the immediate presence of that object makes his meaning completely obvious to me. If we want to speak clearly and the referent is not so obvious from the physical context, we gladly answer questions about the exact meaning of our words. Thus, if Becky (my wife) asks me to bring her a drink from the refrigerator and I discover there a bottle of diet pop and a pitcher of lemonade, I ask her to clarify exactly which drink she had in mind; she replies that she wants pop, making her original reference to "something to drink" narrower and more specific. Clear language supports a sense of order and group cohesion because it shows that we are all able to think and talk about the same things.[3]

The opposite of "clarity" in language is "vagueness." Sometimes we do not communicate as clearly as we might, making it difficult for others to identify exactly what we are talking about. Either because our words are not well chosen or because the context does not point the listener/reader to the thing that we have in mind, or both, our audience cannot determine what we are trying to say. Vagueness represents the most extreme instance of this phenomenon, "situations in which the degree of description provides an inadequate basis for solution." When our language is clear, the listener easily makes a correlation between our words and the single thing that we are talking about; when our language is "vague," the listener cannot connect our words to anything at all.[4] Of course, vague statements can be clarified through further discussion, but once the confusion is resolved, our audience will likely point out that our initial remarks were inadequate; their misunderstanding was our fault, a result of the fact that we didn't communicate very well ("Well, that didn't make much sense"; "Why didn't you just say that in the first place?").[5] Vague language threatens our sense of order by suggesting that we are not thinking on the same wavelength and therefore may not be able to talk about the same things and concerns.

"Ambiguity" in language falls between "clarity" and "vagueness." Most definitions of "ambiguity," at least those that are relevant to our discussion of riddles, suggest that an "ambiguous" statement is one that could reasonably refer to more than one thing at once.[6] For example, W. J. Pepicello and Thomas A. Green, two of the most significant contributors to recent riddle research, define ambiguity as "the situation which obtains in language when two or more underlying semantic structures may be represented by a single surface representation."[7] The "single surface representation" is the text itself, the words and phrases that we actually say or write; the "underlying semantic structures" are the several different things or concepts to which our words could reasonably refer. Similarly, Jack and Phyllis Glazier describe a statement as "ambiguous" when "it [potentially] refers to two or more frames of reference depending on one's interpretation of the term; an ambiguous term can also be one which refers to several or all possible frames of reference" at once.[8] Like "clear" language, ambiguous statements refer directly to the thing the speaker wants to talk about; like "vague" language, ambiguous statements create confusion because they could also refer to something else in the context of the conversation. Oftentimes, the audience of an ambiguous statement cannot even identify all the specific possibilities, much less determine the "correct" one. Yet once the true referent is clarified, we would agree with the speaker that her words really did accurately describe what she wanted to talk about. Our misunderstanding wasn't anyone's "fault" per se, but rather just a reflection of the inherent limitations of language (i.e., a result of the fact that we have only a limited number of words and grammatical structures available to describe the billions of things and ideas that we encounter in the world around us).

Of course, most "clear" statements—statements that obviously refer to one thing or idea—could also potentially refer to several other things, but in these cases the context eliminates the ambiguity by helping the audience weed out irrelevant options. For example, the English noun "punch" can refer both to a beverage and to a tool for making holes (among other things). The question "Where is the punch?" is therefore potentially ambiguous, because it could refer to either of two common items that are completely distinct from one another. But when this question is asked at a party, the audience logically deduces from the context that the "punch" in question is a drink. "Ambiguous" utterances, by contrast, are not set in a context that allows the audience to select one of the several possible meanings without further information. Once such information is provided, however, the ambiguity is eliminated, and the speaker's specific meaning becomes clear: "I am talking about the *punch*, the red stuff in that bowl right there; you see it?" Ambiguous statements are never "clear," but they can be clarified through further discussion as the audience narrows down the range of possible meanings.

But while ambiguous statements are not clear, it is also important to stress that they are not vague, even when they cause confusion. Vague statements (at least for purposes of the present discussion) don't point the audience to anything because they do not describe their referents adequately—they are inherently flawed as acts of communication. Ambiguous statements always point to the right thing; they just also happen to point to several other things that could be described in the same way. It is important to stress this point simply because *riddles are ambiguous statements, not vague statements.*

By way of illustration: as I write this, our daughter, Julie, is about sixteen months old. Julie likes to talk and, being possessed of a remarkable energy for such a small body, speaks often, despite the fact that she knows only about a dozen actual words of the English language. As a result, a high percentage of her comments are difficult to interpret. She may, for example, suddenly run into her room and empty her bookcase onto the floor; then, standing on this pile of literature, she may point to the corner and say, repeatedly, "Ah-wah-dah; ah-wah-dah." Statements of this type are "vague": clearly, Julie is thinking of one specific thing and trying to talk about it, but her lack of skill in the use of language frustrates her efforts. In this instance there are so many possible referents that Becky and I are utterly at a loss to list them all, even after attempting to narrow the field through a series of questions and gestures.

Unable to ascertain the referent of "ah-wah-dah," my wife takes Julie from the room while I proceed to pick up the books. As they make their way down the hall to the kitchen, Becky asks Julie, "Would you like your cuppy?" The child replies, "No-kay." This remarkable word, a hybrid of the polar opposites "No" and "Okay," is beautifully ambiguous: it clearly means either "Yes, I very much want the cup" or "No, I do not want the cup at all," and she variously uses the term with different meanings on different occasions. In this case, however, the context does not provide us with enough data to decide between these two possibilities; we discover the correct referent only when the drink is offered and she responds by either quaffing madly or tearing the lid off and casting the cup to the floor. On this occasion, Becky incorrectly guesses that the child does want the cup; Julie clarifies the true meaning of her words by pouring the milk out on the floor and running into the living room. "Ah-wah-dah" is vague: it is impossible reasonably to identify any limited number of potential meanings for this term, and even if we did figure out what Julie is talking about, we would not necessarily agree that this is the best way to describe it. "No-kay," however, is ambiguous: we all agree that it clearly means one of two things and Becky must guess the correct referent or face a mess.

But while Julie's "No-kay" is clearly an ambiguous statement, and while it is indeed puzzling, it is not a "riddle." Riddles are *intentionally* ambiguous statements that challenge the audience to clarify them by naming the single thing to which the riddler is referring. The riddler and riddlee must know going into the situation that the question is designed to point to more than one answer, and the riddlee must agree that the riddler has authority to determine which of those potential answers is "correct." When Julie says, "No-kay," her word could reasonably refer to more than one thing, but this is not her intention. She clearly has one thing in mind, thinks that she is speaking clearly about that one thing, and becomes enraged when we fail to perceive what it is.

The riddle's "question," then, must be intentionally ambiguous, and its answer must be "reasonable." "Reasonable" here does not necessarily mean that one could "reason out" the right answer, but rather that the "correct" referent must fall within a finite number of possible things or ideas to which the question may reasonably refer—the riddlee must agree that the question really does accurately describe the answer in some way. For example, the question "What has four wheels and flies?" could reasonably refer to several different things, including an airplane, a garbage truck, and a pigeon in a roller skate. The "correct" answer must come from this range of legitimate possibilities; it can't be "tree" or "pencil," because the terms in the question can't reasonably refer to those objects in any use of the English language (at least, few people would agree that they could).

SAYING THE UNSPEAKABLE: AMBIGUITY AND IDEOLOGY

As noted above, riddlers violate normal patterns of language by making statements that are intentionally ambiguous and confusing. If, for example, I were to say to you,

> Though of great age
> I am kept in a cage,
> Having long tail and one ear.
> My mouth it is round
> And when joys abound
> I then sing out wonderful clear.
> [Who am I?]

Thatcher's Glossary of Riddling

Alternative—a riddle that attempts to force the riddlee to choose between two or more proposed answers, none of which is desirable from the riddlee's perspective.

Ambiguous—language that could reasonably refer to more than one thing or idea in the grammatical, physical, or social context of the statement. At least one of the possible referents must be the thing that the speaker actually has in mind, and the audience must agree that the description is reasonable. Riddle questions use ambiguous language.

Answer—the single correct referent of an ambiguous statement, where "correct" means the thing that the speaker is thinking of at the time.

Clear—language that obviously refers to the referent that the speaker has in mind. Riddle questions become clear once the correct answer is provided.

Neck Riddle—a riddle delivered in a riddling session with high stakes; generally, the riddlee must answer correctly or suffer pain, death, or public humiliation. Often included in narratives to heighten dramatic tension and/or emphasize the wit of the protagonist.

Question—the interrogative statement in a riddle, an ambiguous description that asks the audience to identify the single correct referent. Often does not end with a question mark (?).

Referent—the thing, person, or concept to which a unit of language refers; what the speaker or writer is "talking about" at the moment.

Riddle—an interrogative statement that generates confusion through the use of intentional ambiguity and asks for an answer that will render the statement clear.

Riddlee—the riddler's audience; the person who must provide the answer to the riddle.

Riddler—the person who proposes a riddle and who determines the correct answer.

Riddling Session—a social interaction in which riddles are performed, following local cultural guidelines; generally takes the form of a contest between the riddler and the riddlee.

Vague—language that does not guide the audience to any reasonable referent or set of referents, making it impossible for the audience to determine anything that the speaker might have in mind. Even after clarification, the audience does not agree that the description is reasonable. Riddle questions do not use vague language.

Wit—the ability to pose riddles that others cannot answer, or to answer difficult riddles.

you might reply that, in the first place, "I" here obviously does not refer to myself, Tom Thatcher (although it may, for all you know); and, in the second place, that this poem could reasonably describe any number of animals, perhaps most likely an old, deaf parrot. If I then told you that the "answer," the true referent that I have in mind, is "a bell in a church tower," you would doubtless reply that, while the terms of the verse do seem descriptive of a bell at some metaphorical level, this is certainly not a typical way of speaking about that particular object. Yes, the rope on a church bell could be compared to an animal's tail, and the round opening at the bottom of the bell is like an animal's "mouth" in the sense that that's where the sound comes out. This answer is therefore reasonable, but it's still not a normal description of a bell. Or if I were to ask you

> What is put on a table,
> cut,
> but never eaten?

you might reasonably observe that this description could refer to almost any small, nonfood item that can be acted upon with a knife. But when I say that the answer is "a deck of playing cards," you might feel that this response is "clever," simply because it manipulates the English language—in this case the multiple meanings of the verb "cut"—in an amusing fashion.[9] Most leisure-time riddles, and hence most modern Western riddles, operate at this level, exploring the various ways that terms can be indirectly connected to their referents.

But in many cases, riddles violate not only normal patterns of language, but also a culture's ideological norms as well. This is perhaps most obvious in those riddles that use ambiguous descriptions to make the audience think of something disgusting, naughty, or otherwise inappropriate. For example, you must feel a bit uncomfortable when I tell you that

> A layman comes with an iron spoon,
> shoves it in and opens up his mother;
> he salts her, and sews up her skin;
> then he takes his mother's children,
> grinds all their bones,
> and feeds his own children.

Such a statement, left unexplained, can only evoke scenes from *The Silence of the Lambs* or *The Texas Chainsaw Massacre*. But this tension is alleviated when I tell you that the "answer"—the thing that the riddle is really talking about—is "a crop in a field": the "layman" is a farmer; his "iron spoon" is a plow; his "mother" is "mother earth" and her "skin" is the soil; his "mother's children"

is the grain that grows, which the farmer grinds into wheat to make bread for
his family. Viewed from the perspective of the "correct" answer, the riddle is
harmless, its subject utterly mundane. Yet the text uses ambiguity to point the
riddlee to darker topics—incest, necrophilia, murder, cannibalism—that are
completely inappropriate for pleasant conversation at cocktail parties.[10]

Verbal games of this type threaten to transgress social standards; yet such
riddles "play with boundaries, but ultimately to affirm them."[11] They "play
with boundaries" by making people think about things that the rules of society say we should not think or talk about; they "affirm boundaries" by providing answers that anchor even the most dangerous descriptive language in
things that are completely harmless.[12] In the process, riddling becomes a sort
of cultural playground, where "play" refers to "the objectifying and imperson-
alizing of anxiety situations, allowing the free expending of energies without
the threat of social consequence." Every now and then, people need to say and
hear things that challenge the social order and violate ethical norms, and riddles can provide an acceptable outlet for the expression of these antisocial tendencies. Riddles use ambiguity to manipulate standard ways of talking and
thinking, but when this ambiguity is appropriately resolved, both the riddler
and the riddlee are reassured that group values can be maintained.[13]

Yet riddlers need not "play with boundaries" quite so nicely, and in the
process they may transgress group norms at a much more foundational level.
Specifically, many riddles are ambiguous because their questions seem to point
to conclusions that not only violate the audience's sense of propriety but also
in fact challenge the very structure of the group's value system. This aspect of
riddling has been highlighted by folklorists such as Roger Abrahams and Elli
Köngäs Maranda, who describe the riddle as a subversive interactive
metaphor.[14]

Generally speaking, a "metaphor" is a figure of speech that compares two
things on the basis of shared qualities: "he's a beast"; "that joker will never
amount to anything"; "her exams are a breeze." Because metaphors are able
to bring things and concepts
together, they play a key role in the
way the human mind catalogues
information about the natural and
social worlds. As we receive data
from our environment, we attempt
to assimilate new information and
ideas into a hierarchy of mental categories that reflect our cultural values.
These categories are mutually exclusive, because groups tend to order reality
in terms of opposites: male/female, dark/light, right/wrong, clean/dirty, ani-
mal/plant, and so forth. The members of each opposed set, however, share

> "The tendency of social groups is always to domesticate the new by reabsorbing it into what is already known and acceptable."
> —Funk 1993, 532

enough common traits to be reconciled at a higher level of the hierarchy. Thus, at one level men and women may be seen as opposites, but at another level both men and women are "human beings" as opposed to "animals"; white and black are opposites, but at a higher level both are "colors." Metaphors help us sort new data into existing categories by placing unfamiliar terms and items in a "this is (like) that" matrix, making it possible to connect the new to the familiar: "this new thing is like that old thing that I already know about, but it's different from those other two things, so it must go into this box over here." When the new item doesn't fit neatly into any of the existing categories, we simply add a new box at the appropriate level of the pyramid, ideally somewhere toward the bottom.

For example, not long ago I had my first significant exposure to the sport of soccer when I coached my son's team (the fact that a person with no knowledge of the sport could serve as coach indicates the level of competition in this particular league). Faced with this formidable task, and hoping to manage the team with at least minimal effectiveness, I had several meetings with a friend who grew up in South Africa. This individual gave me a crash course in soccer through analogies to other sports with which I was already familiar. His discourse throughout this educational process was highly metaphorical, emphasizing the common traits of different things: "It's just like where, in hockey, you know, you can . . ."; "It's like when in basketball, when the foul is over here, they . . ." My mental category "soccer" was thus, like Frankenstein's monster, constructed from pieces of my understanding of other sports that I already knew about, based on impressions of how soccer is similar to, yet different from, each of them. Abrahams and Köngäs Maranda would suggest that this is typical of the way that the mind uses metaphors to develop and expand its taxonomy of organizational categories for every area of life.

Because all riddles have two parts that bring two things together conceptually, the riddle may be defined as an interactive metaphor. Riddles are *metaphors* in the sense that they compare things from different mental categories: the first mental category is represented by the question and the second category by the answer.[15] Riddles are *interactive* metaphors because the riddler provides one of the terms in the comparison (the question) and the audience has to provide the other (the answer). For example, earlier I cited a riddle that compares a bell to an animal in a cage; according to most ways of thinking, things with long tails that live in cages would not normally be categorized with bells. This riddle is a *metaphor* because its question and answer bring these two sets of things (bells and animals) together; this riddle is an *interactive* metaphor because it takes two people to complete the comparison. I, acting as riddler, provided the description of the animal in the cage; you, acting as riddlee, were supposed to provide the bell.

Yet riddles differ from other types of metaphor in the way that they interact with our hierarchy of ideas and values. Most metaphors unite items from
different mental sets on the basis of common traits in order to highlight some aspect of the thing under consideration, and in the process they may help us put things in their proper categories. Riddles, by contrast, use ambiguous language to highlight common traits in a way

"[A]mbiguity is the business of blurring distinctions and obliterating clear bound-
ary lines."

—Fowler, 197

that challenges our organizational scheme, and in the process they bring "the
whole idea of classification under question."[16] Riddlers can manipulate this
fact to suit their rhetorical purposes, depending on the extent to which they
wish to actually challenge the group's classification system.

To return to the seemingly harmless example above: in a variety of contexts,
it might be appropriate to compare a church bell to a bird by noting that both
"sing out" on joyous occasions, and such a comparison helps us remember that
things we call "bells" are often used in times of celebration. But this riddle does
not seek to reinforce anyone's memory of birds or bells; instead, it points out
that someone can write an ambiguous little poem that can reasonably refer to
two things which are totally different. And the fact that the same silly verse can
accurately describe things in drastically different domains—in this case even
breaching the foundational distinction between living beings and inanimate
objects—inherently raises the question of whether our classification scheme is
legitimate in the first place. Perhaps animals and inanimate objects are really
not so different as we think they are.

John the Baptist's riddle at John 1:15 is another good example of this phenomenon. As I noted in the preface, the Baptist breaks into the Prologue of
the Fourth Gospel to "testify" that "the one coming behind me became ahead
of me because he was before me." In every known culture, people place "things
in front of me" and "things behind me" in two distinct spatial categories. Thus,
when driving down the highway we see many things that fall into the category
"cars," yet we cannot imagine a car that would be both in front of us and
behind us—in two distinct spatial positions—at the same moment. The same
applies to human beings: only in science fiction movies could a person be both
"behind me" and "ahead of me" at the same time. The Baptist's riddle thus
invites the reader of the Fourth Gospel to identify an individual who somehow defies conventional logic by redefining the normal meanings of the words
"behind," "ahead," and "before."

Of course, one might point out that while these riddles—the bell riddle and
the Baptist's riddle—do indeed defy normal schemes of logic, they are not nec-

essarily particularly subversive, or at least do not appear to be insidious. True, it is somewhat odd to describe a bell in terms of a bird, or to describe Jesus as a person who violates normal laws of physics, and as a result these riddles force us to reconsider for a moment some key aspects of the way that we think about things. Yet no one is likely to feel threatened by them. As noted above, their challenge is playful, and the problem is resolved in a way that affirms group values as soon as the answer is provided (in the case of John 1:15, a way that affirms the theological values of the Johannine community).

But some riddles challenge conventional thinking to a much more significant degree, mediating "between [conceptual] sets that are not only different, but in many aspects opposed, and in this way it [the riddle] can form the basis for a differing system of classification, or allow contrasting classifications and conceptual frameworks to co-exist at the same time."[17] The riddler may specifically wish to subvert group values by bringing things from different ideological sets together in a way that cannot easily be resolved, thus forcing a significant redefinition of terms or a realignment of mental categories. A prime example appears at Luke 14:26, where Jesus tells the "large crowds" who are following him,

> If anyone comes to me
> and does not hate (μισεῖ)
> his own father and mother
> and wife and children
> and brothers and sisters
> and even his own soul,
> he is not able to be my disciple.

Since Jesus is apparently perceived by all of his followers to be a rabbi (I shall discuss this issue in a later chapter) and perhaps also by many of them to be a prophet, this shocking statement would be particularly difficult to comprehend. Ambiguity is created by the fact that Jesus' words can reasonably refer to people who should fall into two opposed categories, "disciples" and "lawbreakers"; more specifically here, he says something about his disciples that *should* apply only to sinners. Exodus 20:12 decrees that parents must be honored; Genesis 2:24 says that husband and wife are "one flesh"; Psalm 127:3–5 says that children are a blessing from the Lord; more generally, Leviticus 19:18, apparently one of Jesus' favorite verses (see Mark 12:31), states that God's people are to love their neighbors as themselves. All this being the case, Luke 14:26 describes Jesus' "disciples" in terms that would normally refer to "sinners," people who live outside the strict guidelines of the Law. Put another way: from the perspective of the Hebrew Bible, people who "hate" their parents and spouses and children fall into the category "sinners";

from the perspective of most people in his culture, Jesus falls into the category "rabbi" and/or "prophet," but people in the categories "rabbi" and/or "prophet" do not, by definition, encourage their disciples to be "sinners." Luke 14:26 therefore seems to unite things that normally remain conceptually distinct, in a way that challenges Jewish theological categories at a foundational level.

Modern commentators, aware of the troubling implications of Jesus' "hate" riddle, are generally agreed that its ambiguity is best resolved by redefining the Greek word μισέω. Joseph Fitzmeyer, for example, notes that "*misein* [to hate] has already been used in [Luke] 6:22, 27 to describe the attitude of outsiders toward Christian disciples," but suggests that Jesus is now redefining the term to mean "a willingness to put parents, family, relatives, even one's own

---

Hate, Sin, and Ambiguity: The Hierarchy of Luke 14:26

Luke 14:26 challenges conventional ways of thinking by describing Jesus' disciples, who would theoretically fall under the category "Righteous People," as people who "hate" others, a term normally descriptive of "lawbreakers." In this case, the ambiguity challenges both conventional uses of the word "hate" and also the larger classification scheme that sharply distinguishes between "sinners" and "righteous people."

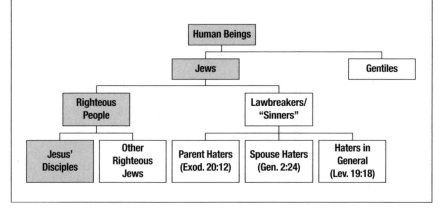

---

life, in subordination to discipleship."[18] Similarly, I. Howard Marshall insists that, while "hate" here has the sense "to leave aside, abandon," the emphasis is "not of psychological hate, but of renunciation."[19] Following this same train of thought, the New American Standard Bible includes a marginal note on Luke 14:26 that does not clarify anything about the translation but instead offers a paraphrase to resolve the ambiguity: "hate," the translators assure us, here means "by comparison of his [the disciple's] love for me." While readings of this type make Jesus' disturbing comment at least minimally palatable, such definitions of μισέω would not appear in any lexicon of the Greek language. Whether the ambiguity lies in the word "hate" or some other aspect of Jesus' radical statement, Luke 14:26 clearly defies conventional ways of thinking and talking about "disciples" and seems to seek to do so. Hence, while Jesus' remark here uses ambiguous language in the same way that a child's joke might, the rhetorical objective is quite different.

Riddles, then, are intentionally ambiguous statements that play with the audience's sense of order and values. They are often difficult to answer, sometimes seemingly impossible, simply because they topple the very hierarchy of ideas that normally allows us to make sense of the world. To resolve them, one must enter into a special mode of thought, and for this reason riddling can play a significant role in a group's sense of identity, as will be seen in the next chapter.

2

"Everybody Knows That One": Ambiguity and Identity

In chapter 1 I defined the "riddle" as an intentionally ambiguous statement which seeks an answer that will achieve clarity. Riddles are "ambiguous" in the sense that they could potentially refer to more than one thing, and their answers "clarify" them by naming the single thing that the riddler is actually talking about. I also insisted that riddles are not "vague," defining a "vague" statement as a flawed act of communication that fails to refer to anything in particular.

Yet this claim—that riddles are always ambiguous, never vague—might be challenged by anyone who has casually flipped through the pages of a book that includes a cross-cultural collection of riddles, such as Mark Bryant's *Riddles Ancient and Modern* (from which many of my examples here are drawn).[1] The reader of such a book will frequently encounter statements that do, indeed, seem "vague," in the sense that she cannot make head nor tail of what the riddle might be talking about. After reading a riddle and checking its solution, we are very often struck not so much by the cleverness of the description as by the fact that we could not possibly have guessed the answer.

For example, Elli Köngäs Maranda, one of the most prominent folklorists of the twentieth century (the American Folklore Society awards an annual prize for Women's Studies in her honor), focused much of her research on traditional riddles from Finland. Her research database therefore includes ambiguous statements like

One pig, two snouts.
[What is it?]

Answer: A double-bladed plow.

17

and a series of riddles based on the following analogy:

> A tree grows in the forest without roots.
> [What is it?]

> **Answer:** A woman.[2]

Upon reading the answers, one can see that the questions in these riddles accurately describe their referents, albeit in a metaphorical fashion. The statement "One pig, two snouts" does seem reasonably to describe a double-bladed Finnish plow: like a pig, the plow digs into the soil as it moves slowly along; also like a pig, the plow uses a protuberance—a blade, like a pig's nose—to do its work. One can easily see that pigs and plows are alike in at least these respects, even though they would otherwise fall into very different categories of things. But before the answer is given, a person who, like myself, is not from Finland, and who, like myself, grew up in the city and saw pigs and plows only on television, and who, further, has never yet seen a double-bladed Finnish plow, nor even a picture thereof—such a person may feel that the question is vague. The statement "one pig, two snouts" could never make me think of a double-bladed plow, simply because I never knew that such a thing existed before I heard this riddle. Similarly, while I must agree that woodland women, like trees, "grow in the forest," and while I must concur that woodland women, unlike trees, grow without roots, I am utterly at a loss to make this connection until Köngäs Maranda points it out to me. This being the case, would not riddles of this type be "vague" (pointing the audience to nothing), rather than "ambiguous" (pointing the audience to multiple possibilities)?

The fact that many (most?) riddles seem vague and therefore virtually unsolvable has been a key sticking point in recent discussions of the genre. Many Western scholars have insisted that an intentionally ambiguous statement can be classified as a riddle only if it meets the "criterion of solvability," meaning that the answer can be deduced from data provided in the question through appeal to common knowledge. According to this rule, questions whose answers "require the possession of special information that is not supplied in the question" should be treated as a separate genre, even when they are identical to "true riddles" in form, function, and subject matter.[3] To some extent, the criterion of solvability is a logical extension of the Western sense of fair play. We use riddles for recreation, and when we are playing a

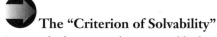

The "Criterion of Solvability"

Any puzzle that cannot be answered by logical deduction and common knowledge on the basis of information supplied in the question is not a "true riddle."

game, every contestant must have a fair chance of winning; it's not fair to cheat and purposefully deceive our opponents. It is therefore difficult for us to concede that the puzzles we see in children's magazines could be inherently "unfair" to somebody; everyone must have an honest chance to answer the question.

While a detailed discussion of the criterion of solvability would take us far afield from the focus of this book, I need to address it briefly here for two key reasons. First, many of the riddles that appear in the Gospels do *not* satisfy this criterion. In fact, all the best sources explicitly state that people outside Jesus' inner circle of disciples found his ambiguous statements to be vague and impenetrable (see Mark 4:11–12; Luke 8:9–10; Matt. 13:13–15; John 10:6; 12:36–40; *Thomas* 1). Actually, even the disciples can't comprehend most of them. According to some theorists, such sayings should not be classified as "riddles" because they are inherently unfair, at least in the sense that most people couldn't figure them out on their own. I therefore need to address this issue, at least to justify the database of sayings I am using for this study, which includes many riddles that do not meet the criterion of solvability. Second, and much more significant to my argument, the problems surrounding the criterion of solvability highlight two key facts about the social dimension of riddling: (a) riddles can be answered only by people who have access to special knowledge and special ways of thinking, and (b) all knowledge and all ways of thinking are "special," in the sense that they are acquired through membership in a group. For this very reason, riddles create a "community of knowledge," a group of people united by their shared ability to pose and answer ambiguous questions.

WHAT YOU NEED TO KNOW TO KNOW

A careful consideration of recent academic discussion of the riddle reveals an interesting trend: while many folklorists have espoused the criterion of solvability, most of them also discuss texts that look and act just like riddles, even though they cannot be answered on the basis of information provided in the question. For example, in his analysis of "dialogue riddles"—riddles that describe a dialogue between two unknown people or things and ask the riddlee to identify the speakers—Archer Taylor notes that often the riddlee must search for clues outside the text itself. For this reason, in one essay he categorizes metaphorical dialogues as "false riddles" because they do not meet the criterion of solvability; yet he elsewhere calls them "true riddles" because they look and function like genuine specimens of the genre.[4] Similarly, Abrahams and Dundes note that the "wisdom question" requires a "learned response" because the correct answer is so arbitrary that it can be offered only by people who have heard it before.[5] Elli Köngäs Maranda refers to one subcategory of wisdom questions as "monk's questions," esoteric inquiries that "ask primarily for a foreknowledge of the answer, especially information about religious tenets and facts."[6] Further examples could be cited, but it is sufficient here to note that many statements that resemble riddles in form and function are not necessarily answerable on logical grounds on the basis of information provided in the question.

This observation has been highlighted by Edgar Slotkin, who goes against the tide of scholarly opinion by arguing that dialogue riddles and wisdom questions actually represent the norm for the genre. In point of fact, *all* riddles require some sort of special knowledge beyond the information provided in the question. This is the case because "few so-called 'true' riddles admit to logical solutions where one and only one answer satisfies the descriptive grid imposed on the riddle topic."[7] Slotkin's maxim carries two important implications: first, not everyone may be able to deduce the logical answer to a particular riddle; second, even when the riddlee can deduce an answer that might be "right," she has no way to determine why other logical answers are "wrong." Both of these points are critical to our discussion, so I shall take a moment to unpack and illustrate them before noting their implications.

To return to an earlier example: the "correct" answer to the riddle,

> Into this world I came hanging,
> And when from the same I was ganging,
> I was cruelly battered and squeezed,
> And men with my blood, they were pleased.

is "a cider apple." Any folklorist would describe this as a "true riddle," because one can easily see how the poem is a fair description of an apple: "hanging" from the tree; picked and "squeezed" in the press to extract the sweet juice, which is represented here as the "blood" of the fruit; "pleasing" in the sense that most people like to drink apple cider. The terms of the metaphorical description line up smoothly with the characteristics of a cider apple, so that the riddlee could, through a process of deduction, eventually identify the true referent. As such, this riddle appears to satisfy the criterion of solvability.

But further reflection reveals that this riddle does not truly meet the criterion of solvability, or at least requires us to significantly redefine that criterion. For, in the first place, while this riddle seems to build on common knowledge and logical deduction, we must ask, Common to whom? and, Logical to whom? And further, in the second place, even a person who might be able to deduce the right answer could not necessarily explain why other possible solutions—say, "a grape"—are wrong. In view of these two problems, it becomes clear that even the most "solvable" riddles can only be answered by people who possess three types of special knowledge: (1) knowledge of the subject of the riddle, the thing that the riddler is talking about; (2) knowledge of cultural patterns of logic and the rules for developing analogies; and (3) in many cases, direct knowledge of the correct answer before the question is asked, meaning that you've heard it before somewhere. The first two types of knowledge make it possible for the riddlee to propose possible correct answers, referents for the ambiguous description; the third type of knowledge makes it possible to determine which of the possible correct answers are wrong. All three types of knowledge are "special" in the sense that they are obtained by membership in a group and would not necessarily be available to people outside the riddler's group.

First, when we say that the answer to a riddle can be "logically deduced" on the basis of "common knowledge," we need to clarify that all knowledge is cultural knowledge, learned by participation in some group. Hence, "common knowledge" is knowledge common to people who are members of a particular group—a family, a church, a business, a city, an academic discipline, a trade, a student body, and so forth. This is the case whether we are talking about the knowledge that is common to the international community of rocket scientists or the knowledge that is common to the employees at a particular Wal-Mart store. While they may be less educated, the Wal-Mart workers doubtless know many things that escape the wisdom of the rocket scientists, such as the aisle in which the shoe polish is located, simply because the rocket scientists are not members of their group and are therefore not as familiar with the layout of their store. For this reason, while the answer to any particular riddle may be obvious to all members of the riddler's group, the very same riddle may appear "vague" to people from other backgrounds, simply because such people may not know much about the thing under consideration.

> **Prerequisite #1:**
> Knowledge of the Subject

To return to the example above: if we say that the cider apple riddle can be answered by appeal to "common knowledge," we realize that such knowledge would only be "common" to people who live in cultures where (a) apple trees grow, (b) the fruit of such trees is used for food, (c) the juice from such fruit is consumed as a beverage, and (d) people enjoy drinking such beverages. Since I live in a country where apple trees and cider are familiar to most people, and in a region of that country where my family can and does occasionally pick apples at local farms with on-site cider mills, I can easily relate to this particular riddle. But I can also easily see why a rocket scientist from, say, the African nation of Togo would be utterly at a loss to identify the correct answer.

Second, it is important to stress that the answer to this simple apple riddle depends not only on special knowledge of its subject matter (apples and their uses), but also, and at a deeper level, on a knowledge of the logic of its presentation. To figure out the riddle, I need to know more than just basic facts about

| Prerequisite #2: |
| Knowledge of the Logic |

apples and cider; I need to know certain rules for making metaphorical analogies. Specifically, I need to know that English poetry can compare the juice of a fruit to the blood of a human being,

and can compare squeezing an apple to the torture of a human being. If I were from a culture that could not make these comparisons, it would be impossible for me to logically deduce the answer to this riddle. The same problem is evident in the very ancient "Riddle of the Sphinx":

> What goes on four legs in the morning
> Two legs in the afternoon
> And three legs in the evening?

The "correct" answer, of course, is "a human being," who crawls as an infant, walks upright as an adult, and hobbles along with a cane in old age. Such seems logical to me. Yet it seems logical to me because I live in a culture where elderly people sometimes walk with canes; where life is viewed as a series of developmental stages; where the stages of life can be compared to the phases of a day, with infancy represented by morning and old age by twilight; where, further, the seasons of life are often characterized in terms of our physical abilities and/or limitations. Yet a person from a cultural group that does not think this way or use such analogies could never deduce this answer, even if she had an IQ of 150. Many researchers have overlooked the fact that the patterns of logic and deduction cherished in Western riddling are themselves forms of special knowledge, learned and culturally determined. As Slotkin observes, "we tend to be ethnocentric in supposing that riddles and riddle contests cross-culturally are supposed to involve principles of deduction rather than memorization or some other mental ability."[8]

Slotkin's observation points to the third type of special knowledge that riddles require: with all riddles, the quickest way to the correct solution is a memorized answer. In fact, "most riddles depend for their solution on either inspired guessing or simply knowing the riddle—which is to say, knowing tra-

| Prerequisite #3: |
| Knowledge of Traditions |

ditions."[9] Because of this third prerequisite, a person who can figure out the right answer to a riddle may not be able to state why other answers are *wrong*. I can explain in detail why "a

cider apple" is the correct answer to the riddle above; I cannot explain why "an orange" is incorrect. Knowing which answers *might be right* is a function of prerequisites #1 and #2 above: knowledge of facts about the answer and knowledge of the logic system the riddler is using. But knowing which possible answers *are wrong* is essentially a function of tradition. You know they're wrong because they just aren't right, and you know this because you've heard the joke (or one like it) before.

The critical role of tradition is highlighted by the cider apple riddle particularly well. Upon reading this metaphorical rhyme, you may have concluded that I was talking about a "grape." The grape, like the apple, is a fruit that "hangs," and grapes are also picked and "squeezed" for their "pleasing" juice; thus, both our knowledge of grapes (prerequisite #1) and our awareness of the laws of analogy (prerequisite #2) may lead us to this answer. But "a grape" is not the right answer; in fact, "a grape" is just as wrong as "a basketball," for reasons that neither you nor I can explain. Put another way: even if you did guess, through a process of analogy and deduction, that "a grape" might be the right answer, how could you have known that it was the wrong answer? Or, if you came to the reasonable conclusion that this riddle could refer to a grape, an apple, a lemon, or an orange, how could you choose between them? And if there is no logical basis for such a choice, who could possibly hope to unlock this riddle? Answer: a person who has heard it before, and who therefore knows the score before the game begins. So if you hear this riddle at a party next month, and if you remember anything from this book, you will no doubt astonish your befuddled friends when you immediately reply, "It's a cider apple." And at that point you'll look just as clever, whether or not you could logically deduce the answer on your own.

IN THE KNOW: RIDDLES AND IDENTITY

Riddles, then, can be solved by people who possess three types of special knowledge: knowledge of the characteristics of the answer, knowledge of the riddler's system of logic, and knowledge of group traditions, which often simply means that you've already heard this riddle (or one like it). Actually, knowledge type #3 overrides types #1 and #2, or at least makes them irrelevant. After someone tells me the answer, I don't need to deduce it logically in the future; I just need to remember it and repeat it the next time the question is asked. It may be fairly said, then, that riddling is dependent on group knowledge and group traditions, and that people who do not share this knowledge and these traditions will not be able to answer even a very simple riddle, regardless of their intelligence quotient.

Because riddles depend on special group knowledge rather than native intelligence, they naturally draw a line between "people who think like us" and "people who don't think like us." The cider apple riddle we've been talking about, innocent as it may seem, ultimately divides the world into two classes of people: those who know the answer and those who don't. As noted in chapter 1, riddles play with a group's core beliefs and values. My ability to pose riddles demonstrates my command of those beliefs and of the boundaries of that value system; your ability to reason out possible solutions or rehearse memorized answers demonstrates that you are also a member of the culture that preserves these same beliefs and values. Riddles thus create a "community of knowledge," a group of people united by the ability to think about the same things in the same way.[10] When I told you the answer to the apple riddle, I initiated you into the Cider Apple Society.

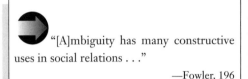

"[A]mbiguity has many constructive uses in social relations . . ."
—Fowler, 196

This aspect of riddling—the use of riddles to demonstrate membership in a group—is perhaps less obvious to people from Western cultures, simply because we use riddles mainly to amuse ourselves, "for the intellectual pleasure of showing that things are not quite as stable as they appear."[11] As a result, our riddles come with very low stakes—at best, a person who knows a lot of good riddles might be dubbed "a right funny bloke" by his buddies at the local pub. But in many traditional cultures, riddles are performed in social settings where the issue of group membership is more explicit: greetings, rituals "involving initiation and death," courtship and wedding ceremonies, and "the educational encounter between teacher and student."[12] In these situations, riddles remind people that they are members of the same knowledge group, even when the group seems to be changing. People greet one another with riddles to demonstrate that they are able to communicate on the same wavelength; they perform riddles at weddings and funerals to show that the change in the family does not threaten the overall unity of beliefs and values that hold society together; teachers use riddles to transmit cultural wisdom from one generation to another. The ability to answer a riddle, especially riddles that seem vague to outsiders, is a mark of membership.

Riddling, then, creates a community of knowledge; yet a community of knowledge is not of the same nature as some other social groups. Specifically, the members of a community of knowledge—at least as I am using the term here—are united *only* by their possession of shared information, regardless of their respective backgrounds. Of course, they may have acquired this shared information through common participation in some other group, like a family, a church, or the student body of a particular school. Thus, the employees of a local Wal-Mart store are both a "group" in the broad sense and a "community of knowledge" in the narrow sense. They are a "group" in the sense that they live in the same area, work in the same building, and have regular interactions with one another; they also know many of the same things about workways at Wal-Mart, and in this sense they represent a "community of knowledge." On the other hand, a great many rocket scientists have never met one another, and many in fact work for governments or corporations with hostile relations. Yet it is still meaningful to speak of "the international community of rocket scientists," even though these individuals are united only by their common knowledge of technical information relevant to the field. Similarly, while the members of the pipefitters' union are united by their common knowledge of that trade, this may be the only thing that unites them; some drive Ford trucks, some Chevrolets; some drink Budweiser, some Miller; some speak English, some Spanish, some French. Communities of knowledge thus transcend the boundaries of other groups.

A community of knowledge, then, may include people from many different groups; it may also exist as a subgroup within a larger society, a collection of individuals who know things that other people around them don't know. For example, "monk's questions" are riddles that require the recall of esoteric theological principles.[13] A riddle delivered by one Irish monk to another Irish monk in a monastery at Maynooth may mystify most of Dublin, but both monks will know the answer if such arcane knowledge is universal *within* the monastery. In this case, what seems vague to most people is clear to the members of a specific subgroup, so that the ability to answer the ambiguous catechetical question is one of several marks that distinguish the Irish monks from the larger population of Ireland. This aspect of knowledge communities is important to our understanding of riddles like Luke 14:26, which seem calculated to redefine key terms and thereby apparently threaten group solidarity. If only ten Jews in Nazareth could unlock Jesus' command to "hate" family and self, these people would not henceforth cease to be "Jews" or "Nazarenes." They would become, at that moment, Jewish Nazarenes who were also members of the community of knowledge whose members understand what it means to "hate" your family, as Jesus uses that term. This community would exclude some of their closest associates and family members, yet include people in other places whom they had never met.

Sometimes, in fact, riddles are used specifically to create subgroups, smaller communities of knowledge within a larger population. Referring to this phenomenon, Elli Köngäs Maranda calls riddles the "underdog's channel," meaning that marginalized people sometimes use them to distinguish themselves from the culture at large. In many cases, riddles are "utilized by those persons to whom other institutionalized expression is denied: women, commoners, unmarried men, and children." As noted earlier, all riddles challenge the group's ideological system, and riddlers can exploit this fact "to 'break' any classifications that come their way."[14]

To conclude, riddle answers are not necessarily "logical," and they are often arbitrary. Most riddle questions can reasonably support many possible answers. Attempts to explain how the answer to a given riddle is "right" generally cannot explain what makes other answers wrong. As a result, "riddles establish worth or identity rather than native intelligence": the ability to answer shows that one is worthy of membership in a community of knowledge.[15]

3

Riddling Sessions:
The Playground of the Mind

Riddles can be fun; they can also be dangerous business. It's fun to stimulate our brains by trying to figure out verses like

> Only to me is it allowed
> to have open intercourse with women
> at the request of their husbands.
> And I alone mount
> young men, grown men, and old men,
> and virgins while their parents grieve.
> [Yet] lasciviousness I hate,
> and the healing hand loves me . . .
> [Who am I?][1]

Answer: An enema.

but it's dangerous to society for individuals to think about taboo topics and blur boundaries too long or too often. Riddles capitalize on ambiguity, play with group norms and values, and thereby seek intentionally to confuse people. Riddles can therefore easily cause misunderstandings and embarrassment; at worst, subversive individuals can use them to create subgroups with secret knowledge, subgroups that may ultimately threaten the security and solidarity of the larger society. As a result, riddling must be carefully regulated, so that it provides pleasure and/or catharsis without doing too much damage.

THE ARENA: RIDDLING SESSIONS

In 1977, I, like many others in my generation, took my first trip to the wonderful world of Middle Earth on the Rankin and Bass cartoon version of

J. R. R. Tolkien's *The Hobbit*. After watching that program, which condensed some 300 pages into fifty-two minutes, I pulled seven hard-earned dollars from my Tootsie Roll bank and purchased a paperback edition of the book with illustrations from the TV show. To this day, my favorite page in that book, and favorite scene from that program, is a depiction of Bilbo's subterranean encounter with Gollum, an episode that is very significant to the larger mythology of *Lord of the Rings*, because it explains how this very average hobbit came to possess "the ring."[2] Only as an adult, after having read *The Lord of the Rings* twice and *The Hobbit* three times, did I realize that Rankin and Bass's interpretation of this scene was my first exposure to a full-fledged "riddling session."

Folklorists refer to the social settings in which intentionally ambiguous questions may be safely posed and answered as "riddling sessions." The communication pattern of a riddling session follows "an implicit set of rules and boundaries," boundaries that are flexible enough to permit ambiguity but rigid enough to protect all parties involved from the consequences of misunderstanding. As a result, the things we say in riddling sessions are "somewhat removed from casual conversation." In "casual conversation," intentional ambiguity and deception are frowned upon, and we quickly learn to avoid people who tend to talk this way. But the riddling session turns otherwise antisocial questions into a form of verbal "play," meaning that the speaker and her audience adopt stereotyped roles that make the exchange impersonal.[3] One person plays the "riddler," the character who poses the ambiguous question and determines the single correct answer; another person, or group of people, plays the "riddlee," the character(s) who must provide that answer. A riddling session may include only one question, a series of questions posed by one riddler, or a back-and-forth exchange in which the participants swap roles, such as the famous contest between Bilbo and Gollum.

As a form of play, the riddle game has well-defined rules, and these rules allow the participants to safely challenge normal ways of thinking without suffering the "real world" consequences of that challenge. The laws of riddling dictate the appropriate times and places to exchange riddles, the appropriate people to exchange them with, and the appropriate rewards and consequences for the ability or inability to answer. In some cultures, for example, it is appropriate to exchange riddles upon a first meeting, but in my culture it is not; on the other hand, my eight-year-old son can ask me riddles all day long, but in other cultures it is inappropriate to pose riddles to one's elders. Whatever the local rules, they must be strictly observed, even when they are not articulated. Gollum could be trusted because, as Bilbo reminded himself, "the riddle-game was sacred and of immense antiquity, and even wicked creatures were afraid to cheat when they played at it"—"afraid" for reasons that Gollum obviously sensed but could not verbalize.[4] To take a well-known example from the Hebrew Bible, Samson clearly thinks that the Philistines have cheated him by forcing his fiancée to tell them the answer to his riddle about the "sweet eater," even though technically no one ever said they couldn't do that. He protests by killing thirty Ashkelonites—a measured response for Samson—yet still lives up to the rules of the contest by paying on his bet to the survivors (Judg. 14:18–19). In a similar, albeit much less violent, instance, the Greek sage Clearchus complained that people who can't answer riddles at parties should not be "penalized" by downing a cup of undiluted wine, because in the old days the rule stated that you had to drink wine mixed with salt water without taking a breath.[5] As is the case with so many social guidelines, people are often most conscious of the unwritten rules of riddling when they sense that they have been broken.

Every player in a riddling session knows the rules of the game; yet how does one know that she is in the midst of a riddling session? Here again, tradition plays a key role at several levels. The members of a group can identify traditional riddle texts as soon as they hear or see them. Even if they don't know the answer, my American readers need no special clues to tell them what's going on when I ask, "What state is high in the middle and round on both ends?"[6] Such a reader immediately and intuitively realizes that we are riddling and presumably knows how to play along with me. In other cases, tradition offers clues in the form of a social setting. If I'm at a party or a

> **Traditional Cues for Riddling Sessions**
>
> 1. You recognize that a certain statement traditionally functions as a riddle (you've heard it, or others like it, before).
>
> 2. You recognize that certain social settings are traditionally appropriate venues for riddling (it's the right place and/or time).
>
> 3. You recognize that the speaker is introducing or concluding a statement with a formula that traditionally introduces or follows a riddle.

concert with my research assistant, Jake, and he is *not* intoxicated, I will suspect that any nonsensical questions he may ask are intended as jokes or riddles, because in my culture, concerts and parties have traditionally been appropriate venues for riddling. Yet if Jake starts talking nonsense when we are at a business lunch discussing some matter relating to a book project or a committee report, I will assume that something else is going on, because according to our cultural traditions, riddles would be inappropriate on that occasion. Tradition thus helps us recognize that an ambiguous statement is a riddle, and/or reminds us that certain social settings are particularly appropriate for riddle performance.

Because we don't like to be misunderstood, we often supplement these contextual clues for riddling with traditional formulae that explicitly warn our audience that they are walking into an ambiguous statement. Americans thus typically introduce jokes or riddles by saying, "Here's one for you" or "Get this," formulae that parallel the old British "Riddle me ree." Köngäs Maranda notes that the Lau people of Melanesia "do not have a marked riddle style," meaning that their riddles don't look or sound inherently different from other types of statements. To compensate for this lack, "the Lau riddle poser announces simply his intention by naming the genre he is about to present": i.e., "This is a riddle."[7] In a similar fashion, Samson does not rely on the Philistines' knowledge that riddles are a typical pastime at marriage banquets. Instead, exercising rare caution, he explicitly says, "Now let me tell you a riddle," and then clearly spells out the terms of the contest (Judg. 14:12). Statements like these help people remember the rules of riddling so that there can be no misunderstanding of the speaker's intention or what the audience is supposed to do.

But it is important to stress that these verbal cues, like the riddles and riddling sessions that they introduce, are traditional, and as such they also vary from culture to culture. As a result, they may not be very helpful to outsiders; that is, people outside the riddler's community of knowledge may not realize that such formulae introduce (or conclude) a riddling session. For example, in Athenaeus's *Deipnosophists*, Daphnus, an Ephesian, quotes an allegorical puzzle by the playwright Crates (fl. 470s BCE) that ends with the question, ἐν Κέῳ τίς ἡμέρα ("What day is it in Keos?"; 3.117). Even at a Phish concert, I would have to wonder what was wrong with Jake's mind if he were to ask me, "What day is it in Keos?" yet Crates obviously assumed that most Athenians would catch his drift and interpret this comment as an invitation to unlock an ambiguous statement. At the same time, I realize that the formula, "Here's one for ya," might not help Crates understand that I want to riddle with him, should he and I ever meet on some other plane of existence. Similarly, I, being from Ohio, would tend to look for riddle collections in the sections of the bookstore marked "Humor" or "Children's," but I can see why a person from, say, Uganda might seek them out in the sections marked Wisdom or Philosophy.

"WHOEVER HAS EARS," LET THEM KNOW THAT WE'RE RIDDLING

Riddling sessions, then, follow traditional formats that vary from culture to culture. These formats include introductory formulae that signal to a knowing audience that ambiguous questions will follow. For purposes of the present study, it will be most helpful to illustrate this principle with examples from the sources for Jesus. Two phrases appear frequently in the Gospels to clue the informed reader that a riddling session is underway, meaning that Jesus is either going to ask or be asked an intentionally ambiguous question—a "question" in the sense that it requests a clarifying answer, not necessarily in the sense that it ends in a question mark (?). The most frequent, and widely distributed, such clue is ὅς ἔχει ὦτα ἀκούειν ἀκουέτω ("Whoever has ears to hear, let them hear"), which highlights riddles in Mark, Luke, Matthew, and *Thomas*. While Matthew likes "Whoever has ears," he also sometimes signals riddling with an alternate formula, τί σοι/ὑμῖν δοκεῖ ("What do you think?"). These phrases are not, of course, the only means of identifying riddling sessions in the sources for Jesus, and I will not try to prove that either of them was actually uttered by the historical Jesus (although I think that they probably were). But their appearance in a variety of contexts at least suggests that several sectors of the primitive church used standardized formulae to underscore ambiguous sayings in their Jesus traditions. The remainder of this chapter will explore the dynamics of several typical riddling sessions that appear in the Gospels, highlighting the ways that these two phrases function to mark statements as intentionally ambiguous.

"Whoever Has Ears" Should Answer

Perhaps because Jesus' riddles do not typically take the form of questions, it is easy to interpret the refrain "Whoever has ears, let them hear" as a functional synonym for the modern maternal admonition "Pay attention!" Donahue and Harrington, for example, say the phrase "is rooted in the prophetic summons, most often addressed to rebellious people, to harken to God's commands." Following this line of argument, they cite Jeremiah 5:21 and 9:20 and Ezekiel 12:2 as precedents for Jesus' usage, a reasonable inference in view of the fact that Jesus quotes Jeremiah 5:21 directly at Mark 8:18.[8] From this perspective, Jesus' use of "Whoever has ears" probably means something like, "You'd better listen up and do what I say this time, or else!"—the tone it clearly carries on the lips of Jeremiah and Ezekiel. This interpretation finds further support in Ben Witherington's observation that Mark prefaces the parable of the Sower with the phrase, "Jesus was saying to them in his teaching, 'Listen' (ἀκούετε; 4:3)," and follows this parable with the statement, "And he was saying, Whoever has ears . . .'" (4:9). Together, "Listen" and "Whoever has ears" seem to form an *inclusio*—a sort of verbal [brackets] that ties the parable nicely into its context—suggesting that the latter phrase means something like "listen attentively."[9] Going behind Mark and into the context of Jesus' ministry, Crossan argues that the saying "focuses on the openness of that [Jesus'] message," and offers the following paraphrase: "You have ears, use them; what I

	"Whoever Has Ears" Will Know That She's in a Riddling Session		

Text	"Whoever has ears"	"What do you think?"	The Riddles(s)
Mark 4:9	✔		follows the parable of the Sower
Mark 4:23	✔		follows the question about whether a lamp should be put under a bed and the statement, "for nothing is hidden except that it should be revealed"
Mark 8:18	✔		stated as a rhetorical question to criticize the disciples' inability to identify "the leaven of the Pharisees"
Luke 14:35	✔		follows a series of "count the cost" statements and the note that salt is worthless once it loses its savor
Matt. 11:15	✔		follows the statements that the Kingdom is suffering violence and that John the Baptist was Elijah
Matt. 13:43	✔		follows Jesus' explanation of the parable of the Weeds, delivered privately to the disciples after they request clarification
Matt. 17:25		✔	precedes Jesus' question, in re the temple tax, "From whom do the kings of the earth receive tribute? From their sons or from strangers?"
Matt. 18:12		✔	precedes the parable of the Lost Sheep
Matt. 21:28		✔	precedes the parable of the Two Sons
Matt. 22:17		✔	precedes the Pharisees' question, "Is it lawful to give tribute to Caesar or not?"
Matt. 22:42		✔	precedes the question, "How can the Christ be the 'Son of David' when David himself calls him 'Lord'?"
Thomas 8:4	✔		follows the parable of the Wise Fisherman
Thomas 21:10	✔		follows the "Thief in the Night" and the statement, "When the crop ripened, he came quickly with a sickle and harvested"
Thomas 24:2	✔		precedes the statement, "There is light in a person of light . . . if it does not shine, it is dark"
Thomas 65:8	✔		follows the parable of the Vineyard
Thomas 96:3	✔		follows the parable of the Leaven

[Jesus] say is as clear and obvious as I can make it. . . . It is not cryptic, hidden, mysterious; it is obvious."[10] In view of these and similar arguments, one can easily see why the Scholars Version generally translates ὅς ἔχει ὦτα ἀκούειν ἀκουέτω with the somewhat colloquial, "Anyone here with two good ears had better listen!"

Yet in most of the contexts where Jesus uses the formula "Whoever has ears," we must wonder what good it would do anyone to "listen attentively" to what he is saying. When Jeremiah tells the Israelites to "hear" in spite of their deafness, he is underlining a disturbingly simple answer to a complex theological question: the people ask, "Why has God destroyed us?" and God replies, "Because you served foreign gods" (5:19). This statement, if not politically correct, is completely unambiguous, as was Jeremiah's proposed solution to the problem (surrender to the Babylonians). In such a context, the admonition to "hear" could reasonably be interpreted, "Do what I tell you!" By contrast, "you've got to have the right kind of ears" to "hear" what Jesus is saying, because the phrase "Whoever has ears" is *always* used in the Gospels to highlight ambiguous statements that "you have to puzzle over."[11] "Whoever has ears, let them hear" thus marks a saying as a riddle and indicates that Jesus expects some response that will clarify what he is talking about.[12]

Mark's three instances of "Whoever has ears" should suffice to illustrate how the Gospels use this phrase to identify riddling sessions, situations in which Jesus asks or answers intentionally ambiguous questions. For sake of clarity—because it's a less complicated example—I will discuss the third instance, Mark 8:18, first, and then move to the somewhat more complex use of the formula in Mark 4. This may be cheating, but I'm not writing a commentary on Mark here, and I want to make my point as clear as possible for readers who may not be very familiar with the issues surrounding these passages.

Mark 8 provides a good illustration of the general dynamics of a riddling session, particularly of the use of verbal formulae to mark statements as intentionally ambiguous. The chapter opens with the story of a miraculous feeding of four thousand people—a different episode from the feeding of five thousand, which has already happened (Mark 6:33–44). After this second exhibition of Jesus' remarkable catering skills, the Pharisees debate with Jesus and "test" him by demanding a "sign from heaven" (8:11). Of course, one could argue that the ability to feed four thousand people with only seven loaves of bread is already fairly impressive (8:5). But maybe the Pharisees were not present to witness that; further, even if they had been there, such a skill could come from the devil, as the scribes have already pointed out at Mark 3:22. They therefore want Jesus to provide "a public, definitive proof that God is with him."[13] Jesus, however, is not particularly concerned to appease them, and replies with his own damning question: "Why does this generation seek a sign? Truly I tell you, if a sign is given to this generation . . ."—well, he doesn't say exactly what will happen then, but it must not be good because he immediately leaves the region in disgust (v. 13).[14] Some scholars feel that Jesus' sweeping reference to "this generation" is a blanket indictment of all people; some limit the term to the Pharisees and others like them who refuse to believe.[15] In either case, it seems clear that the episode to follow is intended to highlight the disciples' "failure to perceive the meaning of Jesus' presence with them"—that is, to show that they don't have a much better understanding of him than anybody else.[16]

Still stewing over the Pharisees' pigheadedness, Jesus sets sail for Bethsaida on the other side of the lake (Mark 8:13, 22). After brooding in the boat for a while, he suddenly cries, "Watch out! Watch for the *leaven* of the Pharisees and the *leaven* of Herod!" (8:15). Now it so happened that the disciples, perhaps due to their hasty departure, had not made it to the bakery that day, and as a result they had only one loaf of bread with them (8:14). Hearing Jesus' comment about "leaven," their eyes slide sheepishly toward the bag that held this slight provision, and they begin to argue about the situation that had aroused their rabbi's wrath. Who was supposed to get more bread in the first place? Not me. But anyway, how could anybody know that he would take off in a huff before they made it to the market?[17] Jesus overhears this discussion and breaks in with a few thoughts of his own on the subject, leading to the exchange at Mark 8:17–21.

Mark 8:17–21

[17]"Why are you discussing that you have no bread? Do you not yet understand or comprehend? Do you have unfeeling hearts? [18]Having eyes, do you not see; and having ears, do you not hear? And don't you remember, [19]when I broke five loaves for five thousand people, how many baskets of leftover pieces you picked up?"

They said to him, "Uh, twelve."

[20]"When [I broke] seven [loaves of bread] for four thousand people, how many large baskets full of leftover pieces did you pick up?"

And they said to him, "Well, uh, seven."

[21]"Do you not yet comprehend?"

Obviously Jesus is frustrated with the disciples and expresses his displeasure by reading them the riot act. This incident is thus yet another in a series of episodes that reveal the disciples' inability to grasp Jesus' true identity and mission (see Mark 4:10, 35–41; 6:45–52). Perhaps because this is a consistent theme in Mark—the disciples never seem to understand what Jesus is all about—modern readers, including most commentators, have tended to overlook or downplay the inherent ambiguity of the comment about "leaven" at 8:15. The "correct" interpretation—that Jesus is using "leaven" as a metaphor for the Pharisees' teaching—is obvious to us; so obvious, in fact, that the disciples seem to be mentally impaired. Lane's analysis of their condition, if somewhat exaggerated, is nevertheless typical. The disciples, in his view, deserved this dressing down because "the dispute among [them] . . . indicated how completely they were absorbed in their temporal preoccupations." One can easily understand "Jesus' sharp condemnation of the lack of understanding in men whose privileged position should have led them to perceive the truth of his person." Jesus' explicit reference to "the leaven *of the Pharisees* and the leaven *of Herod*" should have made it plain that he wasn't talking about loaves of bread, yet the disciples "simply ignored" these words (the words in italics above), so engrossed were they in the pettiness of their blame game.[18]

While it is not my intention to defend the spiritual perception or mental capacity of the Markan disciples, I may exonerate them somewhat by pointing out that Mark 8:14–21 is a riddling session. Because this is the case, although Jesus' statement about "the leaven of the Pharisees" and his subsequent "hints" about the miraculous feedings seem crystal clear to us, they are actually considerably more complicated than Lane's reading would suggest. Nothing in this context would lead the disciples to think that Jesus is not speaking at the most literal level, and Jesus therefore must say, "Whoever has ears," to warn them that he is using ambiguous language. Two aspects of Mark's presentation highlight the complexity of the situation and the need for such a warning.

First, while Jesus clearly is not pleased with the disciples, their initial response to his statement about the leaven—"He's mad because we didn't bring enough bread"—is completely reasonable in its context. Indeed, it is almost the only reasonable conclusion they could come to in such a context. They don't have enough food, so they'll have to buy more as soon as they get off the boat, and Jesus has just had a heated argument with some Pharisees. In that situation, "Watch out for the leaven of the Pharisees and Herodians!" would most logically mean that Jesus "does not want them to buy additional loaves from the Pharisees and supporters of Herod"—he's mad at those people and he doesn't want his money going to them anymore.[19] Or maybe he thinks that the Herodians are going to try to poison him with bad bread. Who knows? Either way, nothing in Jesus' comment suggests that he is not talking about the leaven that would be used to make bread, and several things in the physical context of the remark actually suggest that he *must* be talking about that kind of leaven. One can therefore hardly expect the disciples to realize that Jesus is suddenly speaking metaphorically.

For this very reason—because the statement about leaven refers so obviously to the details of the situation at hand—Jesus provides the disciples with a clue that he has just said something ambiguous. The rhetorical questions, "Having eyes, don't you see? And *having ears, don't you hear?*"—parallel here

to "Don't you understand?" at verses 17 and 21—are signals that Jesus'
remark could potentially refer to more than one thing: it could refer to the
leaven used to make bread; it could also refer to some other kind of leaven.
The disciples initially choose the more obvious, and obviously incorrect,
answer. Jesus wants them to know that they are in a riddling session, and he
uses a variant of the "Whoever has ears" formula to let them know that they
need to look deeper.

The rest of the story plays on the disciples' inability to move from the
wrong referent to the right one; they never give Jesus the answer he wants,
despite his subsequent hints in verses 19–20. After asking them about their
eyes and ears, Jesus proceeds to question the disciples about the leftover baskets of bread at the earlier feedings (Mark 8:19–20; see 6:33–44; 8:1–9). This
line of inquiry appears, to us at least, to immediately clarify the issue. The disciples just saw Jesus feed four thousand people, and in view of this fact we must
ask them: Isn't it obvious that he can make all the bread he wants? And if he
can do that, why would he be complaining that you didn't buy enough bread?
Can't you see that he isn't talking about the "leaven" used to make bread?
Indeed, one "can only wonder how they can possibly fail to comprehend what
is going on around them."[20]

But upon closer examination, these "hints" from the earlier feeding stories
are actually the second reason that Jesus must explicitly warn the disciples that
he is riddling. On one hand, Jesus' questions about the leftovers emphasize the
fact that he can make all the bread he wants, so they won't need to worry about
buying food from the Pharisees anytime soon. The disciples therefore could—
and in Jesus' view should—conclude that the word "leaven" is an ambiguous
term, pointing to more than one possible meaning. Yet the two prior occasions
to which Jesus alludes both involved *loaves of bread*, bread that Jesus had broken and that the disciples had eaten; he talks about bread as a clue that he isn't
talking about bread. As a result, his "clarifying questions" actually lead them
to keep looking for a wrong answer that has something to do with the leaven
used in baking, a rhetorical move that would doubtless draw criticism at a
Pampered Chef party but is very consistent with the communication pattern
of a riddling session. The disciples' simplistic answers to these follow-up questions—"Twelve loaves; seven"—reveal that they have not so much missed the
meaning of Jesus' warning about "leaven" as they have missed the meaning of
his question, "Having ears, don't you hear?" Because they cannot unpack the
latter statement, they see no need to unpack the former, and therefore continue to act as if Jesus had spoken unambiguously.

Of course, my reading here will doubtless do little to defend the disciples
from the criticisms of Mark's modern readers. Even if you concede that Mark
8:15 is a riddle and that "Whoever has ears" at verse 18 explicitly marks the

occasion as a riddling session, the correct answer still seems so obvious that we can scarcely comprehend the disciples' incomprehension. Mary Ann Tolbert has in fact suggested that Mark's portrait of the disciples as "hopeless dimwits" here makes this episode an instance of "situational irony," thus inviting the reader to pass judgment on their misinformed response to Jesus. While Mark may want us to pass judgment, I personally do not think it entirely correct to see this episode as a case of "irony," because literary irony depends on the "joint knowledge and point of view" shared between the reader (us) and the author: we and Mark both know something that the disciples don't know, and together we can laugh at them because of it.[21] This story may make us laugh, but it isn't "ironic," because we (the readers) do not share "joint knowledge" with Mark in this instance. We may think that we do, but in point of fact the "obvious" answer to Jesus' "riddle of the leaven"—the one that commentators expect the befuddled disciples to pick up—*does not appear in the Gospel of Mark at all.* Our ill-founded confidence comes from the fact that Matthew, who didn't believe that we could figure out the riddle on our own, gives us an answer explicitly at the end of his version of the story: "Then they understood that he was not saying to beware of the leaven of bread, but rather of the *teaching* of the Pharisees" (16:12). Matthew thus initiates us directly into his community of knowledge, that group of people who realize that "leaven" can be more than just an ingredient for bread; here as with other riddles, we know the solution through appeal to tradition, because someone has told us the right answer. Mark's unresolved ending to the story—Jesus just says, "Don't you understand yet?" and then it's over (v. 21)—simply indicates that Mark's disciples were not yet members of this knowledge community and therefore did not know how to think correctly.

With Mark 8 in the background, the two occurrences of "Whoever has ears" in the prolonged riddling session at Mark 4 come into sharper focus. The first appears at 4:9, immediately after the parable of the Sower. This story is so ambiguous that the use of an explicit riddling formula almost seems redundant: Mark prefaces the parable with the summary statement "he taught them everything in parables" (4:2); Jesus explicitly states that most people won't understand what he means (4:11–12); even the disciples must request a private explanation later on (4:10); after they ask, it takes Jesus seven verses to unpack the meaning of the story (vv. 14–20); despite this lengthy exposition, scholars today cannot even agree on the focal point of the story—does the parable focus on the sower, the seeds, the soils, or some combination thereof?—much less the correct interpretation.[22] By closing the parable with "Whoever has ears," Jesus "leaves its hearers with the responsibility of discerning and applying its meaning," no small task in view of the fact that it could refer to almost anything.[23]

After explaining the parable of the Sower/Seeds/Soils in detail, Jesus proceeds to ask a rhetorical question about putting a lamp under a bed, and then

> ### Mark 4:21–23
> [21]And Jesus was saying to them, "A lamp isn't brought out so that it should be put under a basket or under the bed, is it? No, but rather so that it should be put on the lampstand. [22]For nothing is hidden except that it should be revealed, nor has anything been hidden away except that it should come to light. [23]*Whoever has ears to hear, let them hear.*"

says, "For there is nothing hidden except that it should be revealed, nor has anything been hidden away except that it should come to light" (Mark 4:21–22). These two analogies—the lamp under the bed and the hidden things coming to light—are clearly parallel, repeating the theme of "revelation" for emphasis. Commentators have focused their energies on the identity of the specific thing that is being "revealed" here, and most conclude that it is "the mystery of the Kingdom of God" mentioned in verse 11. France, for example, suggests that "the light [v. 21] represents the parabolic revelation which is the subject of this chapter"; that is, Jesus is openly revealing God's Kingdom through these parables, so that verses 21–22 are a sort of metaphorical commentary on what is happening in the rest of the chapter.[24] Following this line, Painter makes "Whoever has ears" at verse 23 a minisermon for the disciples, an exhortation to receive this revelation of the Kingdom: "Though they have responded to Jesus the disciples must remain sensitively open because the mystery of the Kingdom of God, though given to them, remains a mystery beyond them to which they must attend as they are drawn on by the light."[25]

All of this seems reasonable to me, and I personally find Painter's commentary inspiring and relevant to my life. Yet for purposes of the present study, which is right now focused on the function of "Whoever has ears" at Mark 4:9 and 4:23, I would note three things. First, I think Gundry is probably correct to insist that there is a shift between verses 20 and 21, so that in verse 21 Mark is picking up where he left off at verse 9; we're now back to Jesus teaching the crowds out in public.[26] Hence, the "lamp" analogy seems to me to be the second thing Jesus told the crowds on this occasion, right after the parable of the Sower/Seeds/Soils, and verse 23 indicates that he followed this second teaching with "Whoever has ears," just as he had done at the conclusion of the parable (v. 9). I do not, in other words, think that the teachings about the lamp and the "hidden things" at verses 21–22 are being delivered only to the disciples at a later time, and I therefore do not see these statements as a commentary on the fact that Jesus has just "revealed" the meaning of the Sower/Seeds/Soils to them, nor as an exhortation to tell others what Jesus has just told them. Jesus' private commentary on the parable, which appears in verses 14–20, was most likely not given until later on in the story, somewhere between verses 34 and 35. Mark has simply put the events out of order for stylistic reasons. The bottom line here is that I see both 4:9 and 4:23 as statements that Jesus delivers to the crowds after saying something ambiguous: "Whoever has ears to hear, let them figure out what the Sower and this Lamp saying and this saying about Hidden Things mean."

Second, while I am calling Mark 4:1–34 a "riddling session," I wish to highlight the fact that the question, "Don't people light a lamp so that it should be put on a lampstand?" (v. 21) is not obviously ambiguous; taken at the surface level, it is common sense. Anyone in the crowd would have to say, "Why, yes, that's true; people do light lamps for that reason." But this observation would not necessarily lead them to conclude that Jesus is pointing to some deeper meaning. They could just as easily interpret the comment as a piece of proverbial wisdom that would apply to their lives in a variety of ways. If someone asks me, "Don't people generally put their socks on before they put their shoes on?" I don't automatically look for some deeper symbolism or hidden subject matter there. I just take it as a piece of common-sense advice about something that I might be doing wrong. Similarly, Jesus' maxim that "hidden things will be revealed" could be taken at face value and applied to any number of practical situations in life. Perhaps Jesus is warning us that our hidden sins will eventually be found out (cf. Pss. 90:8; 101:5; Prov. 9:17–18)? Or maybe he means that God will reward us for the good deeds that we do anonymously (cf. Matt. 6:4–6)? For this very reason—because both of these statements could be treated as simple proverbs—Jesus must follow them with "Whoever has ears" at verse 23 to make it clear that he has just uttered another riddle.[27] This cues the crowds that they are in a riddling session: they need to look deeper for the true point of what Jesus is saying, in this case even the true subject of his remarks. This buried referent, the Kingdom of God, will remain "hidden" behind Jesus' ambiguous language until it is "revealed" by those who are able to identify the correct answer (v. 22).

Third and finally, no matter what is being "revealed" in Mark 4, the "light" is not shining from the text of the parable of the Sower/Seeds/Soils, nor from the parables of the Growing Seed or the Mustard Seed that are about to follow (Mark 4:26–32)—Jesus has just said that those stories are incomprehensible to most people (4:11–12). "The light" is rather to be found in the correct *answers* to these enigmatic sayings, such as the extended explanation of the Sower/Seeds/Soils that the disciples receive in verses 14–20. Without those answers, the specific point of these stories is not obvious; as I noted above, the specific point of the Sower is not entirely obvious even with Jesus' detailed answer. I would therefore fine-tune France's reading of the "hidden things" (v. 22) to specify that, technically, what is "hidden" here are the correct answers to Jesus' riddles; these answers will "come to light" as soon as someone is able

Three Notes on a Riddling Session
Mark 4:1–34

1. In terms of the order of the story, Mark probably means that verse 21 follows verse 9, with verses 10–20 falling between verses 34 and 35. The order of the story is thus: the Sower; the Lamp; the Growing Seed; the Mustard Seed; private explanations of these teachings for the disciples. Jesus says "Whoever has ears" after the first two of these teachings.
2. The "Lamp" and "Hidden Things" sayings (vv. 21–22) could easily be taken as general proverbial wisdom, rather than as comments on the Kingdom of God. Jesus therefore uses "Whoever has ears" at verse 23 to let people know that these are riddles, meaning that they need to look for a deeper reference point.
3. All of Jesus' points about the Kingdom in this chapter are made indirectly: the "revelation" lies in the correct answer, not in his ambiguous questions. Hence, only people who know these answers can really understand anything about the Kingdom (vv. 11–12).

to figure out what he is talking about. Each of those answers will, in turn, illuminate some facet of the Kingdom of God.

These three instances from Mark reflect a general pattern. Overall, while the sources for Jesus never use the phrase "Whoever has ears to hear, let them hear" to introduce a statement that takes the grammatical form of a question, this formula is always associated with intentionally ambiguous statements. Anyone who hears has been fairly warned that Jesus is riddling with them and that he expects them to identify the one correct answer he has in mind. The phrase is therefore functionally equivalent to "Riddle me ree" or "Here's one for you," although the subject matter is obviously more significant than the pub jokes we introduce with those phrases today.

"What Do You Think" about This Riddle?

While Matthew sometimes follows Mark in using "Whoever has ears" to identify riddling sessions, on five occasions he marks a statement as intentionally ambiguous with τί σοῖυ μῖν δοκεί, "What do you think?" This is perhaps most explicit at Matthew 22:15–17, where the Pharisees and Herodians ask Jesus, "Is it lawful to pay taxes to Caesar or not?" The NIV blandly translates the

Jesus Gets Riddled
Matthew 22:15–17

[15]Then the Pharisees came together and conceived a plan of how they might trap him with words. [16]And they sent their disciples to him with the Herodians, saying, "Teacher, we know that you are truthful and you teach the way of God in truth. And no one is of special concern to you, for you do not flatter people. [17]Tell us, then, *What do you think?* Is it lawful to give the poll tax to Caesar, or not?"

introduction to their question as "What is your opinion?" yet every aspect of the context suggests that the Pharisees are not especially interested in Jesus' opinion: they are seeking to "trap" him (v. 15); the exchange is apparently public; the Herodians are present to witness, and subsequently report on, everything Jesus says; the question touches on a dangerous topic, and both of the implied answers–"Yes, pay" and "No, don't pay"–are politically dangerous. Whether or not "What do you think?" is, as many commentators suggest, a redactional addition to Mark's version of the story (cf. Mark 12:14),[28] Matthew is simply underlining what Mark also assumes: that the Pharisees are about to engage Jesus in a riddling contest with high stakes.

On four other occasions, Matthew has Jesus introduce a teaching with the phrase, "What do you think?" and in each case it is clear that he is not asking someone's opinion but is rather seeking an answer that will resolve a potentially ambiguous statement (or using an ambiguous question to stage an answer that he plans to provide). A prime example appears at Matthew 17:25, where Jesus asks Peter a loaded question about a basic principle of taxation: "From whom do the kings of the earth receive customs and taxes?" Jesus' comments here are somewhat overshadowed by the well-known miracle of the coin in the fish's mouth, which immediately follows the riddle and its answer (vv. 27–28). In point of fact, however, the story ends with Jesus' *allusion* to that miracle; we assume that Peter caught the fish and found the coin, but Matthew does not bother to show him doing that. It is therefore reasonable to classify Matthew 17:24–27 as a "scholastic dialogue" rather than a miracle story, meaning that the focus is on Jesus' teaching rather than the fish or the coin.[29] Like many scholastic dialogues in traditional cultures, the exchange is structured as a riddling session.

Kings, Sons, and Strangers
Matthew 17:24–27

[24]But when they came into Capernaum, the people who collect the two-drachma tax came to Peter and said, "Your teacher pays the tax, doesn't he?"
[25]He said, "Of course."
And when he came into the house, Jesus anticipated him, saying, "What do you think, Simon? The kings of the earth, from whom do they receive customs and taxes? From their sons, or from strangers?" [26]When he answered, "from strangers," Jesus said to him, "consequently, the sons are exempt. [27] But so that we should not offend them, go to the sea, throw in a hook, and take the first fish that comes up. When you open its mouth, you will find a stater [worth four drachmas]. When you get that, give it to them [to pay] for me and you."

As the story opens, Jesus and the disciples arrive in Capernaum, and Peter is approached by "those who received the didrachma," the two-drachma tax paid each year by Jewish men in support of the Jerusalem temple (see Exod. 30:11–16). The collectors, apparently unable to find Jesus, ask Peter, "Your teacher pays the tax, doesn't he?"[30] Of course, it comes as no surprise that a tax collector would ask such a question, yet it seems likely that more than two drachmas is at stake. As Donald Senior notes, "the half-shekel [temple] tax also had important symbolic meaning as a sign of solidarity of all Jews both in Israel and the Diaspora." Viewed again this backdrop, "the question raised by the tax collectors is about Jesus' allegiance to the temple and his obligation to support it."[31] Peter would doubtless want to affirm Jesus' support of the temple, whether his rabbi really did pay the tax or not; he therefore quickly responds, "*Nai*—yes, of course he pays that tax."

But after he leaves the tax collectors, Peter is confronted with another question, whose full implications are somewhat less clear. As soon as he enters the

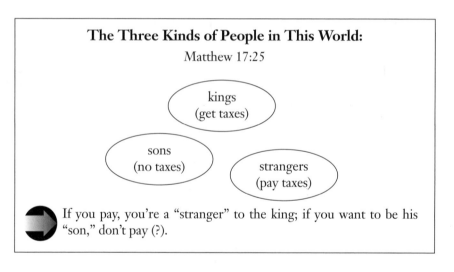

The Three Kinds of People in This World:
Matthew 17:25

kings
(get taxes)

sons
(no taxes)

strangers
(pay taxes)

If you pay, you're a "stranger" to the king; if you want to be his "son," don't pay (?).

house, and before he can even report on what has just happened, Jesus asks him, "From whom do the kings of the earth receive customs and taxes? From their sons, or from strangers?" Compared to many of Jesus' interrogations, this seems relatively straightforward, and with a sigh of relief Peter says, "From strangers." Jesus does not affirm this response, but instead simply completes the thought: strangers pay taxes; the king's children do not.[32] Peter could scarcely doubt the truth of this statement, yet the initial question remains ambiguous because it isn't clear how the answer relates to the situation at hand. "The children of kings don't pay taxes while everyone else does": what does that have to do with Jesus and Peter and the two-drachma temple tax, a tax that is given to God, not to one of the "kings of the earth"? Further, why has Jesus chosen to couch this issue in terms of the difference between "sons" and "strangers" (ἀλλοτρίοι), thus eliminating the more obvious, and much less loaded, answer, "They collect taxes from their *subjects*"?[33] And how can Peter affirm his status as a child of God while avoiding the social ramifications of a refusal to pay the tax? Jesus' question must be ambiguous, reflecting a taxonomy of values that defies conventional ways of thinking and possessing a deeper meaning that presumably has something to do with the issue of whether the disciples should give money to the tax collectors. The phrase "What do you think?" clues Peter to look for this hidden application even before the question is asked.

As Matthew 17:25 illustrates, "What do you think?" like "Whoever has ears" serves as a clue that Jesus is engaged in a riddling session. Matthew uses these two phrases interchangeably to portray statements as intentionally ambiguous and to show that someone is being challenged to demonstrate wit by providing an answer. Of course, this does not prove that the historical Jesus used either of these specific formulae himself. Because "What do you think?" is unique to Matthew, one might easily conclude that it is a distinct feature of his compositional style. But the prevalence of this *type of statement* in the sources for Jesus shows that several sectors of the early church used traditional formulae to mark specific sayings as riddles, and thus to portray the situations in which these sayings appear as riddling sessions.

By this point in the book, I have, I think (hope), adequately explained what "riddles" are and how they work—adequately enough, at least, to serve the purposes of my argument. I have also discussed in some detail the social setting in which people exchange riddles, the "riddling session." Because I assume that most of my readers are interested in Jesus studies, I have freely used examples from the Gospels to illustrate our discussion. I hope this has made the presentation more stimulating, but I am certain that it has led you to wonder exactly which texts in the sources for Jesus would count as "riddles," and what criteria I have used to identify them. The next chapter will discuss these criteria in detail and offer a sampling of the passages that I have in mind.

4

Finding Riddles in Written Texts

My argument to this point has suggested—or, actually, just observed—that riddles were a prominent feature of Jesus' repertoire. They were so prominent, in fact, that I have been able to use familiar examples from the Gospels to support my theoretical discussion of the nature of riddles and riddling sessions. This being the case, you may have asked yourself why most historical Jesus scholars have not noticed these riddles, or at least have not capitalized on their significance in understanding Jesus' message. In my view, the answer to this question does not lie in any disinterest on the part of said Jesus scholars; many of them have intuitively sensed that certain things he says sound like riddles and have referred to these sayings as "riddles" in their writings. Instead, the answer lies in the limitations of the methods that we normally use to identify traditional units of speech in the sources for Jesus. I would, in other words, argue that most Jesus scholars have overlooked riddles, or at least have not fully developed the implications of Jesus' riddling (as I will do in part 2), simply because ambiguous language is so hard to detect, especially when we do not know the local rules of the game. Riddles are difficult to nail down with any level of certainty, and definitely difficult to nail down with the level of certainty that Jesus researchers typically seek to establish. Simply put, riddles can be very hard to find.

KNOWING THE RULES OF THE GAME

Before proceeding to a solution, let me pause for a moment to illustrate the form-critical problems posed by riddling. Suppose that a certain Korean scientist, Dr. Choi, is a renowned expert on the use of lasers in the treatment of eye disease

45

(any similarity to actual persons living or dead is purely coincidental). Dr. Choi is widely sought as a speaker, and already this year has delivered remarkable papers to hushed audiences in London, Tokyo, and Bonn. Everyone who hears Dr. Choi can only comment, in a tone of reverent awe, "The voice of a god, and not a man!" For, indeed, never before has any mortal possessed such keen insight into the workings of the human eye and medical applications of laser technology. Doctoral students crowd around him with eyes cast down, not daring to look upon his glory but wishing only to touch the hem of his lab coat so that perhaps a spark of his genius may illuminate their own dark minds. All readily concede the justice of the fact that Dr. Choi has already received sufficient grants to fund his research, and his condo on Maui, for the next two decades.

On one occasion, Dr. Choi was in Baltimore for a seminar on macular degeneration at Johns Hopkins University, sponsored by the National Institutes of Health and hosted by the U.S. surgeon general. Breaking from his strict regimen of five-star hotels, Dr. Choi was staying at the home of his old friend and fraternity brother Professor Gilligan, lately of the JHU medical faculty but currently a leading researcher for Pfizer. After the day's session, the two scientists sat on the patio by Professor Gilligan's pool, chuckling over fond memories of college drinking sprees and botched eye surgeries. In the midst of this revelry, young Megan Gilligan, the esteemed professor's eight-year-old daughter, appeared in her pajamas for a kiss goodnight. Climbing into her father's lap, she was introduced to Dr. Choi, who inquired pleasantly into the subjects typical of a first encounter between a child and a strange adult: How old was she? Where did she go to school? What was her teddy's name? This repartee successfully warmed the girl, leading her to suddenly pose a question of her own: "What's black and white and red all over?"

Dr. Choi smiled and furrowed his brow, looking askance to his colleague.

"I think it's a newspaper," Professor Gilligan said to Megan. Then he nodded to Dr. Choi, "It's an old kid's joke in America. Did you hear that at school, honey?"

"You're wrong, Daddy," Megan said, looking at the teddy bear in apparent disregard for the adults, "it's a zebra with a sunburn."

Dr. Choi smiled again as she ran off to bed, commending Professor Gilligan on such a delightful child. Only later, while brushing his teeth, did he realize that she was the first person in ten years—the first since his first wife—to ask a question that he could not answer.

There is no sense in which such an incident would discredit the intelligence and erudition of Dr. Choi. Despite his genius, we certainly do not expect him to know the answer to Megan's riddle, nor even to realize that her question was intentionally ambiguous. We do not expect this simply because we realize that *ambiguity is a local phenomenon*. Riddles, in other words, work only if they are not too obvious, and they are almost always obvious only to people who know the way the game is played in a particular culture. As I said in chapter 2, "knowing the game" often means knowing local traditions, which in turn often simply means that you've heard the riddle and its answer before. Dr. Choi, being Korean, could certainly have told Megan the answer to the question, "What has one eye and three legs? [A camera.]" But because he was not familiar with the rules of riddling that prevail among American children, he could not even identify Megan's question as a "riddle," much less provide an answer. This simply illustrates the point I made in chapter 3: not only riddles, but also the rules for riddling sessions, depend on traditional information. If you don't know those traditions, you cannot answer the questions and often can't even tell when a question has been asked.

This fact—that riddles don't necessarily stand out as "riddles" in obvious ways—is the very reason why Jesus scholars have been very careful in their approach to sayings that look like riddles in the sources for Jesus. Riddles generate intentional ambiguity, and this ambiguity can, in turn, be harnessed to serve a variety of objectives (entertainment, teaching, test of wits, etc.). But these objectives do not depend on any particular style or form; as noted earlier, *any* statement of any shape or size can function as a riddle. Riddles come in a wide variety of forms in many cultures (like mine) simply because variety fosters ambiguity; they're more ambiguous if they don't always look or work the same way. For the same reason, riddles do not evidence a consistent content. Even within a single culture, there is usually no narrowly limited set of terms or themes to which they appeal again and again. As an example, the children's book to which I alluded in the preface, Bennett Cerf's *Pop-Up Riddles*, includes questions about ducks, bananas, kangaroos, eggs, 200-pound mice, and a host of other unrelated topics.[1] Riddlers use this license to generate confusion; the more different things a riddle could potentially refer to, the better. Because the form and content of riddles are necessarily inconsistent, specimens of the genre are most easily identifiable by the way that people use them and by the way that other people respond to them. But this makes the task of locating riddles in the sources for Jesus especially difficult, simply because we are not now in a position to ask Jesus or the Pharisees exactly what they were trying to do with their words on various occasions. As a result, riddles have fallen below the radar of the typical criteria utilized in historical Jesus research.

THE QUEST FOR JESUS THE RIDDLER: CRITERIA

Because riddles are not easily uncovered by standard methods of biblical research, the quest for Jesus the Riddler will require other methodological

tools, ones more fitted to the elusive shape of our object of inquiry. For purposes of this study, I have utilized four criteria to detect riddles in the available
sources for Jesus. All the riddles I've discussed so far, and all that will be
addressed in the chapters to follow, meet at least one of these standards. I stress
at the outset that these are *not* "criteria of authenticity"; I do not suggest that
any passage from, say, the Gospel of John that meets one or several of these
guidelines must represent the activity of the historical Jesus. I would, however,
insist that any passage from the Gospel of John that fits these guidelines should
be treated as a riddle, and should therefore contribute to a broad picture of this
dimension of Jesus' teaching style. With this caveat, my criteria are as follows:[2]

1. When *the author directly states* that something a character in the story has
   just said or is about to say is intentionally ambiguous, that statement is a
   riddle.
2. When *the author and/or a character in the story frames a statement* as riddle
   performance, indicating that it was uttered in the context of a riddling session, that statement is a riddle.
3. When *characters in the story respond* to a statement in a way that suggests
   that it is intentionally ambiguous, that statement is a riddle.
4. When a character uses language that seems *calculated to challenge conventional ways of thinking and leaves it to the audience to resolve the dilemma*, that
   statement is a riddle.

I should stress that the phrase, "that statement is a riddle," in each criterion
above is shorthand for, "the author of that document wants us to interpret the
statement in question as an intentionally ambiguous remark that is offered as
a challenge." This reflects my basic definition of the "riddle" as "an interrogative statement that intentionally obscures its referent and asks the audience
to name it." Specifically, any saying attributed to Jesus or any other character
in the sources should be seen as a "riddle" only if (a) it is "ambiguous," meaning that it could possibly refer to more than one thing; (b) it apparently
requests a response, meaning that it challenges the audience to figure out what
the person is talking about; and (c) it meets one of the four criteria above.
Because any one of these criteria would, in my view, mark a statement as a riddle, a brief explanation of each is in order before we proceed.

First, when the author of a source directly states that a character is using
language that is intentionally ambiguous, the saying in question is a riddle.
This criterion reflects my opinion, perhaps naive, that the author of a text
knows his or her own intentions better than I do. Even if the author fails to
achieve ambiguity or ends up just being vague, it is more significant for my
purposes that he was *trying* to portray some question that Jesus asked or
answered as intentionally ambiguous. An obvious example of this phenomenon appears at John 10:6, where the Fourth Evangelist states that Jesus has just

spoken a παροιμία (a "riddle"; NRSV "figure of speech") that the crowds did not understand. This being the case, whatever readers today may think about the parable of the Shepherd and the Stranger at John 10:1–5, the Fourth Evangelist clearly thought that it was some kind of verbal puzzle. Presumably, then, it is safe to treat that saying of Jesus as a riddle, even if the answer seems fairly obvious to us today.[3]

But criterion #1 can also cover references that are not quite so explicit. In some cases, the author may simply clarify that Jesus is not speaking about the most obvious thing in that particular context, thus indicating that his words are ambiguous. Matthew, for example, explains in an aside that Jesus was not really talking about "bread" when he warned the disciples to "Beware of the leaven of the Pharisees and Sadducees!"; instead, he was actually referring to the "teachings" of these people (16:6, 12). Here Matthew does not explicitly say, "Jesus was using a riddle," or "Jesus' words were intentionally ambiguous," but his explanation makes it clear that the remark was calculated to permit of more than one meaning. Of course, authors and narrators are not usually so helpful and typically do not telegraph the speech genres that their characters are using. This is especially true of riddles, because the effect is destroyed as soon as the ambiguity is highlighted: the game is up, as it were,

> **The Four Criteria**
>
> A statement in the Gospels is a "riddle" if . . .
>
> **1.** The author says that it is.
>
> **2.** It happens in a riddling session.
>
> **3.** Other characters are confused.
>
> **4.** It's calculated to challenge normal thinking

as soon as the author gives away the secret. Criterion #1 is therefore extremely helpful to our inquiry, but unfortunately rarely applicable.[4]

Criterion #2 involves clues from the physical context in which a statement is uttered. I noted in chapter 3 that riddles are delivered in special social settings that regulate their exchange and diffuse some of their volatility. The rules for these "riddling sessions" vary from culture to culture, but they always include appropriate framing devices that signal to all parties involved that someone is about to throw out an ambiguous question. In the case of riddles embedded in narratives, the frame in question could be a statement by the author, some aspect of the context that clearly indicates a contest of wits is about to begin, or a formulaic saying by one of the characters. As noted earlier, the most common verbal frames in the Gospels are "Whoever has ears, let them hear" and "What do you think?" When Jesus or another character utters these words, a riddle is sure to be close by. Sometimes, however, the author may forgo such formulae and simply tell the reader that a riddling session is about to begin. Mark, for example, prefaces the Pharisees' question about whether it is lawful to pay poll taxes to Caesar by explaining that they sought to "trap Jesus in a word" (12:13), and John says that Jesus wished to "test" Philip by telling him to provide food for a crowd of five thousand people (John 6:6). Normally, we ask questions to receive clarifying information that will resolve ambiguity; questions that intentionally confuse people in order to "trap" or "test" them are riddles. Sometimes an author will avoid such obvious statements and simply stage an episode as a riddling session, assuming that the reader will realize that a "trap" is being set. Oftentimes, some stereotypical opponent of Jesus—a Pharisee, scribe, chief priest—will suddenly appear and attempt to discredit his wisdom by asking him an ambiguous question in front of a crowd of people. In these and other ways, an author may signal to the reader that a riddling session is about to begin, meaning that some character will be challenged to unlock a difficult saying.

Criterion #3 identifies riddles on the basis of audience response. Sometimes neither the author nor the riddler will indicate directly that a statement is intentionally ambiguous, yet the reaction of the audience reveals that it can be interpreted in more than one way. In the Gospels, this normally means that the characters listening to Jesus are either confused or amazed by something he has just said; they can't determine what he's talking about or don't know how to respond. For example, at Mark 10:23 Jesus tells the disciples, "How hard it is for those who have riches to come into the Kingdom of God." Neither Mark nor Jesus calls this saying a "riddle," but Mark proceeds to say that the disciples "were shocked by his words" (v. 24). They were, in fact, so shocked that Mark mentions it a second time at verse 26, where the disciples proceed to highlight the difficulty of Jesus' comment by asking one another, "Then who can be saved?" Sometimes Jesus' audience may even verbalize the various possible answers as they attempt to reason out his meaning. Thus, when Jesus stands in the temple courts and invites the Pharisees, "Destroy this temple, and I will raise it in three days," they can only highlight the absurdity of his proposition by noting, "This temple has been under construction for forty-six years, and you will raise it in three days?" (John 2:19–20). Clearly, Jesus must be talking about something else, and John makes sure that his reader knows exactly what that "something else" is—"the temple of his body" (v. 21). Criterion #3 assumes, of course, that storytellers do not normally portray characters "speaking nonsense" (unless the character is supposed to be some kind of fool), and particularly that the early Christians would not portray Jesus in this way. If people can't understand what Jesus is talking about, that must be what he meant to happen; it certainly isn't because he made a poor choice of words.[5] Such statements may therefore be interpreted as riddles.

Criterion #4 depends on the fact that riddles, as noted in chapter 1, often do their work by playing with boundaries in the group's belief system. Riddles generate confusion by bringing together words and/or things that are normally kept apart. It is therefore reasonable to argue that any saying that intentionally violates "normal" patterns of thought or language in order to generate ambiguity *may* be a riddle. Criterion #4 applies to the numerous instances in the sources where Jesus makes a statement that obviously requires a redefinition of terms. At Mark 3:33, for example, Jesus asks, "Who are my mother, and who are my brothers?" when in point of fact his mother and brothers are standing right outside the door. Obviously, he is not using these words in the normal, biological sense, as he immediately proceeds to explain. At a deeper conceptual level, this criterion also applies to those sayings that play on one of Jesus' pet themes: reversal of the natural and/or social order. Mark 9:35, for example, shows Jesus scolding the disciples for their aspirations to greatness by informing them that "if anyone wants to be first, he must be last of all and servant of all." Neither Mark nor Jesus nor the disciples explicitly state that this remark is ambiguous; they do not state this simply because there is no need to do so. By any line of thinking, "first" and "last" are polar opposites, making it impossible for anything or any person to stand in both categories at once. Yet this is exactly what Jesus calls his followers to do. In all these cases, the artful manipulation of normal thought patterns indicates a riddling session is underway.

Obviously, criterion #4 differs from the others in that it requires us to appeal to information that may not be explicit in the text under consideration. We must know, for example, that Jesus' associates would normally identify Mary as his "mother" and that people in his culture would normally treat "first" and "last" as distinct categories. We must also understand that it would be unusual for a person in Jesus' time to say that a widow's two mites are worth more than a rich man's treasure (Mark 12:43), that old people in Jesus' society would not normally ask children for advice on spiritual matters (*Thomas* 4:1), and that Jews in Roman Palestine would find it hard to explain how a poor beggar could get into heaven ahead of a rich man (Luke 16:19–31). If we do not know such things, we will not notice that Jesus is asking or answering a question that challenges conventional ways of thinking. Criterion #4 is therefore somewhat more subjective than the first three, in that it requires us to make assumptions about what Jesus, other characters in the story, and especially the author of the source understood to be the "normal" outlook on life. It depends, in other words, on our ability to construct the social world in which Jesus lived. I do not claim to be an expert in that project and have therefore attempted to apply this criterion cautiously, fully aware that my more historically astute readers may challenge some of my assertions and/or (I hope) argue that I have excluded some apparently obvious examples.

A SAMPLE OF SAGE RIDDLES

The four criteria discussed above can be applied to any of the available sources for Jesus to identify instances where he asks or answers riddles. I myself have applied them to Matthew, Mark, Luke, John, and *Thomas* to locate specimens for discussion in this book, and I have included some of the results of my search on the table below. Before you proceed to look at that list, however, I would like to explain two things: why I call this a "table" rather than a "database"; and why I say that this table includes only some, admittedly not even the majority, of the riddles that appear in the available sources for Jesus (or even in the five sources that I've used). Hopefully, the answers to these questions will explain why I have been so selective in choosing texts for consideration and discussion here, all the while highlighting my sincere desire to avoid manipulation of the data in service of my agenda.

First, the table below *is* a "database" in the general sense that it includes all the texts that I discuss in detail in this book (although this book does not discuss every text on the table). It is therefore fair to call it a "database" *for my argument*, the source of the examples that I've chosen to use. But it is *not* a database for my outlook on the historical Jesus; I do not, in other words, claim that the riddles that appear on this table are more likely than others to be historically authentic. As a corollary, my exclusion of any specific riddle from any specific source does not reflect an opinion that said riddle is any more or less historical than any that I have included. It simply reflects the fact that said riddle does not directly figure in my argument. The table below, then, should be viewed as a sampling of texts from some of the available sources that suggest Jesus engaged in riddling as an aspect of his public ministry; as such it may or may not overlap at times with the databases used by real historical Jesus scholars.

Second, the table below is a "sampling" in the technical sense that it includes only some—not all, or even the majority—of the passages from the available sources that meet one of my criteria for identifying riddles. Put another way: all the riddles listed here do meet at least one of the criteria discussed above, but not every passage in the sources that meets one of the criteria appears on this table. I have not excluded these other sayings because they threaten my argument (at least, not at any conscious level), but rather simply because they raise points of controversy that are tangential to our discussion.

Two specific limitations have been imposed on my database. First, the table below only includes riddles that occur during the public ministry of Jesus, meaning that it excludes passages like John 1:15, Luke 2:49, and the many riddles that appear in the Synoptic accounts of the Last Supper and John's Farewell Address (John 13–17). Obviously, this limitation creates some difficulty in the case of the *Gospel of Thomas*, as it is not entirely clear whether the author of that book thinks that some or all of the sayings contained therein were communicated privately to the apostle Thomas (see the prologue). This problem is beyond my power to resolve, and certainly beyond the scope of this book. For purposes of this study, I have decided to treat the Thomasine riddles as "public" because their settings, when indicated, seem to me generally consistent with the portrayal of Jesus' public ministry in Matthew, Mark, Luke, and John. Second, I have included only riddles that the sources use to portray Jesus as a person of unusual wit, thereby excluding passages that involve Jesus' ambiguous predictions of his own death (like Mark 9:9, 30; 10:33–34) and christological statements relating to Jesus' identity and mission (like Matt. 16:8; John 7:34; *Thomas* 13). This does not, again, reflect a belief that no such riddles originated with the historical Jesus; it reflects, instead, my willingness to concede points that are not essential to my argument. As noted in the preface, my conclusions do not depend on the possibility that Jesus uttered or answered any specific riddle, but rather on the likelihood that he used riddles *at all*. This being the case, more is better for my argument, and I would be very happy if you should wish to include other passages that I have left off the table.

I should also note that both the table below and my discussion throughout this book—specifically, my selection of texts for discussion—reflect two further rules of thumb. First, when a saying appears in relatively the same form in more than one source, I have tended to cite and discuss the version available in Mark or, if the unit does not appear in Mark, the version available in Luke. As a result, the table below is heavy on passages from Mark and Luke, with Matthew and *Thomas* cited only where they alone attest to a saying. I leave it to those of you who are interested to look up the relevant parallels. This rule obviously reflects today's dominant theories of literary dependence, which give priority to Mark and use Luke as the default versification for Q. I am not a big supporter of that model—either of Markan priority or, especially, of a fixed Q text—but I acknowledge it here as a concession to those who do favor it. Once again, I will not object to those who may prefer the parallels in Matthew or *Thomas* or the Egerton Gospel, simply because I don't think it will affect my conclusions one way or the other.

Second, a special note should be made on the riddles that appear in the *Gospel of Thomas*. The prologue and logion 1 of the *Gospel of Thomas* portray everything that Jesus says as a riddle, and grant eternal life to those who are able to unlock his puzzles: "These are the secret sayings that the living Jesus spoke and Didymos Judas Thomas recorded. And he said, 'Whoever discovers the interpretation of these sayings will not taste death.'" One could argue, then, that every verse in *Thomas* meets criterion #1 above, because the author seems to explicitly characterize *all* of Jesus' sayings as intentionally ambiguous. I have, however, included only sayings from *Thomas* that can be identified as riddles on other grounds as well, but I would gladly concede to those who wish to include even more texts from *Thomas*. As I said a moment ago, my case gets stronger as the list gets longer.

With all these caveats, I offer the following as a sampling of texts that portray Jesus in riddling sessions—specifically, texts that use riddles to emphasize Jesus' wit and wisdom as a sage without making explicit christological claims.

Jesus the Sage: A Sample of His Riddles		
Source	**Riddle(s) and Answer(s)***	**Criterion/a**
Matt. 17:25	**commenting on the two-drachma temple tax** Jesus said, "What do you think, Simon [Peter]? From whom do the kings of the earth receive customs and taxes? From their sons, or from strangers?" *Answer: "From strangers"; "Therefore, the sons are free" (v. 26).*	Matthew often uses "What do you think?" to introduce riddles. The obvious answer implies that a temple tax inherently treats worshippers as strangers rather than children.
Matt. 21:28–31	THE PARABLE OF THE TWO SONS Jesus said, "What do you think? ... Which of the two did the will of the father?" *Answer: "The first" (v. 31).*	Matthew often uses "What do you think?" to introduce riddles. Jesus' question is difficult because both children disgraced their father, one by lying to him and the other by telling him he would not do as he was commanded.
Mark 2:25–26	**response when told that his disciples should not pick grain on Sabbath** Jesus said to them, "Have you never read what David did when he was in need and became hungry, he and those with him? . . ." *Answer: "The Sabbath was made for people and not people for the Sabbath. Thus, the son of man is lord even of the Sabbath" (vv. 27–28).*	David is not generally seen as a sinner, yet the Scriptures say he flagrantly violated God's ordinances.
Mark 3:4	**question to those who accuse him of breaking Sabbath by healing a man with a lame hand** Jesus said to them, "Is it lawful on the Sabbath to do good or to do evil? To save a life, or to kill?" *Answer: Unstated; Jesus proceeds to heal the man, implying the answer, "to do good" (v. 5).*	The question restates the normal opposition "work/rest" as "do good/do evil" and implies that resting on Sabbath can be evil while working can be good.

*A statement in the Gospels is a "riddle" if: (1) the author says that it is; (2) it happens in a riddling session; (3) other characters are confused; (4) it's calculated to challenge normal thinking.

Source	Riddle(s) and Answer(s)*	Criterion/a
Mark 3:33	**question upon being told that his mother and brothers are looking for him** And answering, Jesus said to them, "Who is my mother, and who are my brothers?" *Answer: "Whoever does the will of God, that one is my brother and sister and mother" (v. 35).*	The question redefines the terms "mother," "brother," and "sister."
Mark 4:3–8	THE PARABLE OF THE SOWER And [Jesus] was saying, "Whoever has ears to hear, let them hear." *Answer: Unstated in the immediate context; in the Synoptics, Jesus provides a lengthy explanation for the disciples later on, defining the "seed" as his message and each "soil" as a type of person who responds to that message.*	Mark says that Jesus was teaching the crowds "many things in parables" (v. 2), and closes the episode by saying that Jesus told them many parables "as they were able to hear" (v. 33). The sources often use "Whoever has ears" to introduce Jesus' riddles. The disciples ask for a private explanation for this and other parables (vv. 10, 34). The size of all three harvest yields is ridiculously large, at least four times what would normally be expected.
Mark 4:30–32	THE PARABLE OF THE MUSTARD SEED "How shall we compare the Kingdom of God, or to what parable shall we liken it? It's like a mustard seed. ..." *Answer: Unstated*	Mark says that Jesus was teaching the crowds "many things in parables" (v. 2), and closes the episode by saying that Jesus told them many parables "as they were able to hear" (v. 33). Defies expectations by comparing the Kingdom to a lowly mustard bush rather than the mighty "cedar" that houses the birds in the Hebrew Bible.
Mark 7:14–15	And calling together the crowd again, Jesus was saying to them, "All of you listen to me and understand. There is nothing outside a man that is able to make him unclean by going into him." *Answer: "Because it does not go into his heart but rather into the stomach, and it comes out into the toilet" (v. 19).*	Jesus introduces the question with the formula, "Listen and understand," and then introduces the answer with, "Are you [disciples] also unable to understand?" The disciples ask Jesus exactly what the statement means (v. 17). Jesus' remark defies the traditional purity standards described at verses 3–4 and also seems to contradict Leviticus 11.

*A statement in the Gospels is a "riddle" if: (1) the author says that it is; (2) it happens in a riddling session; (3) other characters are confused; (4) it's calculated to challenge normal thinking.

(continued)

Source	Riddle(s) and Answer(s)*	Criterion/a
Mark 8:15	**comment to the disciples after feeding four thousand people and debating with the Pharisees over a "sign from heaven"** Jesus was commanding them, saying, "Watch out! Beware of the leaven of the Pharisees and the leaven of Herod!" *Answer: Unstated; Matthew 16:12 says that "leaven" represents the Pharisees' "teachings."*	Mark contextualizes the saying by noting that the disciples had taken only one loaf of bread in the boat, suggesting that "leaven" would most naturally refer to an ingredient for bread. Jesus asks the disciples, "Having eyes, don't you see? And having ears, don't you hear?" (v. 18); "Don't you understand yet?" (v. 21). The disciples are clearly confused by Jesus' words (vv. 16, 19–20).
Mark 9:35	**comment on the disciples' debate over who is greatest** And sitting down, he called the Twelve and said to them, "If anyone wants to be first, he will/must be last of all and servant of all." *Answer: Unstated*	Jesus' comment reverses the normal social order but does not explain how one can be "first/master" and "last/servant" at the same time.
Mark 10:3, 5–9, 11–12	**response to the question "whether it is lawful for a man to divorce his wife"** Jesus said to them, "What did Moses command you?" *Answer: Remarriage is adultery, despite Deuteronomy 24:1–4.*	Mark says that the Pharisees wish to "test" Jesus, indicating that an academic debate is about to begin (v. 2). The disciples question Jesus later about the meaning of his remarks (v. 10). Jesus suggests a contradiction between Genesis 2:24 and Deuteronomy 24:1–4 and resolves this contradiction by dismissing the latter text as a divine concession to human weakness; he then redefines the word "adultery."
Mark 10:14–15	**response to the disciples' effort to prevent children from coming to him** But seeing this, Jesus was angry and said to them, "Permit the children to come to me. Do not stop them, for the Kingdom of God belongs to such as these. Indeed, I tell you, whoever does not receive the Kingdom of God like a child will not enter it." *Answer: Unstated*	Jesus reverses the normal social order by granting Kingdom status to powerless individuals; the phrase "like a child" is then left undefined.

*A statement in the Gospels is a "riddle" if: (1) the author says that it is; (2) it happens in a riddling session; (3) other characters are confused; (4) it's calculated to challenge normal thinking.

Source	Riddle(s) and Answer(s)*	Criterion/a
Mark 10:23–25	Jesus, answering, said to them again, "Children, how hard it is to come into the Kingdom of God. It is easier for a camel to go through the eye of a needle than for a rich person to enter the Kingdom of God." *Answer: Unstated*	The disciples are "astonished" by Jesus' words and left to ask, "How can anyone be saved?" (vv. 24, 26). Jesus defies conventional thinking by stating that wealthy people do not enjoy God's special favor; reverses the normal social order by granting Kingdom status to the poor (note v. 31).
Mark 11:29–30	**response to the scribes' demand to know by what authority he acts and teaches** But Jesus said to them, "I will ask you one question, and should you answer me I also will answer to you 'by what authority I do these things.' John's baptism: was it from heaven or from men? Answer me." *Answer: Unstated; neither option is politically viable for Jesus' opponents (vv. 31–32).*	Jesus specifically states that he wants an answer and then names the stakes in the contest. Jesus' opponents admit that they cannot come up with a good answer (v. 33).
Mark 12:14	And coming to him, the Pharisees and the Herodians say, "… Is it lawful to give tribute to Caesar or not? Should we pay, or should we not pay?" *Answer: "Give Caesar's things to Caesar and God's things to God" (v. 17).*	Jesus notes that the Pharisees are "testing" him (v. 15). The question implies that paying taxes may be unlawful, thus challenging the current social order.
Mark 12:18–23	Sadduccees: "In the resurrection, of which of them will she be the wife?" *Answer: "When they rise from the dead, they are neither married nor given in marriage, but rather are like the angels in heaven" (v. 25).*	Mark portrays the question as insincere by noting that the Sadducees do not believe in resurrection. The question implies that Jesus' belief in resurrection somehow conflicts with a stipulation in the Mosaic Law.
Mark 12:43	**comment after watching a poor widow drop money into an offering box at the temple** And calling together his disciples, Jesus said to them, "Indeed, I tell you that this poor widow gave the most of all those who put something into the offering box." *Answer: "For all of them gave from their leftovers, but she from her shortage gave all that she had, her whole livelihood" (v. 44).*	Jesus reverses normal ways of thinking by suggesting that the widow's two coins are worth more than the "many things" put into the offering box by the rich (vv. 41–42).

*A statement in the Gospels is a "riddle" if: (1) the author says that it is; (2) it happens in a riddling session; (3) other characters are confused; (4) it's calculated to challenge normal thinking.

(continued)

Source	Riddle(s) and Answer(s)*	Criterion/a
Luke 6:20	Jesus said, "The poor are blessed." *Answer: "Because the Kingdom of God is yours" (v. 20).*	Jesus defies the popular association of wealth with divine blessing and reverses the normal social order by granting Kingdom status to the poor.
Luke 10:30–36	THE PARABLE OF THE GOOD SAMARITAN ". . . Which of these three seems to you to have been a neighbor of the one who fell victim to the bandits?" (v. 36) *Answer: "The one doing mercy for him" (v. 37).*	The speaker is a lawyer who wishes to publicly "test" Jesus' insight on key points of the Law (vv. 25, 29). The parable redefines the word "neighbor" and suggests that Samaritans are "neighbors" to Jews.
Luke 12:51–53	"You think that I came to make peace on earth? No, I tell you, but rather division." *Answer: Unstated*	The saying occurs in the midst of a long riddling session that includes several parables and ambiguous statements. The situation Jesus envisions violates ancient Mediterranean family values generally and Exodus 20:12 specifically.
Luke 14:3, 5	**upon healing a man on Sabbath** And Jesus, answering, spoke to the lawyers and Pharisees, saying, "Is it lawful to heal on the Sabbath or not? . . . Which one of you should have a son or an ox fall into a well, and would not immediately pull him out on a Sabbath day?" *Answer: Unstated (vv. 4, 6); context implies that it is lawful to heal on Sabbath.*	Jesus offers both questions as public challenges to the lawyers who are "watching him" (v. 1). Jesus challenges conventional thinking about Sabbath work and healing as a form of "work."
Luke 14:26	Jesus said, "If anyone comes to me and does not hate his own father and mother and wife and children and brothers and sisters and even his own life, he cannot be my disciple." *Answer: Unstated*	The statement explicitly violates Exodus 20:12, Genesis 2:24, Leviticus 19:18, and Jesus' own teachings on marriage elsewhere.

*A statement in the Gospels is a "riddle" if: (1) the author says that it is; (2) it happens in a riddling session; (3) other characters are confused; (4) it's calculated to challenge normal thinking.

Source	Riddle(s) and Answer(s)*	Criterion/a
Luke 15:4–6	THE PARABLE OF THE LOST SHEEP Does he not leave the ninety-nine in the wilderness and search for the lost one until he has found it? *Answer: "There will be greater joy in heaven over one sinner who repents than over ninety-nine righteous people who do not need repentance" (v. 7).*	Luke stages the parable as one of several responses to the Pharisees' accusation that Jesus eats with sinners (v. 2); Matthew 18:12 introduces the parable with the formula, "What do you think?" The shepherd foolishly risks the lives of ninety-nine sheep in hopes of saving one, and his joyful celebration seems somewhat excessive.
Luke 15:11–32	THE PARABLE OF THE PRODIGAL SON [The older son] said to his father, "Look, all this time I have served you and never departed from your command. But when this son of yours, who wasted your money on whores, came, you killed the fatted calf for him . . ." *Answer: Unstated*	Luke stages the parable as one of several responses to the Pharisees' accusation that Jesus eats with sinners (v. 2). The parable portrays God as foolishly naive and depicts both sons as disobedient and disrespectful; in Luke's context, the parable places "sinners" and "table fellows" in the same category.
Luke 16:1–8	THE PARABLE OF THE DISHONEST STEWARD . . . And the master praised the dishonest steward because he acted wisely. *Answer: "And I say to you, make for yourselves friends by dishonest wealth, so that when it fails they would receive you into eternal dwellings" (v. 9).*	A character in the parable is praised for a flagrantly sinful act; the answer challenges the conventional view that wealth is a sign of divine blessing (see v. 14).
Luke 16:19–31	THE PARABLE OF THE RICH MAN AND LAZARUS . . . But it happened that the poor man died, and he was carried by the angels to the bosom of Abraham. But also the rich man died and was buried, and in Hades he lifted his eyes, being possessed of pain, and saw Abraham at a distance and Lazarus in his bosom. . . . *Answer: Unstated; perhaps implied at verse 25, "But Abraham said, 'Child, recall that you received good things in your life, and Lazarus likewise bad things; but now here he is comforted, and you are tormented.'"*	The parable reverses the current social order and defies conventional thinking by equating poverty with eternal reward and wealth with eternal suffering.

*A statement in the Gospels is a "riddle" if: (1) the author says that it is; (2) it happens in a riddling session; (3) other characters are confused; (4) it's calculated to challenge normal thinking.

(continued)

Source	Riddle(s) and Answer(s)*	Criterion/a
Luke 17:20–21	**upon being asked by the Pharisees when the Kingdom of God would come** Jesus answered them and said, "The Kingdom of God is not coming with observable things. Nor will they say, 'Behold! Here!' For the Kingdom of God is among/within you." *Answer: Unstated*	Jesus talks about the Kingdom all the time; the Pharisees now challenge him to explain exactly what and where it is (v. 20). Jesus redefines popular assumptions about the Kingdom of God.
Luke 18:2–6	THE PARABLE OF THE UNJUST JUDGE "… because this widow is a bother to me I will give her justice, because she will wear me out by endlessly coming to me." *Answer: "Shall not God do justice for his elect who cry out to him day and night?" (v. 7)*	The parable compares God, who epitomizes justice, to an unjust judge.
Luke 18:10–14	THE PARABLE OF THE PHARISEE AND THE TAX COLLECTOR Jesus said, "… I tell you, this man [the tax collector] went down to his house having been justified, rather than that one." *Answer: "Everyone who exalts himself will be humbled, but the one who humbles himself will be exalted" (v. 14).*	The parable suggests that fasting, prayer, and tithes cannot secure forgiveness for a righteous person, while confession alone can secure forgiveness for a sinner.
John 8:4–5 (although probably not written by the author of John)	**the scribes and Pharisees question Jesus about a woman caught in adultery** They say to him, "This woman was caught in the act of adultery. In the Law, Moses commanded us to stone such women. So what do you say?" *Answer: "The sinless one among you, let him cast a stone at her first" (v. 7).*	The narrator states that the Pharisees are "testing" Jesus to establish grounds for an accusation. The Pharisees confront Jesus while he is teaching in the temple and use the woman as an illustration to sharpen the public challenge. The question forces Jesus to either condemn the woman or disregard the Law.

---

*A statement in the Gospels is a "riddle" if: (1) the author says that it is; (2) it happens in a riddling session; (3) other characters are confused; (4) it's calculated to challenge normal thinking.

Source	Riddle(s) and Answer(s)*	Criterion/a
Thomas 4:1	Jesus said, "The person old in days won't hesitate to ask a little child seven days old about the place of life, and that person will live." *Answer: Unstated*	Jesus reverses the normal social order by making elders dependent on children for life-giving wisdom.
Thomas 14:1–3	Jesus said to them, "If you fast, you will bring sin upon yourselves, and if you pray, you will be condemned, and if you give to charity, you will harm your spirits." *Answer: Unstated*	Jesus states that standard Jewish acts of piety are in fact spiritually harmful.
Thomas 18:2–3	**upon being asked by the disciples how their end would come** Jesus said, "Have you found the beginning, then, that you are looking for the end? You see, the end will be where the beginning is. Congratulations to the one who stands at the beginning: that one will know the end and will not taste death." *Answer: Unstated*	"Beginning" and "end" are opposites, yet Jesus implies that the two are synonymous.
Thomas 19:1	Jesus said, "Congratulations to the one who came into being before coming into being." *Answer: Unstated*	Something cannot exist before it exists.
Thomas 53:2	Upon being asked by the disciples whether circumcision is beneficial or not Jesus said to them, "If it [circumcision] were useful, their father would produce children already circumcised from their mother." *Answer: "Rather, the true circumcision in spirit has become profitable in every respect"* (v. 3).	Jesus' statement violates normal Jewish thinking about the value of circumcision.

*A statement in the Gospels is a "riddle" if: (1) the author says that it is; (2) it happens in a riddling session; (3) other characters are confused; (4) it's calculated to challenge normal thinking.

All translations from the Greek New Testament are my own, and are intended to highlight the inherent ambiguity of the saying where possible. For the *Gospel of Thomas*, I have followed the translation in *The Complete Gospels*.[6]

Doubtless you noticed, while reflecting on this table, that I have been so bold as to include "answers" to some of the riddles. These were derived from the literary context in which each riddle now appears, and I have noted such answers here to remind you of the way that these ambiguous questions were contextualized by the authors of the sources. Of course, many scholars would immediately question whether these literary contexts were original—whether the sources accurately reflect the setting of specific sayings in the ministry of the historical Jesus. They may or may not, but let me reiterate that I am not even arguing here that these specific riddles originated with Jesus, only that they meet literary criteria that suggest that they are, in fact, riddles. Much less do I wish to argue that Mark's and Luke's and *Thomas*'s proposed answers go back to Jesus. At the very least, the answers that the sources offer or imply represent ways that early Christians—people much closer to Jesus than myself—attempted to understand his puzzles. I would also note that in many instances the sources do not specify an answer ("unstated"), meaning that some early Christians either did not feel compelled to resolve all of Jesus' ambiguous statements or did not know exactly how to resolve them.[7] The fact that some of these riddles are not answered in the sources is itself significant, for reasons that will be explored in chapter 5.

A second observation about these answers is also relevant. In reviewing this table, you may have noticed that many of the "answers" don't actually look like answers: they don't seem to directly respond to a specific term or problem raised by the ambiguous question. For example, the statement, "Let the sinless one among you cast a stone at her first" does not seem to exactly answer the question of whether the Law says that an adulterous woman should be stoned; in point of fact, it looks like Jesus is skirting the issue (John 8:4–7). Of course, it is very possible that in some cases I have not entirely understood the answer a source intends to offer, and have therefore missed the point or made things more complicated than they need to be. But I would also stress that the notion that "answers" should fit smoothly into the terms of the question reflects a modern Western way of thinking, one that arises from the fact that most of our riddles are recreational puzzles that admit of short and simple solutions. The parable of the Pharisee and the Publican is a complex story that confuses several core values in ancient Jewish religious thought, and its "answer" must somehow resolve that challenge by redefining the relevant terms and categories. Such an answer will therefore look quite a bit more complicated than the solutions to the word games that we see every day in the newspaper next to the crossword puzzle. Similarly, the statement, "The master praised the dishonest steward because he acted wisely," does not lend itself to a simple solution in any context where the "master" is obviously God. I am sure that more than one doctoral dissertation could be (or has been) written on the subject. The "answers" to riddles such as these are therefore often somewhat complex and/or indirect, as much as this may bother us today.

Thus far, I have attempted to paint with broad strokes, defining riddles and riddling sessions and discussing criteria for locating riddles in narratives. The chapters in part 2 will narrow the focus to highlight aspects of riddling that are particularly relevant to the sources for, and ministry of, Jesus.

PART 2

Jesus the Riddler

5

The Art of the Absurd: Parables and Puzzles; or "The Kingdom of God Is Just Like That, except It's the Exact Opposite"

In chapter 4, I presented a table of riddles that portray Jesus as a sage, a person of unusual wit who was able both to propose and to answer difficult ambiguous statements. You doubtless noted that most of the puzzles on that table do not take the form of questions; they tend to be propositions ("the poor are blessed"; "the Kingdom belongs to children"), sometimes accompanied by a formula to signal explicitly that the audience is supposed to respond ("What do you think?" "Whoever has ears"; "Don't you understand?"). But once we get past the fact that they are not grammatically interrogative (i.e., that they don't look like questions), modern Western readers can easily see that many of these riddles resemble the brainteasers that amuse us today. Thus, we are well within our comfort zone when Jesus asks whether kings receive taxes from sons or strangers (Matt. 17:25), or how a widow's two mites could be worth more than a rich man's treasure (Mark 12:43), or how the end could be where the beginning is (*Thomas* 18:2–3). All these statements feel like what we call "riddles," and for this reason scholars of the Gospels intuitively refer to them as such from time to time.

But you doubtless also noted that many of the riddles on my table look like something else; that is, some of them don't look like what we call "riddles." Some of Jesus' riddles, for example, play on shock value, implying things that are somewhat disturbing—like insisting that we must hate our children (Luke 14:26), or calling remarriage "adultery" (Mark 10:11–12), or claiming that it's bad to give money to charities (*Thomas* 14:1–3). These aren't nice things to say, and they aren't funny; such statements may not feel like "riddles" simply because we generally think that riddles are supposed to be amusing. Aside from these instances, many of the examples on the table in chapter 4 don't look like riddles because we have tended to classify them as another genre of speech. I am referring here specifically to the nine *parables* that appear on my list. Generally, we think of the parable as a very distinct speech genre, one with its own special themes and rules of argument. This impression is reinforced by our tendency to see parables as the most distinct element of Jesus' teaching style, the thing that really set him apart from his contemporaries. Perhaps for this reason, some scholars have sensed a need to distinguish parables from riddles or at least to discuss them in isolation from one another. Herman Waetjen, for example, insists that Jesus' parables "are ambiguous stories and images. They are not simply riddles!" This is the case because the parables, apparently unlike riddles, are "transparent pedagogical devices" for "those to whom the mystery of God's rule has been given," but at the same time "opaque metaphors that preclude participation" for those who fall outside Jesus' circle.[1] Maybe, then, the criteria that I have used to identify riddles are not tight enough, allowing specimens of another genre to sneak into my database.

I concede the possibility that I may have failed to adequately distinguish two things that should be kept apart. Perhaps the fact that my criteria mark some parables as riddles reveals a fatal flaw in my model. Yet I would make two points in self-defense. First, as I have said several times now, riddles can take a wide variety of forms. A riddle is a riddle because it uses intentional ambiguity and expects an answer, not because it looks or sounds a certain way. Almost any statement can function as a riddle, depending on the context and the speaker/author's intention. I say "*almost* any," but in point of fact I can't think of a single statement that could not be used as a riddle by someone in some situation (please e-mail me if you can think of one). There is therefore no inherent reason why parables could not function as riddles from time to time. Second, the four criteria that I have used to identify riddles in the sources for Jesus—which in my view reflect mainstream folklore research—clearly mark some of the parables as intentionally ambiguous statements that solicit a response (thought not necessarily a verbal response) from the audience. These two facts suggest that there is no reason to think that parables could not function as riddles, and there are many good reasons to think that some of them would.

JESUS PROBABLY USED PARABLES AS RIDDLES

Of course, even if you would concede that some parables could function as riddles, you might also argue that this reflects the literary style of the sources, not the teaching style of the historical Jesus. You might, for example, note that six of the parable-riddles on my table come from Luke, and a number of other

Lukan parables not included there also function as riddles in their respective contexts.[2] Luke, then, clearly likes to present Jesus' parables as ambiguous statements that challenge the audience to respond with some sort of "correct" answer. Has he perhaps skewed his sources and traditions to serve this interest? Because this issue is significant to my overall argument, I will pause for a moment to offer three responses to this line of inquiry.

First, while Luke does indeed like to use parables as riddles, this tendency is by no means unique to his presentation. Mark, Matthew, and John (see 10:1–6) also use parables as riddles, and the parable of the Sower is presented as a riddle in Mark (4:3–8), Matthew (13:3–8), Luke (8:5–8), and *Thomas* (9:1–5). I could, in fact, argue that Mark and *Thomas* implicitly treat *all* of Jesus' parables as riddles. Mark 4—which is widely viewed as the interpretive key to all the parables in Mark—uses the word "parable" in a way that is obviously synonymous with παροιμία, a difficult saying that Jesus is challenging someone to figure out (Mark 4:2, 33–34). Rhoads and Michie have therefore noted that "it is more appropriate to refer to them [Mark's parables] as riddles" because "they must be deciphered by other characters in the story in order for their meaning to be disclosed."[3] According to Mark, only those members of Jesus' audience to whom "the mystery of the Kingdom of God has been given" (4:11) will be able to receive this secret meaning. The *Gospel of Thomas* extends this same challenge to the reader, who is immediately told that she must discover the interpretation of the sayings contained in the book in order to obtain life (1). For those who may find this a daunting task, the Thomasine Jesus assures us that "I will disclose my mysteries to those who are worthy of my mysteries" (62:1). Clearly, however, very few people are thus worthy, for Jesus rarely discloses what he is talking about. Specifically here, Thomas offers no interpretation—not even to the disciples in private or to the reader in an aside—of any of the fourteen parables that he records (with one possible exception).[4] For Mark and *Thomas* as well as Luke, then, parables are "riddles" in the sense that their true meaning is evident only to members of Jesus' community of knowledge. While this fact does not prove that Jesus himself used specific parables as riddles, it does demonstrate that he is portrayed as doing so in a wide range of sources.

Second, while the fact that parables are used as riddles in several different sources does not necessarily prove that Jesus used them this way himself, I would observe that a number of the parables on my table would function as riddles in almost any context in which they might appear. Put another way, I cannot think of any situation in the ministry of Jesus where some of these parables would not be viewed as intentionally ambiguous statements that beg the audience for resolution. The question, then, is not whether Jesus used certain of these parables as riddles, but whether he used them *at all*. If he used them at all, he must have used them as riddles, unless he used them in a form very different from what we see in the Gospels today. A convenient example may be drawn from one of Jesus' best-known parables—indeed, one of the best-known passages in the Christian canon—the parable of the Good Samaritan. The Good Samaritan is particularly significant to my argument simply because scholars almost unanimously attribute at least some version of it to the historical Jesus.

As I noted in chapter 4, the parable of the Good Samaritan (Luke 10:30–35) may be classified as a "riddle" both on the basis of its context and of its content (my criteria #2 and #4). In terms of content, the parable clearly violates conventional thinking by portraying a Samaritan as a "moral exemplar," the savior of a Jew who has been left to die by bandits, a priest, and a Levite.[5] Perhaps for this reason, Luke has contextualized the parable as Jesus' response to the question, "Who is my neighbor?" (v. 29), one round in a lawyer's attempt to "test" his theological insight (v. 25). The lawyer and Jesus agree that observance of Leviticus 19:18 ("Love your neighbor as yourself") is critical to eternal life, but the lawyer wishes to define the scope of the provision by asking exactly who should receive this love. Jesus answers by telling the story, then leaves the lawyer with a counterquestion: "Which of these three [priest, Levite, or Samaritan] seems to you to have been a neighbor of the one who fell victim to the bandits?" (Luke 10:36). The story about the Good Samaritan thus shows a high level of integration into its current literary context, and we could therefore reasonably speculate that Luke has turned a traditional parable into an academic riddle simply because it suited his purposes to do so. It isn't hard to see why Luke might want to demonstrate Jesus' intellectual superiority over a recognized expert in Jewish Law. In support of this argument, we might proceed to point out that Matthew and Mark do not handle the question about the "greatest commandment" in quite the same way. In their versions, Jesus simply quotes Deuteronomy 6:5 ("Love God") and Leviticus 19:18 ("Love your neighbor") himself, creating a much less dramatic scene (see Mark 12:28–34; Matt. 22:34–40). These facts could suggest that Luke has turned a parable into a riddle.

In response to this reasonable line of argument, I would say two things. First, there is no question but that Luke has done a fairly decent job of integrating the parable of the Good Samaritan into the flow of his own narrative; I readily concede this point.[6] But, second, whether Luke's narrative setting does or does not reflect the original setting of that story in the ministry of the historical Jesus, it seems to me that, however you slice it, "the parable itself is intended to provoke."[7] Crossan, for example, senses that there must have been "a totally different, even generically different, meaning to this story at an earlier level [i.e., when Jesus told it] than is now given to it within the interpretive frames of Luke 10." Yet he builds on this claim not to reduce the ambiguity of the story, but rather to underscore the fact that this parable is inherently "provocative" because its "evident idealization of a Samaritan makes this narrative extremely dissimilar from the viewpoint of ancient Judaism"—"dissimilar" in the sense that it utterly defies the way that Jews in Roman Palestine thought about reality. The Good Samaritan clearly blurs the lines between conventional conceptual categories by "put[ting] together two impossible and contradictory words," "good" and "Samaritan." Further, it brings these two impossible words together while at the same time suggesting that priests and

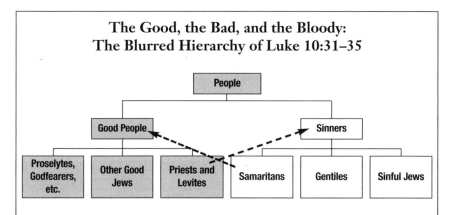

The Good, the Bad, and the Bloody:
The Blurred Hierarchy of Luke 10:31–35

The Parable of the Good Samaritan challenges conventional ways of thinking by describing a Samaritan, who would theoretically fall under the category "sinner," as a "good person," while suggesting that priests and Levites may not be "good people." In this case, the ambiguity challenges both conventional uses of the word "good" and also the larger classification scheme that sharply distinguishes between "Jews" and "Samaritans."

Levites may not really be "good people" after all. It is fair to say that the whole notion of "goodness" is called into question by this story.[8]

My point here is simply that *the ambiguities that classify the parable of the Good Samaritan as a riddle do not derive solely from Luke's application of the story to the context at hand.* These ambiguities are inherent in the story itself, and they would cry out for resolution in any context in which that story might be told—at least in any context where the audience was even vaguely aware of normal relations between Samaritans and Jews. If anything, Luke has actually toned down the ambiguity of the tale by making it at least vaguely applicable to some aspect of Christian living. Thus, if Jesus uttered the parable of the Good Samaritan *at all*, it must have functioned in his teaching as a riddle—an intentionally ambiguous statement that the audience was challenged to figure out.

If it did not function that way in his teaching, the original version must have looked so different from what we see in Luke's Gospel that there is no hope of recovering it.

Of course, all I have said here cannot prove that specific parable-riddles that appear in the sources were actually uttered by Jesus. My point, however, is not to argue that Jesus said any specific thing, but rather to suggest that he used parables as riddles and to explore the implications of that possibility. In my view, this possibility is entirely likely, not only because many sources suggest that he did this and because many of the parables recorded in the sources are inherently ambiguous, but also because parables and riddles, as different as they may seem to us at first glance, actually *do the same things in the same ways*. I noted in chapter 1

**Jesus Probably
Used Parables as Riddles**

1. Many different sources say that he did (Mark, Matt., Luke, John, *Thomas*, etc.).

2. Some of the parables would meet the criteria for riddling in any context in which they would appear (they're naturally ambiguous and challenging).

3. Parables and riddles do the same things in the same ways.

---

that some folklorists have treated the riddle as a type of metaphor; parables may also be treated as metaphors. I also noted earlier that riddles generate confusion by blurring the lines between conventional conceptual categories; many of Jesus' parables do the same thing. Riddles and parables both use metaphorical language to create ambiguity and then play on the rhetorical effects of that ambiguity. To further explore the relationship between these two genres, it will be necessary to examine the ways in which parables, as metaphors, achieve their rhetorical effect.[9]

EMPTY METAPHORS AND APPLIED AMBIGUITY

As you surveyed the table in chapter 4, you may have noticed that many of Jesus' sage riddles are never really "answered"; the sources don't tell us exactly how the ambiguity should be resolved. Sometimes, of course, Jesus will say something confusing and then clarify what he is talking about. He states, for example, that a widow's two mites are worth more to God than a rich man's millions, but immediately clarifies that this is the case because she has given from her need while he has shared his leftovers (Mark 12:43–44). Similarly, at Mark 3:33–35, Jesus confuses the crowd by asking them, "Who is my mother?" while Mary stands at the door, but proceeds to explain that "whoever does the will of God, that one is my mother." Sometimes when Jesus does not offer a specific answer, the author of the source will help the reader along.

Matthew, for example, lets us know that when Jesus spoke of the "leaven of the Pharisees" he was not actually talking about "yeast" but rather about the "teachings" of those people (16:6–12). Yet with all these instances aside, it remains the case that at least fifteen of the entries on my table of sage riddles—almost half of them—are not "answered" by information provided in the source. They are, as it were, simply splattered on the wall for all the world to see, with no attempt to clean up the cognitive mess that they make.

Because the sources provide definitive answers to Jesus' riddles so often, we may be tempted to think that their authors simply assumed that we could just guess the rest of them. Perhaps Mark thought that the answer to the question, "Is it lawful on the Sabbath to do good or to do evil? To save a life, or to kill?" would be obvious, so obvious that there was no need to say it. We always find it redundant, and often insulting, when people state the obvious. Yet, answers are often lacking in the very instances where they are *least* obvious, the points where we would most like to know precisely what Jesus had in mind. Exactly what did he mean when he said that I cannot be his disciple unless I "hate" my parents, spouse, and children (Luke 14:26)? Just how much money would make it more difficult to squeeze me into the Kingdom of God than to push a camel through the eye of a needle (Mark 10:23–25)? How can the first be last, or the end be where the beginning is (Mark 9:35; *Thomas* 18:2)? And how can anyone, without an definitive interpretation from Jesus himself, even hope to *translate* the word ἐντὸς at Luke 17:21, much less to live by this teaching? Is the Kingdom of God "within" the Pharisees (KJV, NIV) or "in the midst of" the Pharisees (NASB) or "among" the Pharisees (NRSV) or "right there in the presence" of the Pharisees (Scholars Version) or "here with" the Pharisees (CEV)? Or is the term being redefined in a way that defies every lexicon? We must know such things in order to apply Jesus' teaching to our lives, yet it is at these key moments that definitive answers elude us. Instead, the sources leave us with unresolved ambiguity, a lingering suspicion that the world may not be as neat and simple as we think, but no clear vision of exactly how it ought to be.

Whether or not Jesus himself used unanswered riddles to leave his audience hanging on a thread of ambiguity—and I would only point out here again that several different sources suggest that he did this very thing fairly often—there can be little doubt that this is exactly what he did with many of his parables. In my view, Jesus' riddles, parables, and parable-riddles all functioned in a similar way: to confront his audience with something ambiguous or absurd, something that would force them to redefine key terms and realign mental boundaries. In some instances, Jesus doubtless resolved this ambiguity himself by offering an interpretation or "answer" to the problem, whether publicly for the crowds or privately for the disciples (the Gospels suggest that he might do

either or both from time to time). But if the sources are at all accurate, it
appears that he was often content to leave the tensions unresolved, forcing his
audience to come up with a viable solution. He achieved this effect by playing
with the ways that parables and riddles work as *metaphors*, figures of speech
that bring two distinct things together. Specifically here, Jesus' parable-riddles
harnessed the power of ambiguity by using metaphors that are "empty," intentionally devoid of any single, obvious reference point.[10]

To explain how "empty metaphors" work, and how Jesus' unanswered riddles and parable-riddles worked as "empty metaphors," I will first need to
define what a "metaphor" is, describe how a metaphor could be "empty," and
then explain how Jesus could exploit this emptiness to make a point. For purposes of our discussion, I will utilize the linguistic theory of I. A. Richards to
define "metaphors" and "empty metaphors."[11] Let me stress at the outset that
my remarks here will be necessarily somewhat brief, and will therefore (a) consciously bypass a number of admittedly significant issues, and (b) fail to interact extensively with previous research on the parables. While my approach is,
in my view, generally consistent with that research (at least the more recent
research), my focus is much narrower. Specifically, I am not seeking here
definitively to define the parable as a speech genre, but rather only to show
that Jesus' parables and riddles could and did function in very similar ways.

Because the metaphor is a figure of speech, any theory about how
metaphors work must begin with a theory about how language works in general—a theory that describes how words are linked to the things and ideas that
they describe. I. A. Richards, like almost all recent language theorists, suggests
that words and things have an indirect relationship: words aren't somehow
naturally connected to what they're talking about, but are instead connected
to their referents indirectly, through cultural conventions. For example, the
thing that you are looking at and reading right now is called a "book" in the
English language. We call it a "book" not because that word has some sort of
cosmic bond with this object, but rather simply because people who speak
English have agreed to use that word when talking about this thing. In a similar way, Germans have agreed to call it *Buch*, while the French prefer *livre*.
The word ("book") and this physical object are thus connected indirectly,
through a set of cultural conventions and personal ideas.

Richards refers to this matrix of conventions and ideas as the "psychological context" of the word, and stresses that the meaning of any word "depend[s]
upon the past history of the organism."[12] You have encountered things called
"books" before, and those experiences have taught you to expect certain
things. If you generally have negative feelings about "books" of this type—say
you find "books" like this one to be boring or difficult to read—then you will
assume that this "book" is also boring and difficult to read. The "meaning" of

what we say or write, then, depends on the relationship that exists between *things*, the *ideas* we have about those things, and the *words* we use to discuss those things.[13] These three points—things, ideas, and words—and the links between them create a semantic triangle.

Significantly, the three sides of the semantic triangle are not the same. The word ("book") and the thing that this word describes (a book) have one kind of relationship, while a different relationship connects the word "book" to your ideas about books and your ideas to the object itself. Specifically, the connections we make between words and things are not solid, a reflection of the fact that "between the symbol and the referent there is no relevant relation other than the indirect one."[14] This simply means, as I noted just a moment ago, that our words don't go straight to the things that we are talking about; our words get to their referents only through our preformed ideas about those things. I call this object a "book" because I live in a culture that does so. This culture has given me not only the word "book" but also a set of ideas about books, what they do and what they are like. To this preformed set of ideas I have added my own beliefs and reflections, based on past personal experiences. On the basis of such experiences, you may have come to think that books like this one are boring and hard to read, and within this psychological context you assume that the book you are now holding will also be difficult.

Such is the way that all language works; let us now turn to the metaphor as a specific type of figurative language. As noted in chapter 1, the metaphor is a figure of speech that compares two things for sake of effect: "he's a stud," "she's a total babe," "kisses sweeter than honey."[15] The subject of the metaphor—the thing that is being discussed—is called the "tenor"; the thing to which that subject is being compared is called the "vehicle."[16] Thus, in the simple metaphor "she's a total babe," "she" (the girl under consideration) is the tenor, while "babe" is the vehicle that describes her. Technically, the girl is being compared to a baby.[17] Yet it is important to note the point on the semantic triangle at which the metaphor does its work. If two young men are speaking about a certain young woman and one of them says, "She's a total babe," obviously that individual is not suggesting that the meaning of either of these English words—"she" or "babe"—should be redefined. He is not, in other words, suggesting that they should henceforth use the word "babe" to refer only to the girl in question, and consequently should no longer call infants "babies." The metaphor does not play with the relationship between the words and their referents; rather, the metaphor operates at the level of the psychological context. Specifically, *a metaphor combines the psychological context of one word with that of another*. Richards therefore defines "metaphor" as "a borrowing between and intercourse of *thoughts*," a figure of speech that mixes elements from different sets of ideas.[18]

To return to my earlier example: imagine, if you will, that a certain girl has been asked to write a review of this book (the one you are looking at right now) as a requirement for a certain college class. But this girl is generally not very interested in books like this one—I know this is hard to believe, but please humor me for a moment—and she finds it difficult to motivate herself to get going with the assignment. She has, in the past, received some poor grades on book reviews, and this fact adds to her discouragement, because she presumes that this book will also be "hard." Now let us further suppose that this girl is sharing her concerns with a classmate who has already read the book (or at least a few pages from the first and last chapters) and finished the assignment. Her friend, in an effort to encourage her, says, "Oh, hey, don't worry about it. *That book was cake.*" These words of assurance are, in fact, a metaphor, one that compares this book to a cake. But obviously, such a statement does not suggest that the object you are now holding should henceforth be called "cake." Rather, this metaphor attempts to *combine the psychological context of the word "book" with the psychological context of the word "cake."*

While the psychological context of a "book review" might evoke thoughts of anxiety, grueling study, and failure, the psychological context of a "cake" is much less threatening. Cakes are yummy and very nice, little to be feared; the metaphor "that book is cake" attempts to mediate the girl's response to the "book" through the psychological context of this much less dangerous entity. This is not to say that the "book" has "become a cake," nor that "cake" is an adjective for "book," nor that the book is full of eggs and flour. The play generated by mingling the psychological context of the one term with that of the other creates a new conceptual entity that shares relevant elements of both— a new entity that will, in this case, hopefully relieve the girl's anxiety about her assignment.

Parables: Ambiguous Metaphors

Before proceeding to discuss how metaphors can be "empty," let me pause to note that Jesus' parables are "metaphors" in the general sense that they compare two things, and that some of them are "riddles" because they make their comparisons in a way that generates ambiguity. As metaphors, parables compare a story (I use the term "story" loosely here to refer to all sorts of illustrations of various lengths and subject matter) to some point that Jesus wants to make—normally a point about the "Kingdom of God" and/or some implication of being a member of that Kingdom.[19] The very name of the genre, "parable," derives from the Greek verb παραβάλλω, which means "throw together" or "throw beside." Jesus' parables throw the Kingdom of God beside some story and ask the audience to reflect on the similarities and differences. In terms of our discussion of metaphors above, Jesus' parables use a story to evoke a particular psychological context—a set of ideas—in the minds of the audience and then metaphorically import that psychological context into "the Kingdom of God."

This principle may be illustrated by the parable of the Mustard Seed, which explicitly compares the Kingdom of God to a simple story about a garden plant in Mark (4:30–32), Matthew (13:31–32), Luke (13:18–19), and *Thomas* (20:2–4).[20]

Jesus' Parables as Metaphors

"How shall we compare the Kingdom of God, or to what parable shall we liken it? It's like a mustard seed. When it's planted in the earth, it's the smallest of all the seeds in the earth, and once it's planted it rises up and becomes the largest of all the plants and bears great branches, so that the birds of the air are able to nest in its shade."

In Mark's version of this parable (4:30–32), Jesus utilizes a metaphor—technically a "simile" because it includes "like" or "as" (ὡς)—that mingles the psychological contexts of the words "mustard seed" (the vehicle) and "Kingdom of God" (the tenor). Of course, the words "mustard seed" might bring a large number of ideas to the audience's mind, some of which could reflect personal impressions that Jesus does not wish to associate with the Kingdom. Psychological contexts can be quite large and layered, depending on one's experiences with the thing in question. As Brandon Scott has stressed, metaphors tap into whole networks of ideas, not just single thoughts.[21] Jesus therefore presents the basic metaphor, "It's like a mustard seed," to evoke a broad psychological context, then specifies the elements of that context that he wishes to apply to the Kingdom: the fact that large mustard plants emerge from very small seeds.[22] This limitation of possible meanings emphasizes the sharp contrast between the Kingdom's humble beginnings and the "great conclusion" that is yet to come.[23] Just as the mustard plant defies its origins by rising to overwhelm the garden, "what has begun in the Galilean ministry of Jesus will, by the power of God, one day prove to be of ultimate significance."[24] As a metaphor, this parable does its work in the interplay between the psychological contexts of the various terms that it employs.

Parables, then, are *metaphors* that transfer qualities from one thing to another; many of them are also *riddles* that generate ambiguity by transgressing the normal boundaries between conceptual categories. This effect is achieved in two ways, one that relates to the psychological context of the vehicle and another that relates to the relationship between the vehicle and the tenor. The former technique is more obvious on the surface level of the text; the latter is implicit, but ultimately more disruptive of normal ways of thinking. For sake of convenience, I will continue to use the Mustard Seed for illustration.

At the most basic level, the parable of the Mustard Seed is an ambiguous metaphor simply because there is something not quite right with the psychological context that it evokes. Such a claim may seem unusual at first because it conflicts with much popular thinking about what parables are and why Jesus used them. Most Christians assume that Jesus' parables were illustrations, and for this very reason parables focus on the familiar. The Kingdom of God, Jesus tells us, is "like" (ὡς) something very common—"common" in the sense that people in his audience would have a well-developed psychological context for the metaphorical vehicles that his parables use. For example, in an agrarian culture like Roman Palestine, most people could immediately evoke a clear psychological context for the phrase, "the sower went out to sow." They also knew what dishonest stewards were, how rich men related to poor beggars, and why a tax collector might call himself a "sinner"; all these images would suggest that the Kingdom of God should be readily comprehensible in terms of everyday experience. For this reason, generations of Sunday school teachers have defined the "parable" as "an earthly story with a heavenly meaning." According to the conventional wisdom behind this well-worn cliché, parables are "heavenly" because they communicate profound theological truth and are "earthly" because they package that truth in simple illustrations from daily experience. Indeed, no less a scholar than C. H. Dodd noted that "in the parables . . . all is true to life. Each similitude or story is a perfect picture of something that can be observed in the world of our experience. The processes of nature are accurately observed and recorded; the actions of persons in the stories are in character"—everything feels familiar.[25]

But while we might be tempted to think that Jesus was trying to bring complex theological problems down to a level that the average person could grasp, most scholars today highlight the *unfamiliar* elements of the parables. As Jeremias notes, Jesus' parables "are drawn from life, but show numerous unusual features"; further, and more significantly, "the element of unexpectedness that they display was intended to indicate where the meaning was to be found."[26] The "meaning" of a parable does not lie in its familiar features, but rather in things that capture the audience's attention because they are so out of place—sometimes a complete reversal of reality, or at least a reversal of what most people assume to be "real." Returning to the Good Samaritan for a moment: people in Jesus' time could of course relate to a robbery on the road between Jerusalem and Jericho (just as we can today), but the point of the story is not that someone was robbed. The point lies in the absurd proposition that a Samaritan would help a wounded Jew, something that was utterly *unfamiliar* because people simply did not behave that way in the real world. Jesus' parables generally contrast the Kingdom of God with the so-called "real world," and in the process challenge people to adopt a countercultural perspective. For this reason, most scholars stress that the "point" of a parable does not lie in the common, but in the uncommon; not in the everyday elements of the tale, but rather in its absurd propositions.

Following this principle, a closer look at the parable of the Mustard Seed reveals that Jesus is bringing together a rather odd set of ideas. To start with, in Luke's version the tiny mustard seeds are planted in a "garden" (κῆπος; 13:19). Scott notes that rabbinic law forbade the planting of mustard in garden plots for purity reasons; against this backdrop, we must wonder, at least temporarily, whether Jesus means that the subsequent growth of the plant should be interpreted as "a divine blessing or a violation."[27] Then there is the rather strange conclusion to the story in Mark. Many scholars speculate that the final clause in Mark's version, "it bears great branches, so that the birds of the air can nest in its shade," alludes to Ezekiel's cedar tree parables (esp. 17:22–24) and/or Nebuchadnezzar's dream of a great tree in Daniel 4.[28] Some members of Jesus' audience—or, at least, some of Mark's readers—would doubtless detect these echoes. But such an allusion would conflict with the psychological context generated by the rest of the story, because bushy mustard plants do not, in fact, grow into anything like a cedar tree. As Scott notes, the "hearer is left to make sense, to fit together a mustard plant that has pretensions to the grandeur of a cedar of Lebanon."[29] On top of all this, it is relevant to note, as Crossan emphasizes, that while the reference to "nesting" has an appealing pastoral ring to modern Westerners, ancient peasant farmers would generally not be especially pleased with a wild plant that "tends to attract birds within cultivated areas where they are not particularly desired"—who wants crows living in their cornfield?[30] In these respects, then, the parable of the Mustard Seed is ambiguous simply because it tampers with the psychological context that the terms of its vehicle would normally evoke. The story introduces an element of the absurd into a relatively familiar situation, thus suggesting that the Kingdom is both like and unlike our everyday world and its expectations.

Of course, one could argue, and many scholars do in fact argue, that the "cedar" theme is a Markan addition to Jesus' original words, and that the "garden" motif is Luke's accommodation to a Greco-Roman audience, who could fearlessly plant mustard in their gardens with none of the Jewish purity concerns. But whether or not this is the case, I would argue that the parable of the Mustard Seed would be inherently ambiguous in almost any form in which Jesus might have used it—that it must have functioned as a riddle if he used it *at all* in his teaching. At best, one could argue that, if anything, Mark and Luke have only toned down the irony of Jesus' story to help their readers make sense of it.[31] These observations lead us to the second, and ultimately more disruptive, means by which parables generate ambiguity.

Parables: Empty Metaphors

The parable of the Mustard Seed has (at least) one major difference from the example of the girl and the book. In terms of a semantic triangle, there is no "thing" to which the term "Kingdom of God" corresponds, leaving a vacancy in the tenor triangle. This void is not accidental. Rather, this void reflects the fact that the parable of the Mustard Seed is an "empty metaphor."[32]

To explore this notion a bit further, let me return for a moment to the sad case of the college student who must write a review of this book for a class assignment. I noted above that the parable of the Mustard Seed is "empty" because there is a vacant space in the tenor triangle—the "thing" to which the words "Kingdom of God" refer is missing. Such a situation might also arise in the context of a conversation between the girl and her friend about the book review. In such a dialogue, the metaphor "that book is cake" might be abbreviated for convenience: the girl's friend might actually say, "Hey, don't worry; *that's cake*." Technically speaking, the English word "that" is imprecise and could potentially refer to anything—there is no specific object to which "that" normally refers. As a result, if we were to diagram this statement as a discrete use of language, something would be missing. We have ideas about what a "cake" is, but no clear and consistent ideas attached to the word "that." We could therefore say that there's a void in the relationship between one of the terms ("that") and its referent that threatens to create confusion.

Technically speaking, then, the statement "that's cake" is an empty metaphor. But of course, it would be senseless to press this point, because we are all aware that in a normal conversation the speaker simply assumes that her audience can supply the missing element from the broader context of the remark. The girl's friend assumes that she has been paying attention and is therefore aware that the word "that" in this case refers specifically to the book. If she hasn't been paying attention, she can simply ask for clarification— "What are you talking about? Oh, the book, yeah, OK"—and the discussion then proceeds without interruption. The metaphor is empty, but the speaker assumes that it will be filled. The speaker in fact depends on the audience's ability to fill it in order for the statement to make sense.

But now I wish to ask: Is this also what is happening in the parable of the Mustard Seed? More specifically, did Jesus assume that his audience could easily fill in the empty space across from the term "Kingdom of God"? Was there some obvious referent that they could import into this parable from the broader context of the conversation? Or did he assume that they would *not* be able to do this, at least not without substantial adjustments to their normal way of thinking?

Let me sharpen these questions a bit, because they are critical to the way in which Jesus' parable-riddles do their work. In the example above, the words "book" and "cake" both refer to tangible entities, things you could touch or set on a table. The pronoun "that" has simply taken the place of one of these tangible entities—in the context of this hypothetical conversation, "that" is obviously just another word for "book," making it easy for the girl to fill in the blank. The term "mustard seed" also refers to a tangible entity, something that some people in Jesus' audience had likely seen and handled. But the words "Kingdom of God" refer to something of a quite different substance, something that cannot be seen or handled very easily. There is, in other words, no obvious entity or institution to which this term seems to point, despite the fact that the word "Kingdom" normally refers to something fairly large that could be easily observed and located on a map. In the sources, people occasionally remind Jesus of this fact by asking him for "signs" of the kingdom's presence.[33]

I would argue that this is not accidental but is rather the foundation of the parable's rhetorical strategy. The parable of the Mustard Seed is an "empty metaphor" in the true sense: an analogy that is not grounded on an obvious referent, where the context of the discussion does not point the audience to what is missing.[34] As a result, this parable generates a psychological context of ideas and experiences and then asks the audience to transfer those ideas to an unknown quantity, thus calling us to look squarely at something that can actually be seen only out of the corner of your eye. "We're talking about the Kingdom of God, OK? Well, that's like a mustard seed, see, because"—but by the time Jesus' audience figures out exactly how the Kingdom could be "like a seed" and why he is comparing the Kingdom to a mustard bush rather than a cedar of Lebanon, they suddenly realize that they don't actually know what Jesus means by "Kingdom." He could mean any number of things, and he obviously means something—the word "Kingdom" is, then, intentionally ambiguous in this context.[35] At the same time, however, Jesus is apparently trying to make a point; the audience is being challenged to identify and understand what he's talking about. The parable, then, seeks an "answer" of some sort. As such, the Mustard Seed is a riddle, an intentionally ambiguous question that asks the audience to respond; its rhetorical impact derives from the fact that no clear answer is provided. Mark does not even tell his readers what this particular parable "means"; he only teases us by saying that Jesus explained it privately to the disciples (4:34). This leaves us in the same position as Jesus' original audience: confronted with an ambiguity that is never really resolved, and still debating its true meaning two thousand years later.

Jesus' parable-riddles generate ambiguity at a variety of levels but never fully resolve that ambiguity. I would argue that all of his parables work this way, although I cannot take time to defend that claim here. I will, however, pause to stress that Jesus seems to have achieved the same effect with other riddles that do not take the form of parables. As I noted earlier, many of Jesus' sage riddles are not "answered" in the sources. They challenge conventional ways of thinking, but the challenge is never fully resolved to a point where we could feel absolutely certain of Jesus' meaning. Mark, for example, never tells us exactly what Jesus meant when he said, "Give Caesar's things to Caesar and God's things to God" (12:17); Luke does not alleviate our concern over Jesus' command to "hate" our parents (14:26); Thomas does not specify how the end could be where the beginning is (18:2). In point of fact, Thomas very rarely specifies anything, even though he opens his book by telling us that our access to eternal life depends on our ability to understand what Jesus is talking

> Jesus' parables "seem designed, within the worldview of the Jewish village population of the time, as tools to break open the prevailing worldview and replace it with one that was closely related but significantly adjusted at every point."
>
> —Wright 1996, 175

about (prologue, 1). In these cases, it could be that the author of the source did not know the exact answer to Jesus' riddle, or that the author did know the answer and assumed that the reader could also answer by appeal to common community tradition—the third and most essential type of "prerequisite knowledge" for riddling that we discussed in an earlier chapter. But it is also possible—and in my view much more likely—that the sources do not give answers to some of Jesus' riddles for the same reason that they do not give answers to some of his parables: because they wish to leave the ambiguity unresolved, both in imitation of Jesus' own teaching style and in order to exploit the rhetorical effect that this strategy produces on the audience.

Both riddles and parables, then, confront us with ambiguities. They point in many different directions at once, and in the process challenge us to realign our conceptual categories and redefine key terms. The sources are doubtless correct to suggest that this is exactly the way that Jesus used both genres, and also correct to suggest that many of Jesus' parables functioned as riddles in the historical context of his ministry.[36]

6

It's Good to Be the Riddler, unless You're Playing with Jesus

Riddles, whether in the form of parables or something else, are potentially dangerous. They often confuse, and sometimes offend, people by playing with social taboos and absurd paradoxes. For this reason, riddles are exchanged in special social settings that diffuse their intensity. "Riddling sessions" follow rules that are intuitive to the riddler and other members of her group, and these rules carry social implications that can be very significant, especially in cultures where riddles serve serious purposes like education and initiation.

This chapter and the next will highlight two social implications of riddling that are foundational to the riddling sessions portrayed in the sources for Jesus. First, just as the rules of baseball inherently favor pitchers over batters (only three strikes and you're out, but four balls draw a walk), the rules of riddling always put the riddler in a superior position. The riddler can ask anything she wants, and she alone is in a position to determine the correct answer; she is, as it were, both the pitcher and the umpire. Second, in every culture, the rules of riddling reward witty people—riddlers who can pose really tough questions and riddlees who can answer them—and punish the ignorant. These punishments may range from shame to alien-

The Two Big Rules of Riddling
- The Riddler Is Always Right
- Witty People Win

ation to death, yet no matter how severe, they are very real for the people who must suffer them. You therefore want to weigh your wit carefully before you challenge someone to a riddling match. Overall, the *authority of the riddler* and the *power of wit* are two of the most notable features of riddling, and both are critical facets of the riddling sessions that appear in the sources for Jesus. The riddler's absolute authority will be discussed in this chapter, while the power of wit will be addressed in chapter 7.

THE RIDDLER'S PREROGATIVE:
THE POWER OF A QUESTION

If you have ever known a three-year-old, you have doubtless been involved in a conversation that went something like this:

> Mom: "Now remember, Aaron, if you have a good day at preschool, we'll go to McDonald's for lunch. OK?"
>
> Son: "Why?"
>
> Mom: "Because you like to go to McDonald's, so that will help you remember to do what Mrs. Wunder tells you."
>
> Son: "Why do I like to go to McDonald's?"
>
> Mom: "Well, because you like to eat food there and play there."
>
> Son: "Why?"
>
> Mom: "Because you like the food there and you like the play place. Don't you like the play place at McDonald's?"
>
> Son: "Yes. But Mom? Why?"
>
> Mom: "Why what?"
>
> Son: "Why do I like the play place?"
>
> Mom: "Well, I don't know why. You just like it."
>
> Son: "Why?"
>
> Mom: "Well, you tell me why. Because it's fun, I guess."
>
> Son: "Why?" ad infinitum

An exchange like this is not a "riddling session," although the child seems to think that everything you say is ambiguous. But such fruitless dialogues do resemble riddling sessions in one key respect: both depend on *the power of a question*. According to the rhetorical laws of American English—not the rules of spelling and grammar, but rather the unstated social rules that govern the use of the language—every question must be answered, even when the question is absurd. Young children learn this rule long before they learn how to ask real questions about real things: so long as Aaron keeps saying,

"Why?" Mommy has to answer him, even when she's so frustrated that she wants to pull her hair out. The same standard operates in riddling sessions: the riddler has full control over the questions, and the riddlee has to provide the correct answer, where "correct" means the exact answer that the riddler wants at that moment. Of course, the "correct" answer can't violate the cultural rules of the riddle game, but in questionable cases the call always goes in favor of the riddler.

The riddler's privileged position is especially evident in instances where *a riddle is seemingly impossible to answer*, and/or where *the correct answer is no more obvious than any other option*. The very fact that riddles of this type may seem inherently unfair simply illustrates the extent of the riddler's power once the game begins. Fair or not, you have to play along.

Locks with No Keys

Riddlers can manipulate the rules to create puzzles that are virtually impossible to unlock. As noted in chapter 2, riddles depend on three types of special knowledge: knowledge of the thing being discussed, knowledge of the channels of logic and analogy that connect the ambiguous question to that thing, and knowledge of traditions. Riddles that can be solved by appeal to knowledge types #1 and #2 satisfy the "criterion of solvability," meaning that someone in the riddler's group could theoretically reason out the right answer (even if she can't say why other answers are wrong). Many riddles, however, depend exclusively on knowledge type #3, knowledge of traditions. Puzzles of this kind can be solved only by people with direct access to inside information (which often just means that they've heard this riddle, or one like it, before). Riddlers can exploit this fact by shrinking the size of the community of knowledge—that group of people who could potentially identify the right answer—to a point where it excludes the riddlee. In the most extreme cases of this phenomenon, the riddler makes this move by speaking metaphorically about something that is known only to herself—some personal insight or experience that no one else, not even other members of her group, could know about. This tactic naturally makes the riddlee totally dependent on the riddler for the correct answer. Three well-known examples of this phenomenon will suffice to illustrate the riddler's absolute authority over the riddling session.

In chapter 3, I noted that Tolkien's portrait of the initial encounter between the hobbit Bilbo Baggins and Gollum is a classic instance of a prolonged riddling session, one that involves a lengthy exchange of questions. Due to the circumstances, Bilbo cannot concentrate as well as he might—he's lost, sitting by a bottomless lake in a pitch black cave, and Gollum wants to eat him—and after a few rounds he finds himself running out of riddles. As Gollum presses him, he fidgets nervously in his pants pocket and, feeling the ring he has just found on the floor, says aloud to himself, "What have I got in my pocket?" The remark was intended for no one in particular, but Gollum interprets it as yet another riddle and demands three chances to answer. It comes as little surprise to the reader when he cannot, because such a question depends on information that would be available only to Bilbo himself (and to readers of the story). All of Gollum's suggested solutions—hands, string, knife—are reasonable and logical, but reason and logic often fall by the wayside in riddling sessions. In a case like this, you just have to know the answer ahead of time. Since no one else has had their hands in Bilbo's pockets that day, this riddle's "community of knowledge" includes only one person (Bilbo), who alone possesses the information that is essential to the correct answer.[1]

If we can sympathize with Gollum's outrage and agree that Bilbo's question was not quite fair, we must also acknowledge that this is by no means a unique instance. The same dynamic is at work in the biblical story of Samson's wedding riddle, which appears at Judges 14:14. As Samson and his parents travel to Timnah to negotiate the terms of his engagement, they are attacked by a lion; à la the Incredible Hulk, Samson is energized by the Spirit of the Lord and tears the beast to pieces. Some time later, he returns to town and sees that a swarm of bees has nested in the lion's carcass. Samson shares some of the honey, but the text states explicitly that no one else knew of its unusual origin (14:9). Despite this fact, Samson feels justified in propounding the following riddle at his wedding banquet: "From the eater came something to eat, from the strong came something sweet." The Philistines, not suspecting that the puzzle refers to such a unique personal experience, attempt to answer through appeal to common knowledge and group logic; when these means fail, they take the less diplomatic approach of threatening to kill the bride if she does not come up with the solution.[2] While I cannot applaud this tactic, one can easily see why Samson's riddle is so frustrating: it reduces the community of knowledge to one member by building on the type of information that could be found only in a person's diary.

Finally, on a somewhat lighter note, the familiar fairy tale "Rumpelstiltskin" includes a riddle similar to those posed by Bilbo and Samson, one that again underscores the riddler's absolute authority, simply because it is so difficult to answer. Once upon a time, a poor miller gained an audience with the king, and wishing to make a good impression, he told the monarch that his daughter could spin straw into gold. The greedy king decided to test this claim, and after calling the miller's daughter to the palace he locked her in a room full of straw and ordered her to spin it all into gold by morning. The girl wept with despair, until suddenly a strange little man entered the dungeon. She shared her wretched plight, and he offered to complete the impossible task in exchange for her necklace (clearly a very valuable necklace). She agreed; he took the necklace and spun until morning, changing all the straw into gold. The king was very pleased and of course rewarded the girl by forcing her to spin twice as much straw the next night. Once again the strange little man saved the day, this time weaving the gold in exchange for her ring. Finally, the king—who happened to be single—promised to marry the miller's daughter if she could repeat this feat yet a third time. On this occasion, the troll offered to exchange the gold for her firstborn son, and she, thinking that he would forget as time went by, accepted the bargain.

Fast forward: a year later, the miller's daughter, now queen, was lying in bed, cradling her tiny newborn son. The maid left the room for a moment, and "Poof!"—the strange little man suddenly appeared to collect his fee. The queen was shocked and afraid; she clung to the child and began to weep bitterly; the troll, obviously a sucker for damsels in distress, felt sorry for her and, to be completely fair, said that she could keep the child—*if* she could answer a simple riddle within three days: "What is my name?" She, having no other choice, accepted the challenge and searched high and low across the kingdom for information on the background and/or whereabouts of this strange individual. But her efforts were vain, and each time the little man appeared to hear her answers she was utterly unable to solve his unusual puzzle.

Now, before we proceed to the climax, I wish to point out that the story of Rumpelstiltskin illustrates two key aspects of riddling. First, we see here again a clear case of the riddler's absolute authority, as evidenced by the obscurity of the question and the high stakes in the contest. Because he was a magical being of some sort, the straw-spinning man's name did not appear in the royal phonebook, nor could it be traced from credit-card receipts at the local Pizza Hut. This information was, in fact, so arcane that even the queen's crack staff of researchers could not find it in their catalogue of unusual names, and real-world folklorists still debate the many possible etymologies of "Rumpelstiltskin." The troll's question could not be "figured out"; it must be answered by appeal to special information. But the number of people who knew this special information (i.e., the troll's name) was exactly one: no one in the entire kingdom had ever seen or heard of him before. According to our modern Western way of thinking, this riddle is inherently unfair, because it does not meet the criterion of solvability. But our heroine did not live in the modern West; she lived in the story world of Rumpelstiltskin, a world where riddlers were more powerful than queens and where princes could be won and lost in contests of wit, no matter how esoteric the questions might be.

Second, I wish to point out that the means by which the story comes to a happy ending—happy for the queen, real sad for the troll—illustrates the only way that riddles of this type can be answered. Late in the evening of the second day of the name quest, one of the queen's messengers returned to the castle and reported a remarkable discovery. While passing through a remote wood, he had heard someone singing, and turning aside he saw a crooked house in a forgotten glen. An ugly little man was dancing around a large fire out in front, singing madly to himself:

> "Today I brew, tomorrow bake,
> And then the little child I'll take.
> For little knows the royal dame
> That *Rumpelstiltskin* is my name."

Armed with this inside information, the queen easily answered the troll's riddle when he appeared the next day to collect the child. Furious, he retaliated by driving his own foot through the floor and then tearing himself in half—a bizarre ending to a bizarre story, the moral apparently being that a miller's daughter who cries a lot can outfox a maniacal dwarf. For purposes of our discussion, however, I wish to point out that the queen outwitted him, not by reasoning out the correct answer, but rather by *stealing* the correct answer from Rumpelstiltskin himself, the same way that the Philistines had to steal the answer to Samson's riddle from his bride. Whether or not any of this is "fair," these instances simply illustrate the fact that, because the riddler always has absolute authority in a riddling session, *the answer ultimately has to come from the riddler*. You know if he tells you; if he doesn't tell you, you can't answer, or at least can't know for sure whether your best guess is right.

Which Right Answer?

The riddler's special privilege is evident not only in extreme cases such as those discussed above, but also in much more common instances where a tradition permits of several correct answers, only one of which is "right" at the moment of a specific performance. For example, the riddle

> There is something
> With a heart in its head.
> [What is it?]

could reasonably refer to a cherry or a peach, the "heart" in each case being the pit/seed of the fruit. Both of these answers, along with several others (a lettuce, an artichoke), have been documented in field reports on the oral performance of this riddle. At any given moment, then, the "correct" choice between these various viable answers is the one that the riddler has in mind; even an informed riddlee from the same community of knowledge could not read the riddler's thoughts to determine which of the well-known solutions was right on that particular day. Similarly, the American children's joke that so confounded Dr. Choi,

What's black and white and red all over?

is subject to at least four common interpretations, any of which may be correct on a given occasion. Thus, on Tuesday, a child may tell this riddle to a friend at a play group and insist that the answer is "a newspaper"; on Thursday, she tells the man who sells ice cream in the park that it's "a cow with diaper rash"; on Friday, she tells Dr. Choi that it's talking about "a sunburnt zebra"; on Sunday, she tells the priest that it's "a frog in a milkshake machine." In these cases, several traditional answers are in circulation, the audience may be aware of all of them, and the "right" one is the one that the riddler wants at that moment. Such are the privileges of being a riddler.

JESUS ALWAYS WINS

I have discussed this principle in some detail because *the riddler's authority is a platform of every riddling session presented in the sources for Jesus.* The sources utilize this dimension of riddling in two distinct ways, both of which are calculated to highlight Jesus' superior wit and wisdom. First, in every case where Jesus is the riddler, type #3 knowledge—knowledge of traditions, special information—is the only kind that works. Which is to say, you know the answer when and if Jesus tells you the answer; if he doesn't, and if you haven't heard this riddle or one very much like it before, you have no hope of getting it right. Jesus' riddles thereby segregate the world into two categories of people: those who are inside his community of knowledge and can therefore answer his ambiguous questions and those who are outside his community of knowledge and therefore can't. The members of the former group "got inside" only by Jesus' invitation. Second, in those episodes where Jesus is the riddlee, answering ambiguous questions posed by someone else, the riddler's inherent advantages are harnessed to ironically illustrate Jesus' superior wit. As noted earlier, the riddler enters every match with a ten-stroke handicap; in most cases, the riddlee can hope for nothing better than a tie. Jesus, however, consistently defies the odds: he not only answers his opponents' challenges, but he answers them in a way that displays so much genius that the riddler generally slinks away in shame, afraid to provoke him further.

The first rule—that you can answer Jesus' riddles only when he gives you the answer—is illustrated by the riddling sessions we analyzed in chapter 3. Thus, in Mark 8 the disciples are left wondering about the "leaven of the

Pharisees" because they cannot, despite Jesus' hints, determine what he is talking about, and Jesus is not inclined to tell them (8:14–21). Similarly, Peter does not know what to do with Jesus' observation that "the sons are free" from the temple tax and must rely on his master to resolve the dilemma by sending him

---

The Riddler's Privilege; or Jesus' Wit Always Wins

 In the sources, the fact that the riddler naturally has the upper hand is always used to demonstrate Jesus' superior wit:

•When Jesus asks a riddle, you can answer only if he gives you the answer; no one figures out his puzzles on their own.

•When Jesus answers a riddle, his response is so clever that it ends the game; people dare not test him twice.

---

to collect the coins from the fish (Matt. 17:24–27). The point of both passages is not so much to stress the disciples' ignorance as to demonstrate that even those people who were closest to Jesus had to wait for his answers.

Jesus' absolute authority as a riddler is perhaps most explicit in Mark 4. After Jesus delivers the parables of the Sower, the Seed and Harvest, and the Mustard Seed, along with the ambiguous statements about the lamp under a bed and the revelation of "hidden things," the disciples ask for a private explanation (4:10). They must do so because the Kingdom of God is a "mystery" that you cannot "reason out" on your own; it involves a subject matter and principles of logic that are known only to members of Jesus' community of knowledge, a community that you enter only when and if he chooses to initiate you. The Kingdom of God is thus "given" to the disciples in the form of the answers to these ambiguous statements (ὑμῖν τὸ μυστήριον δέδοται τῆς βασιλείας τοῦ θεοῦ; 4:11), yet remains "hidden" to those who don't have "ears to hear"—that is, hidden to "everyone who isn't sitting within earshot of me right now while I tell you what I'm talking about." Reason alone will not even reveal that Jesus is talking about the Kingdom of God rather than bread or lamps.[3] Matthew, realizing the significance of this fact, emphasizes that membership in Jesus' community of knowledge is a "blessing" that many prophets and righteous people were not lucky enough to enjoy (13:16–17). Here as elsewhere, Jesus' absolute authority to dispense the correct answers to whomever he pleases is the dominant characteristic of those riddling sessions that he initiates.

Riddlers, then, inherently have an upper hand, a fact that the sources easily exploit when depicting riddling sessions in which Jesus poses ambiguous questions that only he can answer. But the sources also exploit the riddler's privilege to make the very same point in episodes where Jesus must answer questions that are posed by someone else. In all of these cases, Jesus demonstrates an uncanny ability to turn the tables on his opponents and uses their privileged position to make supreme fools of them. A convenient example of this theme may be drawn from Mark 12:13–24. These verses give a play-by-play on the first two rounds of a lengthy riddling session that ultimately concludes with the statement, "and the large crowds were listening to him [Jesus] gladly" (12:37). The people are "glad" to listen to Jesus on this occasion because he is putting on a clinic in riddling and tickling their minds with his wit. The entire chapter, replete with features of an oral world, emphasizes Jesus' sagacity by demonstrating his ability to pose and answer ambiguous questions.

The riddling session opens as the Pharisees and Herodians approach Jesus in an effort to "trap him in a word" (αὐτὸν ἀγρεύσωσιν λόγῳ; Mark 12:13)— a nifty word picture that brings to mind the nets and snares used by hunters and fishermen.[4] The question that they proceed to ask and the context of that question—Jesus has just entered Jerusalem, "cleansed" the temple, and publicly humiliated the chief priests, scribes, and elders with a riddle about John the Baptist (Mark 11:1–11, 15–18, 27–33)—suggest that the "trap" seeks not only to discredit Jesus in the eyes of his followers but also to create grounds for reporting him to the civil authorities.[5] The stakes, then, are very high: if Jesus cannot answer correctly, he will at least suffer public shame and loss of status and at most may also draw the attention of the Romans.

A riddler may contextualize a question in a way that inherently limits the range of acceptable answers, and the Pharisees exploit this privilege to the full as they begin to spread their net at Mark 12:14–15. They preface their puzzle by saying, "Teacher, we know that you are truthful, and you show special concern to no one. For you do not look to the face of men, but rather you teach the way of God in truth." While this is a nice sentiment, in this context it is more than simple flattery. Their compliment implies that "truthful" teachers show disregard for social status and, as a natural corollary, are not concerned with the personal consequences of their words. Those who "teach the way of God in truth," as Jesus presumably claims to do, must make pronouncements on the basis of transcendent ethical principles. Such a teacher would never, of course, say something simply to appease someone, not even a very powerful person. Since Jesus falls into this category, one may assume that he "is not afraid of Caesar, and so will give the revolutionary answer if that is what he believes."[6] Even before they ask the question, then, the Pharisees imply that Jesus should criticize the current social order if he wishes to call himself "truthful."

Having urged Jesus to go the way of Socrates and ruin himself with frank speech, the Pharisees pose a riddle that invites their opponent to "show no special concern" to the most powerful person in the world: "Is it lawful to give the poll tax to Caesar or not? Should we pay, or should we not pay?" (Mark 12:14). The challenge includes two distinct questions, and its genius lies in their interplay. The first question explores the theoretical dimension of taxation: Is it "lawful" to pay? Is such an act consistent with the teachings of Moses and the Jewish faith in general? By itself, this inquiry permits a wide range of answers that could focus on arcane aspects of academic discussion—concerns that would quickly be of no interest to most Jewish peasants or the Roman authorities. Poll taxes were paid only by the subjects of provinces under direct Roman rule, like Judea; Jesus, as a Galilean, was exempt and could therefore easily treat the issue in the abstract.[7] The Pharisees anticipate this avenue of escape, however, and quickly close it with a second question that underscores the bottom line: "Should we pay or not?" If we should pay, are you, Jesus, saying that you support Roman taxation and, by extension, the Roman presence in general? But if we shouldn't pay, do you mean to say that it is inherently unethical for Jews to accept Roman authority? Obviously, either of these answers would be disastrous for Jesus: the first would conflict with his self-posturing as champion of the oppressed; the second would open him to charges of sedition.[8]

The Pharisees' question, then, is foolproof, and apparently permits no safe solution. Mark builds on this fact to highlight the genius of Jesus' escape: "Give Caesar's things to Caesar and God's things to God."[9] This statement is obviously significant to any understanding of Jesus' posture toward civil government, and many theories have been advanced as to its true meaning and implications. The multiplicity of these theories is a direct result of the fact that *Jesus' answer is actually another riddle.* His statement about Caesar and God is, in other words, inherently ambiguous, pointing to numerous possible meanings. "Had he told them to revolt? Had he told them to pay the tax? He had done neither. He had done both. Nobody could deny that the saying was revolutionary, but nor could anyone say that Jesus had forbidden payment of the tax."[10] Jesus' reply is, in fact, so ingeniously ambiguous that none of the sources—not even Matthew, who otherwise generally likes to clear things up for his reader—seems to know exactly what he was talking about; at least, none of them offers an explanation (see Matt. 22:22; Luke 20:26; *Thomas* 100:4).[11] It comes as little surprise, then, that Jesus' interlocutors are left speechless by this comment. Those sources that portray any response at all leave the Pharisees, the Herodians, and the crowds "amazed" at what Jesus has just said and afraid to ask any more questions. Who would dare to challenge such an awesome wit, one that eludes even the most foolproof traps?

So far, the score is Jesus 1, Religious Authorities 0. But the riddling session is not over, as the vanquished Pharisees and Herodians tag out to the Sadducees, who immediately propose a second test of Jesus' wit. Mark does not explicitly state that the Sadducees wish to "trap" Jesus, but he clearly signals that their question is not genuine by framing it with the note that they "say that there is no resurrection" (12:18); this being the case, they can scarcely be concerned with the eternal fate of a bride who married seven brothers. Their question, however, plays ad hominem on Jesus' own belief in resurrection: specifically, it attempts to catch him between this doctrine and the Mosaic teaching on levirate marriage, which they quote as preface to the riddle at verse 19. Moses decreed that a widow with no children should marry her oldest brother-in-law, who the family hoped would sire offspring to stand as his departed brother's heirs (Deut. 25:5–6; see Gen. 38:6–10). Following this commandment, a certain widow married her husband's brother, but he died before they had children; she remarried his next brother, who suffered a similar fate; and so on; and so on, until the unfortunate woman had gone through all seven brothers in the family and, leaving no children, died herself.

The Sadducees' riddle is certainly less volatile than the Pharisees' question about taxation—it's almost playful, maybe even a bit funny (in a macabre sort of way)—yet the goal is no less insidious: to discredit Jesus publicly by presenting a theological knot that he can't untie. The question suggests that Jesus' teaching on resurrection, which Mark assumes here but does not describe, is somehow in conflict with the teachings of Moses, or at least that it does not interface smoothly and logically with the Mosaic Law. As France notes, "Jesus' response to this question will be a matter of complete indifference to the Roman government, but . . . since the questioners seem to assume that Jesus supports the 'Pharisaic' notion of an afterlife, it offers the opportunity to discredit him by presenting him with a reductio ad absurdum of that position . . . and so making him look ridiculous before the crowd."[12] In a culture where shame is worse than death, "looking ridiculous before the crowd" is not much less significant, and certainly much less glorious, than a run-in with Caesar over taxation.

In response to this challenge, Jesus makes three statements that demonstrate both his agility as an interpreter and his intellectual superiority over the Sadducees. First, at Mark 12:24 he prefaces his reply by claiming that his opponents "do not know the Scriptures nor the power of God." This is not a nice thing to say, but in this context it is more than an insult. Jesus is informing the Sadducees that he recognizes both prongs of the dilemma and will provide an answer that at once affirms both the force of Moses' teaching ("the Scriptures") and the validity of his own position on resurrection ("the power of God to raise the dead").[13] Second, he follows this warning with a preliminary answer that requires no reference to Scripture: people don't get married in heaven, anyway, making the question "Whose wife will she be?" irrelevant in the first place (v. 25). Jesus may here be accusing the Sadducees of ignorance of the basic Pharisaic doctrine, or perhaps more narrowly of ignorance of his

own teaching. Either way, they need to come better briefed next time. Jesus'
third statement, Mark 12:26–27, proceeds to a more general defense of his
belief in resurrection, at the same time a critique of the Sadducees' disbelief.
At Exodus 3:6, Yahweh appears to Moses in the burning bush and introduces
himself as "the God of Abraham, the God of Isaac, and the God of Jacob."
Since all three of those individuals were dead in Moses' time, the fact that God
refers to them in the present tense ("I am currently the God of . . .") suggests
that these patriarchs must have remained alive in some form somewhere.[14]

While this response adequately vanquishes the Sadducees, it is easy to see
why commentators have been generally unimpressed with the logic of Jesus'
argument, which "may not appeal to us [modern readers] as particularly
cogent."[15] Even if we wish to be sensitive to the fact that ancient rabbinic
methods of interpretation differed dramatically from our own, we still cannot
help but notice that Jesus' interpretation of the burning-bush episode actually
"says nothing [specific] about resurrection: it could point equally well to [the
general] immortality of the soul."[16] Why did Mark feel it necessary to include
this dubious statement when Jesus has already answered the Sadducees' question at 12:25? Jesus' choice of proof text reflects yet another limitation that the
Sadducees have placed on the range of acceptable answers to their riddle, a
limitation that Mark assumes but does not articulate. The Sadducees deny not
only bodily resurrection (v. 18), but also the canonical status of those passages
from the Psalms and Prophets that might more easily prove Jesus' point.
Against this backdrop, the full scope of the dilemma comes into view: Jesus
must defend his doctrine of resurrection against Moses' teaching about levirate marriage, and he must do this by referring only to other passages from the
Mosaic Law—books that lend very little support to that doctrine. Viewed in
this light, his application of Exodus 3:6 "would have been impressive in its own
time," not only because it is a clever use of that text, but also (and more importantly here) because it turns the tables on the Sadducees and defeats them on
their home court.[17] Small wonder that one of the scribes could only conclude
that Jesus had "answered them well" (Mark 12:28).

The riddler's inherent advantages are, then, everywhere exploited in the sources
to demonstrate Jesus' superior wit and wisdom. Whether posing questions that
can be answered by no one but himself, or by answering questions that are seemingly impossible, Jesus often engages in riddling to demonstrate his intellectual
agility. Because this is a typical function of riddling in traditional cultures, and
because many of the riddling sessions in the Gospels seem calculated *only* to
establish Jesus' qualifications as a theological thinker with no obvious underlying
christological implications, it seems likely that the passages discussed in this chapter reflect a very real and important dimension of the career of the historical Jesus.

7

"Your Answer or Your Life": Caught with No Alternative

A riddler who can manipulate the rules well, or a riddlee who can beat the riddler at his own game, is possessed of "wit," a gift of insight that establishes one's status as a wise or clever person.[1] The social significance attributed to wit is a logical reflex of the three types of knowledge that riddling exploits: knowledge of cultural items, knowledge of group logic systems, and knowledge of community traditions. The witty woman evidences a firm command of such knowledge and thus by extension demonstrates her comfortable grip on information that holds the group together. Riddlers are, in one sense, cultural experts, people who are able to manipulate cherished conceptual boundaries and either reinforce or destroy them. Especially in traditional cultures where riddles regularly appear in connection with significant rites of passage—education, weddings, funerals—wit establishes one's position as a master of the group's order of values. Even in modern Western societies, which prefer to use riddles for recreation, wit is a significant intellectual credential in sports bars, faculty lounges, and (other) designated smoking areas, contexts where "cleverness" is often a major factor in one's social life.

The social power of wit is illustrated by two types of riddle that appear frequently in the sources for Jesus, the "catch riddle" and the "alternative." "Catch riddles" seek to trap the audience in a socially awkward position, using ambiguity to trick the riddlee for the express purpose of making a fool of her. Any riddle in any form can be used as a "catch," depending on the riddler's intention. "Alternative riddles" are ambiguous questions that ask the riddlee to choose between two (or more) proposed answers, A and B, both of which would force her to say something embarrassing or otherwise socially undesirable. Alternatives can easily function as catches because they inherently place the riddlee in a compromising position. Alternatives and other types of catch riddles are used in the Gospels to emphasize Jesus' remarkable intelligence and thus to establish his intellectual credentials, generally at the expense of the various religious authorities with whom he competes for influence over the crowds. Such episodes illustrate the power of wit particularly well, simply

---

Traps and Snares
(or the many perils of riddling)

Catch Riddle—a riddle that seeks to place the riddlee in a compromising position.

Alternative—a riddle that attempts to force the riddlee to choose between two or more proposed answers, all of which would be embarrassing and/or dangerous.

Neck Riddle—a riddle with very high stakes: the riddler must pose a question that can't be answered, or the riddlee must answer a very tough question; failure will lead to serious consequences ("losing your neck").

---

because the stakes in these riddling sessions are always so high. In fact, many of the verbal traps that Jesus sets and springs resemble "neck riddles." The neck riddle is not so much a distinct type of question as a traditional narrative motif, a situation in which the riddler must pose or answer a difficult puzzle to "save his neck"—to avoid loss of status, freedom, or even life.[2] Jesus doesn't kill anybody with his magnificent wit, but he frequently flexes his intellectual muscle to save his own reputation at his enemies' expense.

CAUGHT WITH YOUR MIND DOWN

As I have noted many times now, Westerners are generally most familiar with the use of riddles in recreational contexts. We encounter such verbal puzzles in forwarded e-mails, in electronic trivia games in pubs, while watching *Dora the Explorer* and *The Wiggles* with our children; they seem to be everywhere, and they are almost always innocent and entertaining. Because this is the case, people in my culture generally do not attribute great significance to a person's inability to answer a specific riddle. If, for example, I ask my research assistant, Jake,

What has seven eyes but can't see?

in front of a group of people, he, I, and all those gathered with us can collectively smile at the cleverness of the "correct" answer: "a potato." True, Jake's wit has failed him before many witnesses, but he suffers no loss from this fact because my challenge was impersonal and benign. My riddle sought only to amuse my audience, and the onus falls on me as the riddler if the joke doesn't work.

But a somewhat different dynamic is at work if I ask Jake, while others are watching,

> Yes or no: Do you still pick your nose?

This riddle may amuse my audience, but only at Jake's expense. As worded above, the question would force him to admit either that he presently engages in nose-picking—a socially inappropriate activity in our culture—or, at the very least, that he used to do so ("No, I don't *still* pick my nose," implying in American English idiom that he once did). The focus of this riddle, then, is less on the content of the text than on Jake's embarrassing inability to rescue himself from it. This example illustrates the fact that even leisure-time riddles may be used for the sinister purpose of making a fool of someone in a public place. Because this is the case, the rhetorical moves of my nose-picking question could quickly take us into a very unpleasant confrontation if Jake chose not to play along with me. Most of us have witnessed arguments, or even fistfights, that erupted because someone "with no sense of humor" didn't realize that his or her antagonist was "just joking." The fact that such confrontations do not occur more often than they do is a direct result of our implicit awareness of the cultural rules of riddling sessions. I assume that Jake knows the difference between a genuine insult and a harmless tease (he suffers both from me often), and also that he knows how to play the socially scripted role of "the butt of a joke" when called upon to do so. Such riddles are amusing, but in some cases entertainment comes with a price, generally a temporary loss of honor on the part of the riddlee.

Folklorists refer to verbal games that explicitly victimize the audience as "catch riddles." Abrahams and Dundes define the "catch riddle" as an ambiguous question in which "it appears to be possible to guess the referent of the catch [question]. But, as with all catches, the ease of guessing is simply a device to get the other person to make a move that places [her or] him in a vulnerable and often embarrassing position." The catch riddle is an intellectual snare, with the riddlee as the intended prey. Just as the ease of the unguarded cheese lures a mouse onto the trap, catch riddles use the lure of low intellectual resistance to entice the riddlee to verbalize something that is socially inappropriate or even dangerous. When I ask Jake whether he still picks his nose, the answer is apparently obvious: "No, I do not still pick my nose." But this obvious answer is incorrect, or at least inadequate: I am attempting to lure Jake into a position where he would posture himself as a person who once did, in fact, engage in this shameful behavior. By leading the riddlee to say something foolish or inappropriate, the riddler demonstrates her opponent's intellectual inferiority and/or opens him to ridicule for thinking of the taboo subject.[3]

Of course, the consequences of catches are minimal in the case of leisure-time riddles, such as those described above, where the riddlee often serves simply as a straight man for the benefit of the rest of the group. Jake suffers no real loss of social status by playing the butt of my jokes; indeed, it would be impolite for him to give away the punch lines, even if he knew the solution. Through a strange loophole in our culture's contract for riddling sessions, Jake's social status may even be temporarily enhanced by playing the fool, simply because this role draws the group's favorable attention to him for a moment and provides an opportunity for him to demonstrate his goodwill.

But in other social settings, such as the social settings envisioned in the sources for Jesus, verbal traps are not quite so innocuous. In Jesus' oral culture, wit was a key academic credential, and falling into a trap would inevitably lead to a loss of intellectual status. For this reason, catch riddles in a variety of forms are common in the Gospels, as Jesus and his opponents jockey for position in front of the crowds. This motif may be conveniently illustrated by the well-known riddling session in John 8, the story of the adulterous woman. Here, Jesus and the Pharisees battle for influence by attempting to catch one another in irresolvable verbal puzzles. Jesus' wit is doubly demonstrated by this episode, evident in his remarkable ability to both answer and ask ambiguous questions with damning implications.

Aside from its many text-critical problems—the ancient manuscript evidence suggests that John 7:53–8:11 did not appear in the earliest editions of the Fourth Gospel—the riddling session at John 8 stands out from its present narrative context in a number of ways. In the first place, Jesus' interlocutors are "the scribes and Pharisees" (8:3), a familiar duo in the Synoptics whom John mentions together nowhere else. This is, in fact, the scribes' sole appearance in the Fourth Gospel. Jesus' initial response to their question is also striking: he stoops over and scribbles on the ground, a gesture that is undeniably dramatic but also quite ambiguous in its own right, both because it isn't clear what he's writing and also because the Johannine Jesus does not typically respond to his interrogators in such a passive fashion.[4] Then there is the difficult question of the Pharisees' motive. They drag a woman of ill fame to Jesus and ask him a question about her situation in order to "test him, so that they would have an accusation against him" (πειράζοντες αὐτόν ἵνα ἔχωσιν κατηγορεῖν αὐτοῦ; v. 6). This is, again, fairly standard fare for the Synoptics, but

somewhat awkward in John; the chief priests and Pharisees have just sent offi-
cers to arrest Jesus at the end of chapter 7, implying that they already think
they have plenty of evidence against him. Further, in John, the Pharisees'
attacks are generally much more direct than this, focusing on things like Jesus'
flagrant violations of the Sabbath and his regular claims to deity. Why question his views on adultery when you've already caught him saying things that
border on blasphemy (see 5:1–18)? These and similar considerations, along
with the manuscript evidence, have led most scholars to conclude that John
7:53–8:11 was a free-floating piece of Jesus tradition that was eventually, for
some reason, worked into the text of the Fourth Gospel by a Christian copy-
ist.[5] I mention these facts not because they impact my reading of John 8:4–6,
but rather because they further affirm the basic thesis of this book by adding
yet another independent witness to the list of sources that portray Jesus in riddling sessions.

The story of the adulterous woman opens with Jesus teaching a crowd in
the temple. The setting, then, is public, and Jesus is posturing himself as an
expert on the Law. To challenge his competence, the scribes and Pharisees
suddenly show up with a woman whom they claim was caught in adultery, perhaps meaning that she was soliciting for prostitution (John 8:4).[6] Using her as
a case study, they "test" Jesus' wisdom with a riddle that builds on two indis-
putable facts. First, they stress that "this woman was *caught in the act* of adultery." This being the case, Jesus cannot weasel out of the dilemma on a
technicality by questioning the evidence; she is obviously guilty and apparently does not deny the charges. Second, they remind Jesus that, "in the Law,
Moses commanded us to stone such women." Jesus can hardly dispute this
claim, because Moses did in fact say this very thing on two separate occasions
(Lev. 20:10; Deut. 22:22). The Pharisees' actual question—"What then do you
say?"—simply invites Jesus to state the inevitable consequence of these two
undeniable realities: she played, and now she must pay.

By all appearances, the Pharisees have exploited their riddler's privileges to
the full, leaving Jesus in a no-win situation. There is no denying the crime, the
Law is absolutely unambiguous on the sentence, and the rules of riddling say
that you have to provide an answer once a public challenge is issued. Jesus must
either affirm the Law and assert that the woman should be killed, or rule in
favor of the woman and deny the force of Moses' regulation. The latter option
would obviously threaten Jesus' public status as a teacher, while also implying
that he takes a lax stance on sexual sin. The former would uphold the Law, but
only at the expense of Jesus' "well-known compassion for the broken and dis-
reputable, his quickness to forgive and restore, and his announcement of the
life-transforming power bound up with the new birth."[7] The Pharisees' riddle
is, then, not only ambiguous (open to at least two answers), but also dangerous,

because both suggested solutions would ruin Jesus' public image. To escape from this dilemma, Jesus must somehow identify a third option, one that will save the woman's life without minimizing the seriousness of adultery or suggesting that Moses was misguided.

Against this backdrop, the genius of Jesus' response—"Let the sinless one among you cast a stone first"—lies in the fact that it accepts everything that the riddle affirms but neutralizes its application, all the while turning the horns of the dilemma back onto the Pharisees. Their riddle tries to trap Jesus in an inevitable *verdict*; he affirms that verdict, but undermines it at the point of *execution*. The woman should be killed per Moses' decree; Jesus insists only that the executioner must not be a "sinner" himself. This simple condition, however, renders the preceding discussion utterly hypothetical: no one can carry out the prescribed sentence, because Moses everywhere assumes that all people are sinners. Of course, the Pharisees could quickly counter that Moses generally calls for the accused to be executed by the entire community or, in a few cases, by the witnesses to the crime (see Deut. 17:2–7; 22:20–24). The Law nowhere stipulates that only sinless people may carry out a death sentence. Yet such an observation would immediately spring the very trap that they had set for Jesus. Dare they state publicly that Moses says the woman can be stoned by anyone at all? Obviously meaning that they themselves would reject the way of mercy and demand her execution? Thereby implying, further, that the crowd should take matters into their own hands and kill her on the spot? And that they, as recognized religious leaders, will answer any questions that the authorities might subsequently raise about the incident? The Pharisees' silent departure from the scene is an admission that Jesus has caught them in their own trap, turning the riddler's advantage into yet another proof of his magnificent wit.

NO GOOD ALTERNATIVE

In terms of function, the Pharisees' riddle at John 8:4–5 is obviously a "catch," an ambiguous question that seeks to trap Jesus in a compromising situation and thereby destroy his credibility with the crowds. In terms of form, the riddle of the adulterous woman is an "alternative." "Alternatives" are riddles that force the riddlee either to violate conventional categories of thinking or to accept a negative consequence for affirming those categories. The ambiguous question proposes two or more logical answers, all of which would lead the riddlee to say something embarrassing and/or taboo.[8] The example we discussed earlier in this chapter, "Yes or no: Do you still pick your nose?" is a classic alternative: the riddlee is invited to say either "yes" or "no," but both of these responses carry damning implications. Similarly, the Pharisees offer Jesus two potential responses to the riddle of the adulterous woman: "yes, kill her to support the Law," which would destroy his image as a gracious person and risk the ire of Rome; "no, let her go," which would imply a lax stance on sexual sin and a disregard for Moses. As these instances illustrate, *the "correct" answer to an alternative is never one of the proposed solutions.* The witty person will be able to come up with a third possibility—"Your mother picks her nose"; "Let the sinless person cast a stone first"—that deconstructs the dilemma by introducing a third term that neutralizes the dangers of the obvious suggestions.

As a matter of course, the sources never allow Jesus to fall prey to a trap. But on numerous occasions he humiliates his opponents by posing alternative riddles to publicly catch them in a compromising position. One of the most effective instances, at least in terms of its present literary context, is the riddle of John's baptism at Mark 11:29–30. Here as elsewhere, Jesus uses an alternative to establish his own academic credentials while temporarily stripping the chief priests, scribes, and elders of theirs.

Jesus' puzzling statement about the Baptist appears in all three Synoptics in the aftermath of the temple incident (see Matt. 21:23–27; Luke 20:1–8). Whether Jesus' actions were intended as a "cleansing" of the temple or a symbolic forecast of its destruction, the religious authorities could scarcely ignore his accusation that the sacred precinct had become a "robbers' den" (Mark 11:17).[9] Their options for dealing with him, however, were limited by his popularity: after this event he was surrounded by a crowd every time he appeared in public (11:18; Luke 19:47–48). Realizing the difficulty of an arrest, and perhaps hoping to defuse the situation without recourse to violence, the chief priests attempt to discredit Jesus by publicly challenging his authority. Indeed, Jesus' "authority" to act and speak as he does is the lynchpin of this episode: the word ἐξουσία appears four times in these seven verses. To determine what ἐξουσία means in this context, and how the riddle of John's baptism relates to Jesus' "authority," it will be helpful to address two key questions. First, what is the purpose of the chief priests' initial inquiry? They could have dealt with the problem of Jesus in a variety of ways; what did they seek to gain by asking him who had authorized his teaching? Second, in what sense, if any, does Jesus' retort about John the Baptist answer their questions? Is he really addressing the issues that the chief priests have raised, or simply skirting them with clever sophistry? The answers to both sets of problems become clear when Jesus' counterquestion is treated as an alternative catch riddle.

On the first question above, one can scarcely disagree with France that "Mark's telling of the incident [11:27–33] suggests a hostile approach [by the chief priests] rather than an open-minded request for information."[10] The terms of their interrogation and the context in which it is delivered reveal their strategy to discredit Jesus. Earlier in Mark's narrative, Jesus had established his "authority" with the crowds in Galilee through charismatic teaching, healing, and exorcisms (Mark 1:21–28; 2:10–12), and the chief priests apparently realize that it would be futile to debate these points. They choose, instead, to attack Jesus where he is most vulnerable, and certainly most inferior to themselves: he does not possess official academic credentials.[11] The authorities "design their questions to embarrass Jesus, to leave him defenseless, to expose him as an imposter" who "has no official status here in Jerusalem," the metropolis of Judaism.[12] Mark underscores this motive by situating the confrontation in the temple courts, where Jesus is "walking about" and teaching the Passover crowds (11:27); many people, the chief priests hope, will witness Jesus' shame, effectively limiting his influence. The episode thus reflects the inherent tension between two types of authority claim, one that Jesus cannot defend and another that his opponents cannot deny. Specifically, the chief priests ignore Jesus' well-established charismatic credentials and instead challenge his status on the basis of an institutional model of intellectual authority. The riddle of John's baptism should be understood as Jesus' answer to this challenge.

It is safe to say, then, that the chief priests wish to discredit Jesus by highlighting his lack of formal credentials; most scholars are agreed on this point. But this conclusion naturally leads to another, more significant problem: In what sense is Jesus' ambiguous inquiry about the Baptist a response to their challenge? Recent answers to this second question have generally been guided by a particular understanding of the relationship between Mark 11:27–33 and its broader context. Before proceeding to offer my own solution, I will digress for a moment to outline this majority position and its implications. Indeed, I must do so, because the majority position would tend to suggest that Mark 11:29–30 is what I have called a "mission riddle" in the introduction to this book, one that seeks to assert something about Jesus' unique messianic identity. To the contrary, I will contend that this saying is a "sage riddle," one that functions primarily to demonstrate Jesus' remarkable wit.

Most commentators read ταῦτα at Mark 11:29 ("by what authority do you do *these things*") against the immediate backdrop of the temple incident. Indeed, France is hesitant to extend the chief priests' inquiry even back to the triumphal entry (Mark 11:1–10): "We may suppose that they have also heard something about the way Jesus had approached the city and the welcome given him by the pilgrim crowd. But the events of the previous day alone are quite enough to provoke their concern and to demand an explanation."[13] Carrington boldly asserts that Jesus' exchange with the priests "can no more stand by itself than the severed half of the fig-tree story [Mark 11:12–14, 20–21]; each narrative has been split, and the severed halves interlaced or alternated with one another in the Marcan manner." It is only, then, by an accident of Mark's

literary style that 11:27 does not immediately follow 11:19, as a necessary conclusion to the events in the temple.[14] While most scholars would not go quite
so far, the riddle of John's baptism is commonly read against the backdrop of
the temple incident, with some acknowledgment that the authorities may also
still be suspicious of Jesus' earlier antics. The chief priests' question at Mark
11:28 may thus be paraphrased, "By what/whose authority did you do what
you just did in the temple?"[15]

While the conclusion that the chief priests' question refers primarily to the
recent temple incident is certainly reasonable, its implications are more significant than first appears. Many scholars who subscribe to the paraphrase
above also interpret the temple incident in terms of Mark's larger agenda to
establish Jesus' messianic identity. This reading, in turn, supports the conclusion that the counterquestion, "from heaven or from men?" invokes the image
of the Baptist primarily in order to establish Jesus' own christological credentials. To take a notable example, N. T. Wright says that the chief priests' challenge "is obviously a question about Messiahship. Someone doing what Jesus
was doing [in the temple] provokes the thought that he is acting as a would-
be Messiah; if so, he is presumably claiming that YHWH has given him this
authority." Building on this assumption, Wright proceeds to argue that "Jesus'
riddle goes deeper than a mere verbal fencing-match." By alluding to the ministry of the Baptist, Jesus is implicitly making two claims: first, "to be the true
successor of the last great prophet," John; second, that he is "in fact the Messiah," the one who had been anointed with the Holy Spirit at his baptism by
John in the same way that David had been anointed with oil by Samuel. Thus,
Jesus "had the authority to act as he did [in the temple] because YHWH had
given it to him," as Messiah, "in and through John's baptism."[16] Following
Wright's approach, then, the riddle of John's baptism and the temple incident
are cut from the same cloth: the former establishes, albeit in veiled terms, the
basis for Jesus' messianic authority; the latter shows that authority in action.

A christological reading of the riddle of John's baptism provides an easy
explanation for the stunned reaction of Jesus' opponents at Mark 11:33. When
they first approach Jesus, the chief priests evidence a confident command of the
situation, fully expecting that he cannot meet their demands; by the end of the
story, they are reduced to a stupefied "we don't know" in response to a relatively simple question. In Hurtado's view, this is yet "another [Markan] example of people confronted with Jesus' authority being unable (and unwilling) to
perceive the true nature of his mission." The chief priests here are more unwilling than unable, having shown "that they do not really want to be confronted
with God's revelation" by their prior refusal to hearken to the Baptist's call to
repent. They have rejected John, and now they are rejecting Jesus; hence,
both their initial inquiry and their refusal to answer Jesus' counterquestion are

insincere.[17] Similarly, Witherington concludes that the Jewish leadership is "both calculating and prepared to lie, for when they say that they don't know whether John's baptism is of God or not, they are simply refusing an answer"; that is, they know that it wasn't from God but are afraid to say what they truly think.[18] According to this reading, the chief priests are well able to answer Jesus' obvious question; the fact that they will not simply reveals the hardness of their determination to destroy the one whom God has authorized as Christ and to protect their own interests (à la John 11:49–50).

It is fair to say, then, that the "majority position" suggests that Mark 11:27–33 serves three basic purposes within the larger narrative. First and least, Jesus "proves himself a debating champion" by "placing his opponents on the horns of a dilemma that allows them no escape without losing face." But we must not stop with the conclusion that Jesus' question is a "purely evasive" "rhetorical ploy," for the pericope is clearly "an important element to the developing christology of this part of the gospel [of Mark]."[19] Second, then, Mark's true purpose is to situate Jesus' recent action in the temple against the backdrop of the Baptist's prophetic ministry. Third, in the process of associating himself with John, Jesus can claim a divine, messianic authority for himself, while couching that claim in terms so ambiguous that he can live to fight another day. One can easily understand why the chief priests are hesitant to answer the question: driven by a refusal to compromise their own authority, they cannot publicly acknowledge the hand of God at work in John and Jesus, yet they fear the political ramifications of a flat denial of his (and John's) charismatic credentials. One can also easily understand why the Jesus Seminar concludes that this entire sequence of events, driven as it is by Mark's literary and theological concerns and centered around Jesus' christological riddle, is "plausible" but entirely unhistorical.[20]

The "majority reading" of Mark 11:27–33—and I stress that my summary here is a composite image, not necessarily representative of the specific opinions of any single person, living or dead—is, in my view, quite interesting, and since I know very little about the Gospel of Mark I would not be in a position to refute it definitively, even if I desired to do so. It appears to me to be a very clever way of interpreting the riddle of John's baptism against Mark's broader christological agenda. But in terms of situating this riddle in the context of the life of Jesus—which is my present purpose—I must confess that I feel that the majority approach does not frame the issue in the most helpful way, and in the process it assumes a great deal about Mark's intentions that is not obvious from the data available in the passage itself. This is not to say that Mark, or even Jesus, was oblivious to the possible christological implications of this episode, only that a christological reading seems to overlook the basic dynamics of such an exchange in an oral culture. As such, the majority position sig-

The "Majority Position" on Mark 11:27–33

(a summary of many that may not reflect the specific views of any one)

1. Jesus' question outwits his opponents, but his remarks must be more than just a clever ploy, because . . .

2. His true purpose is to connect his ministry to that of John the Baptist, because . . .

3. Such a connection would provide the prophetic/messianic credentials necessary to justify what he did in the temple, thus answering the chief priests' initial question, but . . .

4. Of course, the chief priests don't acknowledge the revelation of God in either John or Jesus; yet they're afraid to say so in public, so they refuse to answer in order to protect themselves.

On the basis of all this, some reasonably conclude that . . .

5. The entire episode is a Markan creation to "demonstrate Jesus' [messianic] authority, on the one hand, and, on the other, to prepare the way for his eventual arrest and execution."

—Funk 1998, 124

nificantly complicates the second key question noted earlier: in what sense, if any, does Jesus' retort about John the Baptist answer the chief priests' question about his credentials?

Douglas Hare notes that "interpreters disagree about whether Jesus' question [about John's baptism] is merely a rhetorical ploy, intended only to embarrass his questioners publicly, or a genuine response to their challenge."[21] Hare's summary accurately reflects the state of research reflected in the preceding outline of the majority position: the "real issue" behind Mark 11:30 is Jesus' messianic authority, borrowed here from the Baptist's reputation; for some reason, maybe to explain why Jesus wasn't arrested on the spot, Mark has chosen to couch that claim in a strange little verbal game. But I wish respectfully to suggest that this way of framing the issue creates a false dichotomy between Jesus' rhetorical strategy and his response to the challenge that the chief priests have raised. Specifically, I would suggest (a) that Jesus' "rhetorical ploy" is, in and of itself, "a genuine response to their challenge," and (b) that Jesus' ability to "embarrass his questioners publicly" is, in fact, the very seal of authority that they have demanded. These facts become apparent as soon as we abandon the notion that Jesus' words inherently carry some deep christological significance, and choose instead to read them in terms of the way that alternative riddles can be used in an oral culture to establish academic credentials. For sake of convenience, my counterreading of Mark 11:27–33 will turn on the axis of two specific points from the exhaustive discussion in Robert Gundry's 1993 commentary.

First, I cannot accept Gundry's assertion that ταῦτα, "these things," in the authorities' original question at Mark 11:28 must refer exclusively to the recent temple incident.[22] Of course, that event would be foremost in the minds of the religious authorities at that moment in Mark's narrative. But I would also observe (a) that this particular challenge from this particular group would be completely unsurprising at any moment in Mark and (b) that there is nothing about this episode, aside from its present literary context, that inherently ties it to the temple incident. On point (a), Rhoads and Michie and, more recently, Elizabeth Struthers Malbon have effectively demonstrated that Mark portrays the Jewish leadership "in a consistently negative light" as a group of people who systematically oppose Jesus.[23] The scribes, who appear with the chief priests and elders here at 11:27, had already begun to challenge Jesus' authority as early as chapter 2, over a christological claim that was much less ambiguous than Jesus' actions in the temple (cf. Mark 2:1–12 with 11:15–18). One may therefore reasonably assume, as many commentators do, that the scribes' question at 11:28 refers not only to the temple incident and the triumphal entry but also to "all his teaching and healing activities," which are now moving from the remote villages of Galilee to take center stage in the temple during Passover.[24] This being the case, on point (b) I see no particular need to tie the content of this story exclusively to the temple incident, and can envision, contra Carrington's hypothesis, a number of settings in the early church where it might have been cited on its own for purposes of preaching, teaching, or anything else. John 2 makes it quite clear that at least some early Christians did not feel that the temple incident needed this particular episode for clarification. In summary, Jesus' exchange with the chief priests and scribes, when taken as a self-contained unit, is completely typical of his encounters with the Jewish authorities on a variety of occasions. Mark 11:27–33 would thus be entirely coherent in any of the first ten chapters of that Gospel and at least bears verisimilitude to a large number of incidents in the career of the historical Jesus.

Second, on the basis of the preceding observations, I must agree with Gundry that, even if the canonical evangelists saw the temple incident as critical to the messianic identity of Jesus, it does not necessarily follow that Jesus' messianic identity is at the forefront of the events described at Mark 11:27–33. By which I mean, I do not know that the point of this particular story, even from Mark's perspective, is to prove something about Jesus' messianic status. In my view, it would be more accurate to say that, if anything, Mark simply assumes Jesus' messianic status here as the backdrop to an episode that does not, and could not, prove any messianic claim in and of itself. While Gundry may go too far in saying that "the whole dialogue has to do with nothing deeper than saving and losing face," I would affirm his conclusion that Jesus is primarily concerned here to "impale the Sanhedrin on the horns of an embarrassing dilemma."[25] His ability to do this, and their tacit acknowledgment of this ability, is the platform on which this episode builds an answer to the question of Jesus' "authority."

As Gundry and a number of other commentators have noted, Jesus' question about John's baptism creates a "dilemma" for the chief priests. It does so because it is phrased as an alternative catch riddle, one delivered in the very public setting of the temple courts (Mark 11:27). The subject is John's baptism, and the alternatives are these: Do you chief priests say that John's baptism was "from heaven," in the sense that it was authorized by God? Or do you say that John's baptism was "from men," essentially something that John made up in his own mind, meaning that the ritual lacked divine sanction and, therefore, spiritual efficacy? Neither answer is good and, as is often the case with alternative riddles, the most obvious answer is the least attractive: the chief priests did not authorize John's activity and perhaps resisted it (see John 1:19–25), but they dare not say definitively that God had no role in the Baptist's ministry, especially in front of the Passover crowds who hold John in esteem (Mark 11:32). Their response, "We don't know," is not a stubborn refusal to answer Jesus' question, but rather *an admission of their inability to answer*. As noted earlier, the "correct" answer to an alternative catch riddle is always a third proposition that bypasses the unpleasant consequences of the proposed solutions: when I ask Jake, "Do you still pick your nose?" his only safe answer is, "*You* do," a response that effectively springs the trap back on me. Similarly, the "correct" answer to the riddle of John's baptism would be any response that could assert that John's work was "from men" while also avoiding the wrath of the crowd. The chief priests, in attempting to locate such a response, do not betray a lack of integrity; they betray a lack of wit. The Jewish authorities, in other words, are not culpable here because they are hardhearted or dishonest; they are culpable because they have been completely outfoxed on their home court by a rube from Galilee who has no real academic credentials.

Viewed against this backdrop, Jesus' concluding statement, "Neither will I tell you," is not a childish refusal to answer the chief priests' question. It is, rather, a simple observation that he has met their demand for proof of his credentials. They wish to know who has authorized his teaching, and now they have found out: "Neither will I tell you" means, "Nor do I need to," because *"you* just gave me the authority to do these things by admitting that you can't untie my knots and, thereby, submitting to my superior intellect"—a cultural reality that the chief priests cannot deny and do not challenge. Jesus does not need to borrow any prestige from John the Baptist here, nor does he need christological claims to defend his right to "walk about the temple" courts teaching the people. His stunning demonstration of wit is sufficient in itself to establish the academic credentials that the chief priests wished to see. An alternative catch riddle is particularly effective for this purpose because it demonstrates both the riddler's wit and the riddlee's ignorance at the same time.

Before moving on, I should note that this reading of Mark 11:27–33 justifies, in my view, the assertion that Jesus' question about John's baptism is a "sage riddle." The question establishes Jesus' intellectual authority as a teacher, but does not, in any obvious sense, attempt to establish his authority as a messianic figure who would have some right symbolically to cleanse/ destroy the temple. This is not to say that Mark did not believe that Jesus possessed such messianic authority, nor that Mark did not structure his version of the temple incident to reflect this claim. It is to say, however, that I do not think we can reasonably assume that this episode is not historical simply because it is christological; it isn't inherently christological, and it must be "historical" at least in the broad sense that it represents a type of encounter that probably occurred frequently in the life of Jesus. Any christological value that Mark attributes to the incident would only build on the extended implications of Jesus' remarkably superior wit. As such, I feel justified in including this text in my database of "sage riddles."

By any account, the alternative riddle at Mark 11:29–30 appears in a context that exudes hostility. Jesus and the religious authorities are locked in a battle for authority, with each side pulling out its heaviest intellectual guns. The same may be said of several other alternative riddles that we have already discussed, such as the poll-tax riddle, the riddle of the woman with seven husbands (both Mark 12), and the riddle of the adulterous woman (John 8). But aside from such agonistic encounters, the sources suggest that Jesus sometimes used alternatives to present his disciples (and neutral audiences) with paradoxes, then displayed his wit by providing a solution that transcended the obvious, yet incorrect, proposed answers. In this respect, it appears that Jesus sometimes used ambiguous questions as a teaching tool. The riddle of the temple tax at Matthew 17:25, which was briefly discussed in an earlier chapter, may serve as a convenient example.

After Peter's encounter with the collectors of the two-drachma temple tax, Jesus asks him, "From whom do the kings of the earth receive taxes? From their sons, or from strangers?"[26] This question frames the issue in a somewhat unconventional way, one that dramatically complicates the relatively simple matter of paying the tax by forcing Peter to choose between two undesirable options. If Peter pays the tax, he shows support for the temple but thereby ironically classifies himself as a "stranger" to God; if he doesn't pay, he classifies himself as a "son," but only at the risk of offending most Jews. Peter cannot resolve this dilemma on his own, so Jesus provides a third alternative that falls outside the scope of the proposed solutions and thus avoids the disadvantages of both: a "son" can voluntarily pay the tax so as not to offend the "strangers" who have no choice (17:27). This makes it possible for Peter, and other disciples, to classify themselves with Jesus in a fourth category: sons who *choose* to pay the tax, even though they are technically exempt. Peter may enter this special group, however, only after Jesus has invited him to do so—he doesn't even know that it exists until his master tells him.

Because it is ambiguous, Jesus' question about kings, sons, and strangers could potentially apply to a large number of situations. Commentators are therefore naturally divided on its original setting. Jesus' point seems to be that "the sons are exempt," but who are these "sons" and exactly what "tax" is he talking about? If Matthew 17:25 goes back to the historical Jesus, the "tax" in question would obviously be the two-drachma temple tax mentioned above, and the "sons" would be "God's true children[, who] should not have to pay tax to him."[27] Jesus, however, voluntarily paid the tax to avoid "the impression that he rejected the temple and all that it stood for."[28] But some scholars argue that, while the passage is indeed talking about the temple tax, Matthew developed this story as "an instruction to the community in the guise of a narrative," so that the "sons" in question are actually second- and third-generation Jewish Christians. Before the destruction of the Jerusalem temple in 70 CE, Jewish Christians faced the dilemma of whether they should still pay the tax in support of the cult. Matthew wished to remind these believers "of the freedom given them as God's children, which, however, requires regard for particular circumstances"—that is, as Christians they are technically exempt from the tax, but they should continue to pay so as "not to cause unbelieving Jews to [be offended and] reject the gospel."[29] A third group of scholars, however, envision a much different scenario. When the Romans destroyed the Jerusalem temple, the emperor Vespasian continued to collect the temple tax, yet dedicated the funds to the reconstruction of the temple of Jupiter Capitolinus in Rome, which had been recently ravaged in a civil war. It is this "tax" to which Matthew refers, so that the "king" is the emperor and the "sons" of Jesus' riddle are post–70 CE Christians who were not sure whether they should give money to support a pagan temple. Matthew, like Paul (Rom. 13:1–7), advises believers to pay the tax as a gesture of obedience to the civil authorities.[30]

The specific origin of this saying, and the precise problem that Matthew thought such a teaching would resolve for his community, are beyond the scope of this book. For my purposes, it suffices to note that this episode is structured as a riddling session; that the phrase "What do you think?" explicitly warns Peter that this is the case; that Matthew 17:25 plays with taboos and blurs conventional boundaries of thought; and, especially here, that *this riddle would function as an alternative catch for any of the proposed audiences described above*. Jesus' riddle suggests that there are three kinds of people in the world: kings, who receive taxes; their families and friends, who don't have to pay them; everybody else, who does. The question, with its two suggested answers, forces Peter to say that people who pay are in the same category as aliens (ἀλλότριοι) to the king; the fact of paying taxes, whether to the temple in 32 CE or to Vespasian in 82 CE, means that one is being treated as a "stranger" by the powers that be, a dangerous proposition anytime and anywhere in the first century.[31] Hence, whether the question originated with Jesus or Matthew or some other unknown individual, the temple tax riddle introduces a complex problem of the highest order of importance, one that would call any first-century audience (and many twenty-first-century audiences) to move beyond the obvious alternatives.

Riddling, then, can be serious business. We could argue this point from the Gospels alone, even if folklorists had not found ample evidence elsewhere for such a claim. Because this is the case, the sources for Jesus frequently portray him in riddling sessions that highlight his intellectual credentials as a sage. Even when Jesus is at a significant disadvantage, his superior wit always prevails; enemies fall before him like autumn leaves, and even his closest disciples must wait for him to provide suitable answers. Riddling is a social game, but it's a very dangerous game when you're playing with Jesus.

Up to this point I have, I think, adequately defined the riddle as a speech genre and have located and discussed a variety of different sage riddles in a wide ranges of sources for the historical Jesus. I have also noted general trends in the ways that the sources use such riddles to make their points about Jesus and his message. The next three chapters will apply this analysis to two key issues in Jesus research: the social posture of the historical Jesus; and, Jesus' conception of the Kingdom of God.

8

The Messianic Ambiguity

Up to this point, I have focused my remarks on riddles themselves: what they are, how they work, and what they mean for our understanding of a number of key passages in the sources for Jesus. I now wish to explore what all of this riddling might tell us about two central problems in historical Jesus research, but before I do so let me summarize the main contours of our discussion thus far.

1. "Riddles" are intentionally ambiguous questions that seek to confuse the audience by blurring conventional boundaries of thought and/or language. The riddlee is asked to identify the "correct" answer among two or more reasonable possibilities, where "correct" means the one that the riddler wants at that moment.
2. Riddles can take a large number of forms and styles, across cultures and even within one culture. Any statement that can be used to create intentional ambiguity can function as a riddle.

Let me pause for a moment to review a significant implication of point #2, at least for the present study. Because riddles are defined mainly by their function rather than their form—that is, they are defined by what they do (create ambiguity) rather than by how they look—they can be difficult to detect in written narratives. Specifically, the riddles in the sources for Jesus cannot be detected by conventional form-critical criteria, which depend on formal and verbal consistency at the surface level of a saying. Riddles are, however, easily ascertainable in the Gospels (canonical and noncanonical) through the application of literary criteria that identify intentional ambiguity, such as those that we discussed in chapter 4. Now let us proceed with our summary.

111

3. Because riddles can potentially create confusion and embarrassment, they are performed in carefully scripted social settings. The rules for these "riddling sessions" vary from culture to culture, but the local guidelines are well known, at least intuitively, to the members of each specific group.

4. To answer a riddle, the riddlee must appeal to at least one of three types of cultural knowledge: knowledge of cultural items (people, places, things); knowledge of cultural patterns of language, logic, and analogy; knowledge of traditions, which very often simply means that you've heard this riddle, or one like it, before. People who do not possess such cultural information will not be able to answer the riddle, regardless of their IQ. Note that the word "cultural" here is essentially synonymous with "group," and that this principle applies to groups of all sizes, ranging from large, complex societies to tiny subunits within those societies.

5. "Wit" is the ability to apply one or several of the three types of knowledge mentioned above to a specific riddle in order to answer it. Witty people demonstrate their firm command of cultural/group information and traditions by their ability to ask and answer riddles.

6. Those individuals who share common wit form a "community of knowledge," a group of people who are united by the possession of information that is unknown to others. This is a logical extension of points #4 and #5 above: those people who share knowledge of things and traditions, and command of specific patterns of logic and analogy, may be thought of as a "group" on the basis of this common intellectual property.

This much I have said about "riddles" per se, and in many instances I have simply used examples from the Gospels to illustrate these theoretical points. Now, however, I will proceed to two more focused observations that have emerged thus far in our study. These observations will take us into the two central problems in historical Jesus research that I mentioned above.

➤7. Many sources show Jesus engaged in riddling sessions, asking and answering ambiguous questions. The riddling sessions in the sources emphasize both the inherent advantages of the riddler and the power of wit in order to demonstrate Jesus' remarkable intellect. In such passages, *Jesus uses riddles both as a teaching tool and as a means of establishing his academic credentials.*

➤8. In the sources Jesus often uses riddles to discuss key elements of his teaching: purity regulations, Sabbath observance, imperial and temple taxes, divorce, wealth, social responsibility, prayer, humility, and so on. Overall, it is fair to say that *Jesus' riddles are closely tied to his concept of the "Kingdom of God,"* a fact that is perhaps most explicit in the Kingdom parables that function as riddles.

Essentially, then, I conclude that *Jesus often used intentionally ambiguous questions both to establish his credentials and to communicate key elements of his message about the Kingdom of God.* Put another way, riddles were central both to the way that Jesus postured himself for public consumption and to the very nature of the Kingdom that he proclaimed. Many sources reflecting a variety of theological perspectives make this assertion. Hence, I think it reasonable to suggest that Jesus' riddling can help us to answer two key questions in historical Jesus research: (1) How was Jesus perceived by his contemporaries? (Apocalyptic prophet? Cynic sage? Radical rabbi? Magician? Christ?) and (2) What did Jesus understand the Kingdom of God to be? These two issues are closely related, and I think it obvious that neither is insignificant to our understanding of Jesus and the Gospels.

In the remainder of this book, I will attempt to show, in a very preliminary way, how my profile of Jesus the Riddler might help us answer those two questions. You will quickly discover that my remarks are programmatic rather than exhaustive, and I confess at the outset that they must be so at this stage of my own journey. I present my conclusions as an invitation to future reflection rather than as a fixed portrait of Jesus, a series of dots that could be connected in any number of ways to create a variety of different images.

JESUS WAS A RIDDLER

Point #7 above suggests that *"sage riddles" were a key element of Jesus' social posturing, a rhetorical device that he used to position himself and his message*. Obviously, this conclusion begs us to ask, "What does Jesus' riddling tell us about the way that he was perceived by his contemporaries?" What type of person did they think that he was—rabbi, philosopher, prophet, exorcist, M/messiah, lunatic, or some or all of these at once? My short answer to that question would be, "By themselves, the riddles don't tell us enough to come to any firm conclusion," which is simply to say that I don't think the sage riddles can really tell us anything definite about Jesus' identity apart from other aspects of his activity. The same would be true even if we extended this discussion to include the christological mission riddles that appear in the Gospels from time to time: the *content* of the mission riddles, if we accepted their claims, might help us to understand Jesus' self-image, but the fact that such content is communicated through riddling would not, in and of itself, take us much further. In traditional cultures, riddles function to establish wit and, thereby, intellectual credentials, but intellectual credentials might contribute to several different public profiles in the context of Roman Palestine. Of course, this problem is not unique to the riddles: most of what Jesus does in the sources—including his exorcisms, healings, and table fellowship—could support several different identities, depending on your point of view. This fact should perhaps make us wary of any attempt to assign Jesus to a single, exclusive category. But with these caveats, I shall be so bold as to make a few comments that I hope will at least underscore the potential value of Jesus' riddling for more detailed considerations of his social posture.

At the most basic level, I think we can be completely certain that *Jesus was a riddler*, both in the sense that he consciously postured himself as such and in the sense that his contemporaries thought of him this way (I hope this claim does not surprise you at this point in the book). To conclude otherwise would require us to reject information from all the best available sources, even where such information is not obviously tied to christological claims, theological biases, or literary style. But while this conclusion is certain, its implications are limited. As I noted in an earlier chapter, the designation "riddler" describes a scripted role in a cross-cultural social game, the riddling session; "riddler" does not, except in *Batman* comics, designate a specific identity that a person might hold in a traditional society (unlike, for example, "trickster"). Specifically here, ancient Palestinian Jews would not have recognized a social category of people called "riddlers"—at least, I am not aware that they did. They would, however, recognize that people who consistently trump their opponents in public riddling contests are "witty." We may therefore confidently suggest that Jews in Roman Palestine would think that *Jesus was a person of unusual wit*—that is, a person who demonstrated a remarkable knowledge of cultural items, logic, and traditions—and that they would have come to this conclusion because he did and said certain things that fit this profile.

The firm conclusion that Jesus' riddling led his contemporaries to conclude that he was "witty" allows us to revise and expand our first key question as follows: how would Jesus' contemporaries interpret his consistent displays of remarkable wit, and what type of person would they associate with such displays? Put another way, if a Jew in Roman Palestine wanted to categorize Jesus, how would Jesus' wit inform any decision about which category to choose? I do not know how to answer those questions conclusively, although I am convinced that they must be asked if we want to understand how Jesus postured himself. But to illustrate the problem and, I hope, to open avenues for further dialogue, I will briefly discuss how Jesus' riddling and wit might interact with three categories from his own culture that are frequently mentioned in both the sources and modern Jesus research: "rabbi/teacher," "prophet," and "messiah/christ." Would a recognition that Jesus portrayed himself as an unusually witty person, capable of manipulating ideological boundaries to either affirm or destroy them, lead people to conclude that he was one of these three types of person? Let me proceed from what I judge to be the most certain possibility to the least certain.

A RIDDLING RABBI?

Not infrequently, the sources refer to Jesus as "rabbi" or "teacher," terms that appear to be synonymous—John, in fact, twice tells his readers that "rabbi" is synonymous with the Greek διδάσκαλος (1:38; 20:16), suggesting that he sees no meaningful difference between these words. Many of these references appear in stories that do not meet the criteria of authenticity normally utilized in historical Jesus research, but as far as I can tell, there is no obvious pattern that would link either term to the peculiar ideological tendencies of the sources. Luke, it is true, seems to avoid the word "rabbi" (cf. Mark 9:5 with Luke 9:33; Mark 14:45 with Matt. 26:49//Luke 22:47–48), and *Thomas* rarely uses any title for Jesus, but neither of these observations point to an obvious theological bias.[1] Two consistent trends are, however, very evident across the sources in those passages where "rabbi" or "teacher" appears: Jesus does not use these titles of himself; other people very often do. On the former point, Jesus never calls himself "rabbi" and refers to himself as "teacher" in only two passages, both times imitating what the disciples might call him (Mark 14:14; John 13:13–14). In two other passages, Jesus flatly states that "I am not your teacher," criticizes those who like to be called "rabbi," and tells his own followers that they must never accept either designation (*Thomas* 13:4; Matt. 23:6–10). Yet if the historical Jesus did not prefer these titles, the sources suggest that his associates entirely missed the point. In the Gospels, Jesus is called "rabbi" or "teacher" at least fifteen different times by his disciples, and even more often—at least twenty-one different times—by opponents or people who do not seem to know him very well.[2]

Whether or not they misunderstood his intentions, it is relevant to note that characters in the Gospels call Jesus "rabbi" or "teacher" in the types of situations where such titles would be entirely appropriate: when the disciples ask him a question, when other religious experts want to engage him in debate on some theological point, when strangers solicit favors or ask his opinion about something. Thus, the disciples call Jesus "rabbi" before asking him why a certain man was born blind (John 9:2); the Pharisees, Sadducees, and a scribe all call Jesus "teacher" before drilling him with theological questions about taxation, resurrection, and the greatest commandment (Mark 12:13–34); a person in a crowd calls Jesus "teacher" before asking him to make his brother divide an inheritance (Luke 12:13). In all these instances, the people whom Jesus encounters seem to assume that he does things that a rabbi/teacher would do.

For purposes of the present study, it is relevant to note that Jesus' frequent riddling and the remarkable wit that he thereby displayed would be entirely consistent with this portrait, especially since so many of his riddles touch on the Scriptures or theological principles. It is easy to imagine that Jews in Roman Palestine would refer to a person who is gifted at posing and answering difficult questions about biblical and ethical issues, and who often does this in public settings, as "rabbi/teacher." One may therefore confidently conclude that Jesus used riddles to display his wit, and that he did this in order to posture and credentialize himself as a rabbi/teacher, even if he did not like the implications of those titles.[3]

But this conclusion leads us to ask, "*Only* as a rabbi?" In other words, Does the category "rabbi" exhaust the possible implications of Jesus' riddling for a discussion of the way that he was perceived by his contemporaries? Specifically here, could Jesus the Riddling Rabbi also, and at the same time, be perceived as a "prophet" and/or a "messiah"? These questions are, in my view, much more difficult to answer, and here I will simply point out the kinds of problems that would have to be addressed before we could come to a definitive conclusion.

A RIDDLING RABBINIC PROPHET?

In considering whether Jesus' contemporaries might conclude that he was a *riddling prophet*, it is first relevant to note that characters in the Gospels do not necessarily think of Jesus as a "rabbi" in the same sense that most modern Jews think about their rabbis. Both ancient and modern Jews would, of course, expect their rabbis to exhibit a firm command of biblical and theological principles, and an ability to relate those principles to practical situations in a way that would both challenge and confirm popular thinking. But the Jews who appear in the sources for Jesus seem willing to apply the title "rabbi" to people who can do quite a bit more than this. Thus John the Baptist, whom the Gospels everywhere portray as a "prophet," is called "rabbi" by his own disciples (John 3:26) and "teacher" by a group of tax collectors (Luke 3:12). In a similar vein, people sometimes call Jesus "rabbi/teacher" in contexts where they clearly expect a display of what modern readers would call "supernatural" power. Thus, Jairus's servants tell him not to bother "the teacher" about healing their master's daughter because she has already died (Mark 5:35), and a man calls Jesus "teacher" before asking him to exorcize the demons that have severely afflicted his son (Mark 9:17). This expanded use of the word "rabbi" is perhaps most striking in the Gospel of John, where Nicodemus calls Jesus "rabbi" before admitting that "no one would be able to do the signs that you do unless God were with him" (3:2), and Nathaniel, even more remarkably, tells Jesus (upon their first meeting), "Rabbi, you are the Son of God, you are the King of Israel" (1:49). In modern idiom, the designations "Son of God" and "King of Israel" would make the title "rabbi" at least a bit pale, if not entirely redundant. From these and other examples, it appears obvious that the authors of the sources did not feel that the designation "rabbi" necessarily excluded other acclamations, including exorcist, healer, prophet, and "Christ." Hence, I would argue that we cannot necessarily conclude that Jesus was *not* perceived as a prophet, exorcist, healer, or messiah just because he was perceived as a riddling rabbi. He was certainly perceived as a riddling rabbi, but perhaps also as these other things as well.

Against this general backdrop, let us consider the specific value of Jesus' riddles in determining whether he postured himself as, and/or whether his contemporaries understood him to be, a "prophet"—a *riddling rabbinic prophet*. The riddles alone cannot, in my view, bring us to a firm conclusion on this point, but I will briefly highlight three points that might be fruitful for further discussion.

First, I have noted several times now that "wit" demonstrates command of cultural logic and traditions. But in many—I want to say "most," but statistical documentation is not available—traditional societies, cultural logic and traditions carry an aura of the sacred (perhaps another reason why riddles are sometimes performed in conjunction with funerals and initiation rites). Oral cultures can therefore easily view unusual wit as a form of giftedness, a sort of supernatural endowment. Applying this principle to Jesus' setting, cultural logic and traditions were certainly viewed as "sacred" in Roman Palestine, a society that derived—or at least thought that it derived—its basic belief system and social structure from the sacred texts of the Hebrew Bible. In such a context, Jesus' remarkable mastery of puzzling theological questions and difficult Scriptures could easily be understood as a divine endowment, establishing him as a prophetic sage. This conclusion would explain both specific texts where Jesus is called "prophet" by representatives of the masses (Matt. 16:14; 21:11, 46; Luke 7:16; 24:19; John 4:19; 9:17) and the sources' more general suggestion that Jesus' credentials were charismatic/informal rather than institutional/formal. It may be, in other words, that in Jesus' cultural milieu unusual wit was interpreted as a gift, especially when such wit was regularly used to successfully undermine the institutional powers of religious authority. I wish to underline the words "*may be*" in the preceding sentence, because I am certainly not prepared to argue the point in detail here. For now, I would simply note that Jesus the Riddling Rabbi could also have been perceived to be a prophet, depending on how people understood the source of his magnificent wit.

Second, the question of the perceived source of Jesus' wit immediately reminds us, as Crossan has argued so forcefully, that one man's prophet is another man's magician.[4] Which forces us to ask, If Palestinian Jews in Jesus' time did interpret unusual wit as a supernatural endowment, would they necessarily view it as a *prophetic* endowment, or would they interpret such wit as a *demonic* endowment, especially in view of the fact that Jesus so often used his wisdom to explode cherished theological principles? We would probably have to answer that question somewhat ambiguously, noting that different people would likely respond to Jesus' wit in different ways. If we wished to be bold and predict a trend, we could perhaps compare Jesus' riddling to his skill as an exorcist. At Mark 1:21–27, Jesus' ability to cast out demons leads a crowd in Capernaum to conclude that he brings a new brand of authoritative teaching; later on, the Jerusalem scribes cite such activity as evidence that "he is possessed by Beelzebul" (Mark 3:11–12, 20–22). I can easily imagine the same sort of bifurcated response to Jesus' riddling: the masses, impressed with his charismatic credentials, conclude that Jesus' wit is a divine gift; the religious authorities, uncomfortable with the implications of his message, argue that his unconventional wisdom comes from the devil. I imagine this scenario, yet I am not in a position to prove it right now, so I will only note here that the tension between miracle and magic would probably need to be considered in any attempt to determine whether Jesus' riddling could have led his contemporaries to conclude that he was a prophet.

Finally, before we could firmly conclude that Jesus' contemporaries interpreted his wit as a gift of prophetic/demonic insight, we would have to address a third, and perhaps more essential, question: Can we establish that first-century Jewish prophets/magicians were witty? Can we, in other words, show that people who were called "prophet" in Jesus' time sometimes credentialized their claims through public displays of wit? Again, I have no firm answer, but to illustrate the problem I will close this section by using John the Baptist, the first-century Jewish prophet who was closest to Jesus and in whom the authors of our sources were most interested, as a point of comparison.

To focus the problem of "prophetic wit" on a single, convenient point, let us briefly consider the way in which the sources portray the respective interactions of the Baptist and Jesus with Herod Antipas. If Josephus's comments about the Baptist are original, he agrees with Mark that Herod killed John for fear of his influence over the masses (*Antiquities* 18.116–19). Mark, however, goes beyond Josephus in explaining why Antipas might have reason to fear such influence: "John was saying to Herod," and presumably to other people about Herod, "it is not lawful for you to have your brother's wife" (Mark 6:17–18; cf. Lev. 18:16, 20:21). John's approach seems entirely consistent with the Jewish prophetic tradition, which cherished the memory of brave people who had ruined themselves with frank speech before wicked kings. But at the same time, one can scarcely call John's pointed remark "witty," simply because it is utterly lacking in ambiguity. The Baptist's message to Herod is completely clear, and its political implications are also completely clear: no "Jewish" king should be permitted to flagrantly violate God's Law.

But a very different picture emerges when we consider Jesus' comments about Herod at Luke 13:32. For unspecified reasons, Herod apparently wishes to kill Jesus, prompting some sympathetic Pharisees to urge him to leave the area. Jesus responds by saying, "Go and tell that fox, 'I cast out demons and heal today and tomorrow, and the third day I will be finished.'" Exactly how would these Pharisees, and Herod himself, interpret such a statement? Is "fox" an insult, or an acknowledgment of Antipas's political shrewdness? Further, what does Jesus mean when says that he will "be finished" on "the third day"? Finished healing, or finished causing trouble, or what? And what's he going to be doing four days from now? However we answer these questions, Jesus' comment about Herod is considerably more ambiguous than that of the Baptist. My point here is not disabled by the fact that Luke 13:32 is a mission riddle with obvious christological implications; right now I am talking about the way that "prophets" and "riddlers" might be respectively portrayed in the available sources for Jesus. John the Baptist, a prophet by any count, is portrayed as frank, but not witty, in his comments about Herod Antipas; Jesus the Riddling Rabbi is portrayed as sly and ambiguous.[5] I believe that I could extend this comparison, with similar results, to the cases of other heterodox prophets whom Josephus mentions in the late Second Temple period. I am therefore unprepared to say that we can know with certainty that people called "prophet" in Jesus' day used, or were expected to use, wit to establish their credentials, although it is theoretically possible and culturally feasible that they would have done so.

A RIDDLING RABBINIC MESSIAH?

Finally, let us briefly consider the role that Jesus' riddles might play in future considerations of his messianic identity. I can conveniently summarize my own thoughts on this issue as follows: (1) in terms of *faith*, I would personally understand Jesus to be the Christ; (2) in terms of *history*, I think it reasonable to argue that at least some of Jesus' contemporaries understood him to be a messianic figure, although he did not encourage this line of thinking; but (3) in terms of *this book*, nothing that we have been talking about could directly support my beliefs as stated in #1 or #2. On a scale of 1–10, where 10 represents "historical certainty" and 1 represents "we can't be sure," I would probably give the christological question a rating of about 2. This rating reflects not only my cynical personality, but also the fact that the connection between riddles and Christology seems to me to be very difficult to establish. I will, however, proceed to outline two points where Jesus' riddling might intersect the thorny problem of messianic identity, one relating to methodology and another to a specific type of data that is available from the sources. Neither of these observations will bring us to a definite conclusion on the issue, but both might open interesting channels for further discussion.

First, as a point of *research method*, I would argue that the mere fact that Jesus was a riddler cannot take us directly forward on the christological issue. The whole question of what ancient Jews expected the M/messiah(s) to be seems incredibly complicated and almost impossible to resolve, and I am not sure how we would even begin to determine whether Jesus' contemporaries expected the M/messiah(s) to be "witty." Of course, the *content* of many of Jesus' riddles in the sources—those that I have called "mission riddles"— might speak directly to the christological issue, the questions being (a) whether we can accept the historicity of what they say, and (b) what their claims would have meant in a first-century context, unencumbered by the decrees of the later church councils. These are important questions, but the fact that the sources sometimes communicate their christological claims through riddles will not necessarily answer them for us.

To illustrate the problem, I would like to review briefly a riddle that was *excluded* from the database for this study, John 10:34–36. This text closely resembles many of the sage riddles discussed here, but I left it out because it very clearly contributes to the broader Johannine Christology. While we can fairly say that the *content* of this riddle portrays Jesus as Christ, its *rhetorical moves* portray him only as a rabbinic expert on the Hebrew Bible.

John 10:34–36 is a good example of a "neck riddle," a situation where the protagonist must answer or pose a difficult question in order to "save his neck" with wit. Jesus shocks the Jews at the Feast of Dedication by claiming that he is one with the Father (10:22–31); they respond by collecting stones to punish his blasphemy. Realizing that things aren't going very well, Jesus tries to curb their wrath by posing a riddle that appeals to Psalm 82:6–7, where God warns Israel's wicked judges that they themselves will be judged: "I say, 'You are gods, children of the Most High, all of you; nevertheless, you shall die like mortals'" (NRSV). Jesus cites this passage and then points out that "the Scripture cannot be broken" to remind the Jews that the terms of the psalm must be accepted without debate; the riddle proceeds to set this irrefutable sacred text against their proposed course of action. How can they condemn him for calling himself "God's son" when the Bible sometimes refers to human beings as "gods"? Jesus' clever ploy, typical of many of the riddles discussed in this book, creates ambiguity by driving a wedge between popular theology and an apparent loophole in the Hebrew Bible; also like many of the sage riddles, it challenges conventional thinking at a moment when Jesus' public image, and here even his life, is clearly at stake. The Jews cannot resolve the proposed dilemma, a fact that clearly demonstrates Jesus' superior wisdom.

But while John 10:34–36 is similar to the sage riddles in that it challenges established theological beliefs and verifies Jesus' academic credentials, its present literary context suggests that the Fourth Evangelist is primarily interested in what this ambiguous statement says about Jesus' identity. Chapter 10 opens with the "Good Shepherd" discourse, which includes two "I Am" sayings and connects Jesus' sacrificial death to his unique mandate to pasture God's people and bring them abundant life (10:1–18). Jesus builds on these claims to inform the Jews that they cannot enjoy the eternal benefit that he provides because "you are not my sheep" (10:22–29). The episode closes with an altar call, as Jesus invites the Jews to repent and accept that "the Father is in me, and I am in the Father" (10:37–38). Against this backdrop, one must conclude that the Fourth Evangelist is using the Psalm 82 riddle to portray Jesus as God's "son" in an exclusive sense. Hence, while John 10:34–36 looks and acts like a sage riddle, it is clearly concerned primarily with Jesus' unique messianic identity.

We may, then, confidently assert that John 10:34–36 is a mission riddle, meaning that its content explicitly promotes the Fourth Evangelist's christological vision. This assertion does not exclude our recognition that the saying generates ambiguity in the same way that many sage riddles do—by playing with an apparent tension in the Hebrew Bible to manipulate ideological boundaries. But the latter observation does not contribute to the former assertion: the riddle displays Jesus' wit, but this display does not, in and of itself, enhance the christological content of the saying. Deity claims are a dime a dozen in the Fourth Gospel, and the fact that this one takes the form of a riddle adds very little to its luster.

As a point of *method*, then, Jesus' riddling cannot help us to determine whether he or his contemporaries thought of him as a messiah, even if we extended this study to include ambiguous sayings that include explicitly christological content. But the fact that Jesus used riddles so often may tell us something rather important about a *specific type of relevant data* that is available from the sources: the data associated with the so-called "messianic secret."

Narrowly defined, the messianic secret is a running theme in the Gospel of Mark, where Jesus plainly reveals himself as Christ to his closest disciples but commands them not to share this information with the world at large until after his death (see Mark 8:27–32; 9:9, 30–32; 10:32–34). More broadly defined, the theme of "secrecy" appears in a variety of forms in different sources. Following this motif, the Gospels often suggest that Jesus' activities and teachings were inaccessible to the masses of people, with only a smaller and more intimate audience grasping their full significance. The secrecy motif thus emerges in the Synoptics in passages like Mark 1:44; 5:43; 7:36; 8:26; and their respective parallels, where Jesus performs a dramatic healing and then orders the patient and/or bystanders not to tell anyone what he has done, and Mark 4:10–12//Matt 13:13–17//Luke 8:9–10; 10:23–24, where Jesus tells the disciples that they are uniquely privileged to receive special information about God's Kingdom. The secrecy motif also appears in the Fourth Gospel's persistent theme of "misunderstanding": no matter how explicit, the teachings of the Johannine Jesus are almost completely incomprehensible to all other characters in the story, and he finally admits to the disciples that this has been the case because he has spoken "in riddles" (ἐν παροιμίαις; John 16:25–30). The *Gospel of Thomas* goes a step further, characterizing all of Jesus' sayings as secrets and promising that those who discover their meaning will never taste death (prologue; 1). My point here is simply that "secrecy," broadly conceived, is not a uniquely Markan motif. The notion that Jesus gave some people special teachings and insights that the masses were not privileged to receive emerges throughout the sources in a variety of ways.

What, then, can this secrecy motif tell us about Jesus' identity as a *riddling messiah*? If I am correct to assert that Jesus was a riddler, it seems very likely that the sources' general portrait of Jesus as a rabbi/teacher who revealed secret wisdom to select people was very likely grounded in historical reality. The secrecy motif—both the narrower Markan version and the broader theme—builds on the notion that Jesus' teachings were sometimes obtuse, and that only those who were closest to him and most aligned with his way of thinking could fully understand what he was saying. Is it possible that Jesus revealed special information about his self-image, his personal sense of identity, to some people but not to others? Or, more specifically here, is it possible that his public statements about his self-image were ambiguous, and that he clarified these statements privately for his disciples? Mark 8:32 and John 16:29–30 both claim, in entirely different contexts and apparently completely independently of one another, that Jesus began, at a certain point in his career, to speak παρρησία ("plainly") to a select group of followers about his ultimate destiny. I would suggest—and I can offer no more than this very limited suggestion—that there is no obvious reason why Jesus could not have spoken about his identity to the disciples in a less ambiguous way than he spoke to the masses, exactly as Mark and John and *Thomas* seem to suggest. In summary, Jesus' riddling supports the historical veracity of the overall "secrecy" motif and thus might indirectly support the claim of various sources that he secretly discussed his self-image with his disciples. At the very least, I would have to conclude that Mark's portrait of Jesus the Riddler is in no way inconsistent with his portrait of Jesus the Secret Messiah.

9

An Unbrokered Kingdom of Nobodies: Eating and Drinking with the Crossanian Jesus

I began chapter 8 with a summary of the points made in this book thus far about riddles generally and Jesus' riddling specifically. You may recall that the last two points in that list, #7 and #8, were as follows:

7. Many sources show Jesus engaged in riddling sessions, asking and answering ambiguous questions. The riddling sessions in the sources emphasize both the inherent advantages of the riddler and the power of wit in order to demonstrate Jesus' remarkable intellect. In such passages, Jesus uses riddles both as a teaching tool and/or as a means of establishing his academic credentials.
8. In the sources, Jesus often uses riddles to discuss key elements of his teaching: purity regulations, Sabbath observance, imperial and temple taxes, divorce, wealth, social responsibility, prayer, humility, and so on. Overall, it is fair to say that Jesus' riddles are closely tied to his concept of the "Kingdom of God," a fact that is perhaps most explicit in the Kingdom parables that function as riddles.

On the basis of these two points, I summarized my conclusions as follows: *Jesus often used intentionally ambiguous questions both to establish his credentials and to communicate key elements of his message about the Kingdom of God.* Chapter 8 proceeded to discuss several questions this conclusion might raise for our thinking about Jesus' social posture—how he presented himself to, and/or how he was perceived by, his contemporaries (point #7 above). In this chapter and the next, I will explore what issues Jesus' riddling might raise for our understanding of his teaching on the Kingdom of God (point #8 above). This is a complex issue that could be approached from a number of different angles, so let me begin with a basic caveat and an outline of the discussion to follow.

First, the caveat: please note that I simply assume, and therefore will make no specific effort to prove, that the Kingdom of God was not *a* topic of Jesus' teaching; rather, the Kingdom of God was *the* topic of Jesus' teaching. Let me be absolutely clear on this point: I think that the Kingdom was more than just a central issue or a core value for Jesus; rather, I think that everything Jesus said and did was a revelation of some aspect of this reality. Thus, I interpret Jesus' call to repent as instructions about how to enter this Kingdom; I interpret his "ethical teachings" as reflections on what it means to live as a citizen of this Kingdom; I interpret any comments he might have made about his own identity as credentials to announce the presence of this Kingdom—it's all about the Kingdom. I believe, in other words, that Mark is completely correct to summarize Jesus' message as, "the time has come and the Kingdom of God is near; repent and believe the good news" (1:15); I believe that Luke is completely correct to suggest that Jesus explicitly tied this proclamation to his and his disciples' healing ministries (9:1–2, 11; 10:9); I believe that Luke is also completely correct to suggest that Jesus explicitly postured his exorcisms as signs of the Kingdom's presence (11:20). These beliefs are not directly related to my conclusion that Jesus was a riddler, and what I will say in the remainder of this book would not necessarily depend upon them, but for sake of clarity please note that when I say "Kingdom of God," I am essentially using that term as shorthand for everything that Jesus was about. Jesus was, in my view, all about bringing people into a life under God's sovereign rule.

Second, the outline for this chapter and the next: let me first summarize my position, and then explain how the remainder of the discussion will proceed. Throughout this book, I have been arguing that Jesus was a riddler, and in chapter 8 I explored how that conclusion might impact our thinking about his social posture. My discussion there was fairly focused, but here I will begin with a general observation that would hold true whether Jesus was perceived to be a rabbi, prophet, Christ, or all three and then some. The observation is this: while Jesus no doubt made himself readily available to unclean people, sinners, whores, and tax collectors—again, I assume this and therefore will not argue the point—the evidence suggests (to me) that *the accessibility of his person was not necessarily matched by the accessibility of his message*. By which I mean: while the sources indicate that almost anyone could sit down for a meal with Jesus, the sources do not indicate that everyone who ate with him could understand what he was talking about. In fact, the sources indicate that almost no one who ate with him could understand what he was talking about. Most people would find Jesus' ambiguous discourse to be confusing, if not entirely incomprehensible, and as a result few tax collectors would leave Jesus' table with a completely coherent—or even barely coherent—comprehension of his vision and program. This was the case because *the Kingdom of God that Jesus envisioned is a community of knowledge,* the total number of people in all places and social situations who could understand his riddles and parables and who could then apply that type of thinking to a variety of situations in their own lives. As a result, the Kingdom that Jesus envisioned could manifest itself in an almost infinite number of ways.

In order to unpack the summary above and explore its implications, I think it will be helpful to highlight the points of contact between this book and the larger field of study by relating my conclusions to those of a real Jesus scholar. For sake of convenience, I will structure my discussion of the Kingdom as a dialogue with the research of John Dominic Crossan. I focus particularly on Crossan's work for three reasons: first, because his theory is comprehensive and covers most of the issues and themes that historical Jesus scholars underscore when discussing the Kingdom (although of course many do not agree with his conclusions); second, because Crossan's model of the Kingdom is built from a database of Jesus sayings very similar to the one that I have utilized in this book;[1] and, third, while he would perhaps be horrified by some of the things I am going to say, Crossan's conclusions nevertheless intersect with mine at several key points. In this chapter, I will begin by briefly summarizing Crossan's understanding of the Kingdom of God, then in chapter 10 develop my own remarks through comparison and contrast with his conclusions.

In Crossan's view, any consideration of the "Kingdom of God" must begin with a basic vocabulary lesson. Specifically, modern Western readers of the Bible tend to interpret the word "Kingdom" in political or institutional terms, "some geographically delineated location on earth." In Jesus' idiom, however, βασιλεία refers more broadly to "power and rule, a state much more than a place," where "state" means a "way of life or mode of being."[2] The Kingdom of God, as Crossan understands it, is essentially a "mode of being" characterized by unwavering recognition of God's sovereign authority over the universe generally and over one's own life specifically. Indeed, "the Kingdom of God is what the world would be if God were directly and immediately in charge," how we would think and act if we pretended that God rather than Caesar were on the throne in Rome.[3] Consistent with this definition, Crossan's discussion of the Kingdom focuses on the world-denying message and lifestyle that Jesus advocated. Jesus' radical teachings and actions—calculated to subvert and dismantle ancient Mediterranean social standards—essentially created a "Kingdom of nobodies," a characterization that is relevant to Crossan's reading of Jesus at two distinct points. First, Jesus' invitation to participate in the Kingdom was thoroughly inclusive, meaning that all people of every social status—the "nobodies" and "undesirables" of the world—were welcome to come. Second, and equally significant, those who entered God's Kingdom remained "nobodies" in the sense that Jesus did not envision any form of rank or privilege among members. "For Jesus, the Kingdom of God is a community of radical or unbrokered equality in which individuals are in direct contact with one another and with God, unmediated by any established brokers or fixed locations."[4]

Crossan's conclusions about the Kingdom are supported by a complex analysis that essentially follows a three-step outline. Crossan begins by situating Jesus' vision on a rubric of ancient Jewish speculation about the Kingdom of God; he then proceeds to examine the significance of Jesus' teachings and actions within the framework of that rubric and against the backdrop of ancient Mediterranean society; on the basis of this analysis, he describes Jesus' Kingdom as "sapiential" and "brokerless." This is, of course, a fairly simplistic overview of a very sophisticated set of arguments, and I hope that I have not misrepresented Crossan's position. I think, however, that my outline covers most of his concerns; so for sake of convenience my review of his position and my subsequent dialogue with his approach will follow this three-step model.

A KINGDOM OF WISDOM

Crossan begins his discussion by attempting to situate Jesus' teaching about the Kingdom within its broader historical context. Ancient Jewish thinking about God's Kingdom may be categorized "by crossing the thematic distinction of apocalyptic and sapiential with the class distinction of retainers and peasants."[5] Crossan's model thus situates Kingdom speculation on two axes: "theme," which essentially refers to the *time* when the Kingdom will appear; and social class, which determines the *type of action* that an individual will take on the basis of the theme that she adopts. Thus, for example, in analyzing John the Baptist's beliefs about God's reign, Crossan would attempt to identify the dominant theme in the Baptist's teachings—apocalyptic/futuristic or sapiential/contemporary—and then reflect on how a person in John's social situation would express those beliefs. Both elements are critical to our understanding of how Jesus and his contemporaries thought about the Kingdom and acted on that thinking.

In terms of "theme," the "apocalyptic" approach, in its various manifestations, sees the Kingdom of God as a future reality, "a coming act of transcendent divine power that, having destroyed all evil and pagan empires, would establish a rule of justice and a dominion of holiness in which humanity would dwell forever." By contrast, the "sapiential" outlook "underlines the necessity of wisdom . . . for discerning how, here and now in this world, one can so live that God's power, rule, and dominion are evidently present to all observers."

Essentially, then, the apocalyptic approach situates the Kingdom in the future, while the sapiential approach sees the Kingdom as "a present ethical . . . realm," a lifestyle that reflects submission to God's authority[6]—note that the English word "sapiential" comes from the Latin *sapientia*, which means "sense/understanding/wisdom." Because it looks ahead, the apocalyptic posture is essentially passive: the Kingdom will come through an act of divine power, and believers can only watch and pray for it to appear.[7] By contrast, the sapiential vision calls the faithful to imagine "how one could live here and now within an already or always available divine dominion." Both visions of God's Kingdom are essentially countercultural: the apocalyptic sees present society as hopelessly corrupt, unjust, and in need of divine purging; the sapiential "challenge[s] contemporary morality to its depths" through its rejection of the dominant way of thinking and its promotion of an alternative lifestyle.[8]

Either view of the Kingdom—apocalyptic or sapiential—could produce varying responses, depending on the social class of the individual believer. Apocalyptic Jews in the "retainer" class—essentially the bureaucrats who managed the political, financial, and religious institutions of Roman Palestine and who thereby acted as an interface between the wealthy rulers and the peasant masses—responded to this vision by "writing and proclaiming," thus leaving the fascinating documents that we now find in volume 1 of James Charlesworth's *The Old Testament Pseudepigrapha*. Illiterate apocalyptic peasants, being unable to express their hopes and revenge fantasies through pen and paper, "marched and performed" ritual actions that reenacted the victories of Moses

Crossan's Four Kinds of Kingdoms		
Theme	**Class**	
	Retainer (literate)	**Peasant** (oral)
Apocalyptic (cosmic cataclysm)	**Time:** later **Actor:** God **Response:** write/read apocalypses and wait for God to act **Example:** *Psalms of Solomon*	**Time:** later **Actor:** God **Response:** preach, perform ritual actions, and wait for God to act **Example:** John the Baptist
Sapiential (life of wisdom)	**Time:** now **Actor:** believers **Response:** contemplation and the pursuit of divine wisdom **Example:** Philo	**Time:** now **Actor:** believers **Response:** teach and practice an alternate lifestyle that defies current social norms **Example: Jesus**

and Joshua in anticipation of God's future victory.[9] The sapiential outlook also generated two responses. For retainers, the sapiential Kingdom was an empire of philosophers, a divine rule "that wise, just, and virtuous sages . . . could enter into here and now"—Crossan cites Philo and the author of the Wisdom of Solomon as prime examples.[10] The fourth category of ancient Jewish Kingdom speculation—peasant response to the sapiential vision—is best illustrated by the ministry of Jesus. The remainder of Crossan's discussion outlines "what the here-and-now [sapiential, peasant] Kingdom of God meant for Jesus" as he brought it into existence through his deeds and words.[11]

GOD'S WORLD VS. THIS WORLD; OR "THE KINGDOM IS WHAT I DO AND WHO I TOUCH"

In Crossan's view, Jesus intended to build his sapiential, here-and-now Kingdom on the ruins of normal society. For this reason, Jesus' *teaching* was characterized by statements calculated to undermine the social structure of Roman Palestine. Ancient Mediterranean culture was organized into two interlocking groups, "the familial and the political, kinship and politics"; Jesus opposed both with "biting aphorisms and dialogues." Indeed, Jesus "very, very often" entered into "an almost savage attack on family values," specifically the oppressive values associated with patriarchal rule.[12] This emphasis is evident, for example, at Luke 12:51–53, where Jesus says that homes will split over his proclamation—"son against father, daughter against mother, daughter-in-law against mother-in-law." Commenting on this passage, Crossan points out that Jesus does not just envision a varied response to his message, but rather a division between generations: it is "the normalcy of familial hierarchy that is under attack," making Jesus' prediction a challenge to the androcentric patriarchialism of his day.[13] But this subversion of traditional family values was, ultimately, a commentary on the larger social order, since "the family is society in miniature." Jesus occasionally attacked this larger social order directly, as evident in statements like "Blessed are the poor" (Luke 6:20), a remarkable beatitude that defied all norms and values with its "stark and startling conjunction of blessed poverty and divine Kingdom." Against the sharp stratification of ancient Mediterranean society, Jesus called for the emergence of an "ideal group . . . an open one equally accessible to all under God."[14]

Yet we must not stop with Jesus' radical teaching if we wish to fully comprehend the substance of his message. Crossan insists that "the historical Jesus had both an ideal vision and a social program"—that is, both a sapiential image of what the Kingdom should be and a blueprint for building that Kingdom in Roman Palestine.[15] Broadly speaking, Jesus' Kingdom "vision" is evident in what he said (his radical teaching), while his "social program" is reflected in what he did. These two modes of proclamation, words and deeds, were completely united in Jesus' ministry; they must therefore be read against one another and cannot be disentangled or prioritized.[16] Jesus "enacted" the Kingdom in three very significant ways: open commensality (i.e., eating with sinners and unclean people); healings and exorcisms; and radical itinerancy. Each of these activities invited people to experience God's sovereign rule in defiance of cultural norms. Specifically, whereas Caesar's Kingdom was sharply stratified on the basis of patriarchy, patronage, honor, and, in Palestine at least, religious purity, God's Kingdom would be open, accessible, and egalitarian, completely devoid of rank. Everything Jesus did complemented his radical message by underscoring the inherent differences between the Kingdom of God and normal society.

Before proceeding to discuss these symbolic deeds individually, it is important to outline briefly Crossan's understanding of the rhetorical strategy behind Jesus' activity: how would eating with sinners or healing a leper make a theological point about the Kingdom of God? Crossan's answer to this question relies heavily on sociological models that emphasize the symbolic relationship between the bodies of individuals and the larger body politic. "Indeed, *body to society as microcosm to macrocosm* undergirds . . . my entire understanding of the historical Jesus." Viewed from this perspective, bodily practices like eating together or touching someone "are not simply private operations between individuals but social miniatures that can support or challenge, affirm or negate a culture's behavioral rules or a society's customary codes."[17] This model, which in my view generates Crossan's most interesting insights, is foundational to his understanding of two key aspects of Jesus' ministry. First, Crossan interprets *Jesus' own bodily practices* as illustrations of his social program: the things that Jesus did with his body were tangible expressions of the Kingdom of God. Hence, when Jesus ate without washing his hands or mingled with crowds of unclean people, these actions did not simply create a venue and an audience for Jesus' teaching; they were, rather, a central element of that teaching. Second, Crossan similarly interprets *Jesus' actions on the bodies of other individuals* as commentaries on the current world order. Thus, when Jesus exorcized demons, he did so to protest the damaging effects of imperial oppression; when he told his disciples to proclaim the Kingdom from house to house and to eat whatever was offered with whoever offered it, he was undermining the ancient Mediterranean systems of patronage and purity; when he blessed children, he was denying the validity of unmitigated patriarchal power. No act of Jesus was incidental; everything he did announced the outbreak of God's Kingdom.

Jesus' countercultural message was perhaps best illustrated by his *open commensality*, his practice of eating with all sorts of unclean and sinful people without discrimination. Just as the human body is a microcosm of the body politic, the dinner table, as "the place where bodies meet to eat," is a microcosm of society and its "vertical discriminations and lateral separations."[18] Jesus' innovative table practices may therefore be interpreted as an attempt to create an alternate social order: by eating with people of all social classes, Jesus challenged the idea that social classes should exist in the first place. Crossan focuses here on two bits of data, the parable of the Banquet (Luke 14:15–24//*Thomas* 64) and the accusation that Jesus was a glutton and a drunkard (Luke 7:31–35). Jesus' original version of the Banquet, somewhat obscured now by the sources, envisioned a situation where people from a wide range of backgrounds freely dine together: "anyone could be reclining next to anyone else," regardless of sex or social status. The accusation of gluttony likely arose from the fact that Jesus himself frequently shared in meals of this type. He "lived out his own parable," and in the process failed to make socially "appropriate distinctions and discriminations" in an effort to illustrate the egalitarianism of the Kingdom.[19]

Jesus' egalitarian vision was also promoted through his *healings and exorcisms*. These activities may be lumped together not only because ancient people frequently associated illness with demonic oppression, but also because Crossan again reads Jesus' response to both conditions through the principle that the human body is society in miniature.[20] Crossan sharply distinguishes Jesus' "healings" from medical "cures" on the basis of a further distinction between "disease" and "illness." "Disease" refers to the biomechanical, clinical aspect of sickness, an irregularity in the physical body and/or its operations; "illness" refers to the psychosocial implications of a physical irregularity, such as the ostracization of AIDS victims. Jesus did not, in Crossan's view, "cure diseases"; rather, Jesus "healed," and in the process he made calculated comments about the social values normally attached to illness.[21] For example, at Mark 1:40–44 a leprous man begs Jesus to remove his infirmity: "If you are willing, you are able to make me clean" (1:40). In Roman Palestine, leprosy was a physical irregularity (a "disease") that carried a complex of social implications based on Jewish purity standards (an "illness"). Jesus touched the leper (v. 41) precisely in order to unravel these social implications: "I [Crossan] presume that Jesus, who did not and could not cure that disease [leprosy] or any other one, healed the poor man's illness by refusing to accept the disease's ritual uncleanness and social ostracization. . . . Jesus heals him . . . by taking him into a community of the marginalized and disenfranchised—into, in fact, the Kingdom of God."[22] Jesus' healings, then, were not just simple acts of compassion or evidences of supernatural power, but rather an attack on the social stigma reflected in ancient thinking about disease and demon possession.

Finally, Jesus embodied his social program in a lifestyle of *radical itinerancy*. The sources suggest that Jesus moved from place to place quite often and that he instructed at least his closest followers to do the same. Crossan insists that this mobility was not only practical, but also programmatic: Jesus did not travel simply to carry his message to new audiences; Jesus traveled because traveling was, in and of itself, a central aspect of his message, the "geographical equivalent" and "symbolic demonstration" of the Kingdom's egalitarianism.[23] To develop this claim, Crossan offers a detailed analysis of the "commission of the 12/70" at *Thomas* 14:2//Luke 10:4–11//Mark 6:7–13, which he sees as a general description of the Jesus movement rather than an isolated event.[24] The equipment, modus operandi, and proclamation of the missionaries were all calculated to promote Jesus' Kingdom vision. Jesus sent his disciples to visit peasant houses, where they would heal the sick and cast out demons; they were to take no money or food supplies, so that they would be forced to accept whatever was given to them. Their acceptance of food must not, however, be interpreted as "a strategy for supporting the mission" or a payment for healing. "Commensality [eating together] was, rather, a strategy for building or rebuilding peasant community on radically different principles from those of honor and shame, patronage and clientage. It was based on an egalitarian sharing of spiritual and material power at the most grass-roots level."[25] Thus, when the missionaries told their new friends at the open banquet that "the Kingdom has drawn near" (Luke 10:9), they were not talking about a future event but rather naming what had already come into existence before their very eyes.[26]

Crossan's Key to the Sign Language of Jesus

Jesus' Activity	Jesus' Objective
Radical Teaching	• announce the presence of an egalitarian, brokerless Kingdom in the here and now
Eating with Sinners	• defy social stratifications supported by popular notions of shame, patronage, and purity
Healing/Exorcism	• defy social stratifications supported by popular notions of the stigma of illness, and challenge the validity of colonial power
Itinerant Ministry	• defy popular notions of spiritual brokerage by creating a community based on mutual dependence, open commensality, and free healing

In summary, Crossan insists that Jesus saw the Kingdom of God "not as an individual dream but as a corporate plan."[27] The dream was evident in Jesus' radical teaching; the plan was actualized in his alternate lifestyle; the two together subverted almost every core value of Jesus' culture and, indeed, even the social frameworks that gave those values structure and meaning.

NO BROKERS

According to Crossan, then, Jesus promoted a sapiential vision of the Kingdom of God through teachings and deeds that were intended to create an egalitarian community among the peasant population of a sharply stratified traditional society. Indeed, Jesus' agenda was so different that the word "egalitarian" is not even adequate to describe it. Crossan frequently uses the term "radical egalitarianism," which he defines as "an absolute equality of people that denies the validity of any discrimination between them and negates the necessity of a hierarchy among them."[28] This emphasis supports Crossan's well-known characterization of the Jesus movement as a "*brokerless* Kingdom of nobodies and undesirables."[29]

Within the patronage system of ancient Mediterranean society, a "broker" was an individual with patrons above him, friends around him, and clients below him on the social pyramid.[30] In fact, the word "broker" is essentially synonymous with "patron," the only shade of difference being that "broker" emphasizes the patron's role in securing aid and favors for his clients. By characterizing the Jesus movement as "brokerless," Crossan wishes to stress that Jesus did not simply replace the current class system with another one; rather, Jesus abolished the notions of class, status, and honor altogether, so that everyone in his movement was completely equal. As a result, there were no individuals who functioned as "brokers" in the Kingdom of God; nobody needed to ask some important person for help in order to enjoy benefits and favors. Everyone was equally important—or unimportant—and no one had special access to God, Jesus, or anything else.

To illustrate the point, Crossan offers Mark 1:16–38 as a snapshot of Jesus' brokerless Kingdom. At the beginning of this sequence, Jesus calls his first disciples from their fishing nets and takes them to a synagogue, where he casts out a demon.[31] Following this remarkable display, which generates considerable regional interest (1:28), the group proceeds to the home of Simon Peter, where Jesus heals Peter's mother-in-law of a deadly fever (1:29–31). As word of these wondrous events spreads, large numbers of the sick and possessed flock to the house; indeed, "the whole city gathered together at [Peter's] door" (1:33). Crossan notes that this state of affairs would logically lead people to conclude that "Peter's house is becoming a brokerage place for Jesus' healing, and Peter will broker between Jesus and those seeking help."[32] Peter should, in other words, start charging admission and selling T-shirts; soon, only people who play on Peter's bowling team will be able to schedule an exorcism. Yet, to the surprise of everyone (and perhaps to the disappointment of Peter), Jesus rises the next morning and says that he is ready to move on to other towns so that he may proclaim his radical vision there also; at 1:39 he proceeds to do just that by embarking on a preaching tour of Galilee. This itinerant program reflects, in Crossan's view, Jesus' rejection of anything that smells like a brokerage system. "The equal sharing of spiritual and material gifts, of miracle and table, cannot be centered in one place because that very hierarchy of place, of here *over* there, of this place *over* other places, symbolically destroys the radical egalitarianism it announces."[33] No person anywhere deserves special treatment; everybody everywhere stands before God on completely equal terms; the spiritual brokers are therefore out of business.

Such, then, is Crossan's view of the Kingdom of God proclaimed by Jesus. If my summary of his position has been inaccurate, I very much hope that it has at least been fair, because I enjoy Crossan's work and find myself strangely charmed by his conclusions and his style of public speaking, despite my rejection of his source-critical methodology. As noted above, I will close this book by building my own image of the Kingdom on Crossan's outline. I hope that this comparison and contrast will highlight both the points where my conclusions align themselves with mainline Jesus scholarship and the junctures where Jesus the Riddler might point us in new directions.

10

The Empire of Wit; or
Maybe Peter Really Did Have the
"Keys to the Kingdom"

In chapter 9, I outlined John Dominic Crossan's view of Jesus' brokerless, sapiential Kingdom. I will now use Crossan's argument as a framework to discuss my own understanding of the Kingdom of God as proclaimed by Jesus the Riddler. Before we proceed, I should probably confess that, for me personally, this chapter is the payoff for the whole book. For some time now I've struggled to get a handle on Jesus' talk about the Kingdom of God, and have always found it odd—and, on a more personal level, frustrating—that he would be so vague about something so central to his message. My current thinking is that he was not so much being vague as ambiguous and that the key to the Kingdom lies in the very fact that only certain people could understand it. I do not claim to be one of those people, but I do think that my portrait of Jesus the Riddler can give us a sharper sense of exactly who they were/are and how these witty people, taken together, could make up a Kingdom of God in the midst of this fallen world.

A KINGDOM OF WIT

I begin with Crossan's claim that Jesus viewed the Kingdom of God "not as an apocalyptic event in the imminent future but as a mode of life in the immediate present."[1] This quote epitomizes Crossan's belief that Jesus did not tell people to sit back and wait for God to do something remarkable on the third of Nisan in 43 CE. Rather, "one entered the Kingdom as a way of life, and anyone who could live it could bring it to others." This is what Crossan means when he says that Jesus' vision was "sapiential," oriented toward wisdom and ethics, rather than "apocalyptic," oriented toward cosmic cataclysm and the end of the world.[2] Jesus called people to do something here and now in response to their recognition of God's present sovereignty, rather than, say, to wait in a bomb shelter with a stockpile of canned beans until God sets things right by blowing the whole world to hell.

Clearly, my claim that Jesus frequently used riddles (including parable-riddles) would affirm Crossan's sapiential model. The fact that Jesus regularly used ambiguous questions to challenge conventional ideas suggests that he wanted to help people develop a new mode of thinking in the here and now. As more and more people accepted this new paradigm and began to act upon it, the Kingdom of God would grow up within Caesar's kingdom in the form of individuals who could grasp, or at least appreciate, Jesus' unconventional wisdom. Of course, Jesus may have also foreseen some future culmination of the Kingdom, yet this would not diminish the urgency of his call to experience God's reign in the immediate present.

I would, however, probably want to slightly abridge Crossan's proposal by pushing Jesus a bit closer to what he calls the "retainer response" to the sapiential vision. Obviously, Jesus didn't write abstract philosophical treatises or allegorical political poems—he probably couldn't write at all, or at least very little—and he directed his rhetoric primarily to the peasant masses rather than the literate elites. But at the same time, Jesus' vision of the emerging Kingdom placed a very heavy emphasis on wisdom and wit, on thinking alongside doing. I would therefore revise Crossan's quote at the beginning of this section as follows: "one entered the Kingdom as a way of *thinking*, and anyone who could *think this way and apply that thinking to real-life situations* could bring that same *vision* to others." Crossan would perhaps agree with this statement in the most general sense—actions imply some sort of prior thought process—but I wish to emphasize that the revision above reflects my view that Jesus' version of the Kingdom of God is best understood as "a community of knowledge."

I have said many times now that riddles and parables—genres of speech that Jesus often used to discuss matters pertaining to the Kingdom—can be answered only by people who possess the necessary prerequisite knowledge of cultural items, cultural logic, and cultural traditions. The answers to riddles often appear arbitrary to people outside the riddler's group; even very educated individuals may not be able to unlock a riddle unless they know the correct solution beforehand. Thus, when Jesus defied all conventional wisdom by telling people the parable of the Good Samaritan or by casually informing his followers that "the first will be last," he must have been aware that most of his audience would have no idea what he was talking about. They would, of course, know about the city of Jericho, and highway robberies, and why Samaritans are bad; they would not necessarily know how to handle the idea that a Samaritan would rescue a Jew after his own people had abandoned him, or exactly what this might have to do with ethical living or the inbreaking of God's kingdom. Jesus must also have been aware that a person who could not locate the correct referent for his ambiguous words would not be able to actualize them in her life. You can't live by a teaching that you don't understand in the first place. Does the parable of the Sower mean that we should be more careful about throwing seeds on the road, so that we don't waste the things that God has given us? And when Jesus says that "there is nothing outside a man that is able to make him unclean by going into him" (Mark 7:14–15), does he mean that I can eat anything I want, or that I can have free sex with prostitutes at the Serapis banquet with no fear of moral contamination? These interpretations are reasonable, but I doubt they would fall within the range of Jesus' intentions. I also doubt that he was ignorant that most people would struggle to understand what he was saying.

Presumably, those people who spent a good deal of time with Jesus would eventually come to some deeper insight, either by reading his riddles through the lens of his clearer remarks and actions or by simply asking him privately to explain what he was talking about. The total number of individuals who obtained such insight would become Jesus' community of knowledge, that group of people who understood his special logic and traditions and who could appeal to such logic and traditions to unpack his ambiguous statements. But I would further argue that the phrase "Jesus' community of knowledge" is essentially synonymous with "the Kingdom of God," because (a) Jesus' riddles and parables often point directly to the Kingdom of God (or to his symbolic actions that point to the Kingdom), and (b) Jesus must have understood that only those who could think the way he did would have access to his special understanding of the Kingdom. If you can figure out what Jesus is talking about and put that into practice, then you may enter his community and Kingdom; if you lack wit, you can't get in.

I will develop the implications of this conclusion—that the Kingdom of God is essentially Jesus' community of knowledge, the total number of people who can think the way that he thinks—as I continue my dialogue with Crossan, but for now let me make two preliminary observations. First, I think it very highly likely that Jesus assumed that participation in the Kingdom would require a substantial "change of mind," a reconfiguration of conceptual frameworks that would allow a person to understand his riddles and parables. This is, I think, the correct way to read the verb μετανοέω ("repent") at Mark 1:15//6:12—you cannot grasp Jesus' proclamation of the Kingdom until you change the way that you process information, simply because that proclamation often takes the form of riddles, parables, and, following Crossan's analysis, ambiguous actions that could be understood only by people who think against the cultural grain in a particular way. In this respect, Jesus' message of "repentance" was somewhat different from that of John the Baptist, whose apocalyptic vision of the Kingdom called for people to purify themselves before God comes to earth to settle the score (see Mark 1:4; Matt. 3:2). John's proclamation seems to touch primarily on inner moral reform, the need to return to a more thorough obedience to God's Law; hence the ethical tone of his exhortation at Luke 3:7–14, and Josephus's presentation of the Baptist as a moral philosopher at *Antiquities* 18.116–19. Of course, Jesus also surely thought that repentance would lead to a visible change in behavior, but people who could not understand his ambiguous speech would never feel the force of this call.[3] The full weight of his proclamation would rest on those who could "repent"—who could change their way of thinking—and who could act on/out this new perspective.

My second implication here relates to the essential difference between knowledge communities (such as the Kingdom of God) and other types of groups (such as a cricket club or a Red Hat society). As I noted in chapter 2, the members of a community of knowledge are united *solely* by their possession of common information, regardless of their backgrounds or geographical locations. Fans of *Harry Potter* are spread out far and wide across the globe, as are experts in Aramaic and people who follow Formula-1 racing; yet all these people, regardless of their heritage and station in life, share common information. Hence, we find a remarkable demographic distribution at any given *Star Wars* convention, and many of the people who gather there to celebrate their common passion would never otherwise come together in one location. Further, these convention-goers share the same mythological insights as other *Star Wars* enthusiasts whose schedules and incomes (and perhaps spouses) will never allow them to attend a fan club meeting. Yet all these *Star Wars* fans in every location—whether they ever meet one another or not, and regardless of their personal backgrounds and social status—may be thought of as a "knowledge group," as the marketing people at any company that makes collectible figures will tell you.

When I apply this model to the Kingdom of God, Crossan's reading is affirmed in the sense that Jesus the Riddler's vision and program completely transcended geographical and social boundaries. Like all other communities of knowledge, the sapiential Kingdom that Jesus envisioned was a-temporal and a-geographical, located not in any specific future time or place but rather in the lives of those who could understand him. People in Nazareth and Sepphoris and Jericho and Jerusalem could all participate equally in God's Kingdom, and they could do so whether they ever met one another at an open banquet or not. The Kingdom is present everywhere we find a person who can figure out Jesus' puzzles and think the way that he thinks. Such people share a common tradition, even if they live in relative isolation from one another day to day.

THE KINGDOM IS THIS WORLD
TURNED INSIDE OUT

To continue the dialogue: Crossan suggests that Jesus' radical teaching and actions were a culturally appropriate expression of his sapiential vision, the natural intersection of Jesus' theory and his social reality. Specifically, Jesus' teachings and actions functioned to undermine that social reality and replace it with a whole new order, one founded on very different principles of human relations. My portrait of Jesus the Riddler would substantially affirm this aspect of Crossan's analysis. Jesus' ambiguous statements about the Kingdom, and also the rhetorical gestures behind his dining policies, free healing, and itinerancy, were all calculated to disrupt normal ways of thinking and to force people to substantially reconsider foundational assumptions. Riddles and parables were useful tools for Jesus simply because they blur mental boundaries by apparently mixing words and/or things that polite society wants to keep separate.

I believe that Crossan would agree with what I have just said—that Jesus' ambiguous statements blurred the lines between mental categories—but I think that he would also rightly observe that the above paragraph is not entirely accurate, simply because it does not go far enough. As I noted in chapter 1, Elli Köngäs Maranda has argued that riddles "play with boundaries, but ultimately to affirm them."[4] Some of Jesus' riddles and parables may have done that, but most of his ambiguous statements did not just "play with boundaries"; they completely *erased* boundaries by disabling the polar oppositions that support the very notion of "mental categories." By "polar oppositions" I mean terms that most people would view as natural opposites: white/black, day/night, true/false, rich/poor. Once we decide that two words are opposites, we henceforth assume things that bear these labels can never mingle: white cannot be black; good cannot be evil; male cannot be female; fire cannot be ice; liberal cannot be conservative. Yet the sources suggest that Jesus frequently mixed oil and water by reversing (white/black ➔ black/white) or equating ("white is black") opposite terms, forcing his audience either to develop a new perspective or to abandon all hope of understanding him. In some cases, Jesus achieved this effect by making statements that radically conflicted with conventional wisdom and/or values ("taboos"); in more extreme instances, he made statements that seemed to be inherently self-contradictory ("paradoxes"). Both types of riddles asked his audience to redefine key terms and realign foundational concepts in order to explain how the statement could be true—if not "true," at least coherent and conceivable. In the process, Jesus invited his listeners temporarily to step outside their normal, everyday perspective and look at the world in a new light. To emphasize this aspect of his teaching and its implications, let me briefly review how Jesus used both taboo and paradox in service of his proclamation of the Kingdom.

The sources suggest that Jesus often challenged his audience to respond to an ambiguous statement that was logically coherent in its own right, yet impossible from the perspective of the majority worldview. These riddles, like many of the parables, would be especially striking to Jesus' contemporaries simply because they seemed to be absurd—sometimes not only absurd, but also shocking and offensive. For example, Jesus' disciples are astonished when he tells them that it is "hard for a rich person to enter the Kingdom of God"— harder, in fact, than pushing a camel through the eye of a needle—because they "live in a culture that interpreted wealth as a sign of God's blessing."[5] Such a statement is, in fact, so alien to conventional ways of thinking that the disciples initially take Jesus to mean that it would be impossible for anyone to be saved; it does not occur to them that his riddle might require them to sever the conceptual thread between money and salvation (Mark 10:23–27). A person who cannot cut this cord could only point out that the Lukan beatitude, "The poor are blessed" (6:20; also *Thomas* 54:1), is utter nonsense, regardless of whether we translate μακάριος as "blessed," "happy," or "fortunate." Poor people are not "happy" because they are not "fortunate," and popular theology would say that this is the case because they have not been "blessed." And because they do not enjoy God's blessing, poor people do not get into Abraham's bosom ahead of rich folks (Luke 16:19–31), any more than a tax collector could have his sins forgiven more readily than a pious Pharisee (Luke 18:10–14). One can only wonder exactly what kind of "kingdom" Jesus is talking about.[6] Apparently, a "kingdom" of children, because one must clearly "receive the Kingdom of God like a child" (Mark 10:14–15; see *Thomas* 4:1), a claim that is entirely inconsistent both with the legal status of children in the ancient world and with the fact that Jewish religious culture emphasized the wisdom of age. In the real world, rich people get into heaven ahead of poor people, and children follow adults; not so in the Kingdom of God as proclaimed by Jesus the Riddler.

Jesus' riddles, then, often reversed the current social order simply by making claims that challenged conventional ways of thinking. They were ambiguous, and perhaps shocking, because they seemed to point the audience in unexpected directions, often toward cultural or theological taboos. But according to the sources, many times Jesus was not content simply to contradict conventional ways of thinking: sometimes he made statements that seemed inherently *self*-contradictory. Riddles of this type generally equate terms that appear to be polar opposites and then ask the audience to explain how the tension can be resolved. The Thomasine Jesus thus tells us that "the end will be the beginning" (*Thomas* 18:2–3), a proposition that is impossible whether we take "end" and "beginning" in the spatial sense ("here and there") or in the temporal sense ("past and future"). Such metaphysical maneuvers are prominent in the *Gospel of Thomas*, which includes the remarkable beatitude, "Blessed is the one who came into being before coming into being" (19:1)— we can only ask how it is possible to exist before we exist. Mark, being of a somewhat more practical bent, includes riddles that disrupt not only the metaphysical order, but also the social order. Thus, if the disciples wish to be "great" or "first," they must become "slave of all" (Mark 10:42–44), a concrete application of Jesus' refrain, "the first will be last and the last will be first" (Mark 9:35).[7] I would emphasize that Jesus does not say here that there will be no slaves in the Kingdom; he literally says that slaves will be kings and that people on the bottom rung will also be on the top rung *at the same time*, thus envisioning an impossible state of affairs that undermines the very notion of a social ladder. In all such instances, Jesus' words do not just contradict common ways of thinking; they seem to contradict themselves, and in the process they challenge not only current mental classifications but even the very notion of classification. Riddles of this type present a paradox that must be resolved, and in the process suggest that the Kingdom of God will remain incoherent to those who cannot provide an answer. Without debating whether any of the specific paradox riddles mentioned above originated with the historical Jesus, I would simply note here that a wide range of sources claim that he used this type of speech on a fairly regular basis.

Many of Jesus' riddles, then, did not just *challenge* the validity of conventional beliefs; they flagrantly *contradicted* conventional beliefs and eliminated the conceptual frameworks that made such beliefs coherent and meaningful. In order to comprehend God's Kingdom, one must reconsider the conceptual boundaries of significant terms like "age," "wealth," "status," and "salvation." Returning to our discussion of parables in chapter 5, one might say that Jesus asked his followers to develop a new "psychological context" for these words. For those who were not able to do this, Jesus' riddles, and the Kingdom to which they pointed, would remain ambiguous and probably also offensive, and this offense would begin long before they ever saw Jesus drinking wine with lepers while whores washed his feet with their hair.

Of course, I do not claim that my observations here are novel. They are, in fact, extremely old hat. True, most scholars have not treated Jesus' ambiguous statements as "riddles" in the technical sense, but the world was not waiting for me to reveal that there was a strongly countercultural element in Jesus' teaching. Crossan himself often highlights this aspect of Jesus' message, and the preceding paragraphs could easily appear as an appendix to the next edition of his *The Dark Interval*. One of my favorite quotes about the parables specifically and Jesus' Kingdom teaching generally comes from an article that Crossan wrote more than thirty years ago: "The literal point [of the Good Samaritan] confronted the hearers with the necessity of saying the impossible and having their world turned upside down and radically questioned in its presuppositions. The metaphorical point is that *just so* does the kingdom of God break abruptly into a person's consciousness and demand the overturn of prior values, closed options, set judgements, and established conclusions."[8] My conclusions about Jesus the Riddler also resonate with Crossan's claim that the parable of the Leaven (Luke 13:20–21//*Thomas* 96:1) must have been "immediately shocking and provocative" because it violated so many norms of Jesus' day, and with his observation that the parable of the Treasure in a Field would have been very disturbing because it asked Jesus' audience to condone "actions neither socially acceptable nor morally approved within their [social] environment."[9] These and similar statements reveal strong points of intersection between Crossan's model and my portrait of Jesus the Riddler.

BROKERING THE BROKERLESS KINGDOM

As noted above, I would essentially affirm many aspects of Crossan's reading of Jesus' radical teaching and would argue that my conclusions tend to support his claim that Jesus was building the Kingdom of God on the ruins of the kingdom of Caesar. While I have limited the scope of my analysis to sage riddles and parables, it is relevant to mention that my approach would also tend to support Crossan's interpretation of the rhetorical moves behind Jesus' deeds: open commensality, healings, exorcisms, and itinerancy were all ambiguous actions that would ask the observer to find a solution. But now I will address what seems to me to be the most substantial difference between Crossan's proposal and my emerging portrait of Jesus the Riddler: the sapiential Kingdom of God that Jesus promoted could not have been "brokerless" in the strict sense of that term.

As we begin to explore the notion of "brokerage," let me first state that I agree with Crossan that Jesus freely and frequently ate with marginalized people and that the parable of the Banquet illustrates this practice and makes it normative for the Kingdom of God. Crossan proceeds to argue that Jesus' open commensality reflected his complete disregard for Jewish purity regulations: "he ignored them [such regulations], but that, of course, was to subvert them at the most fundamental level."[10] Paula Fredriksen has challenged this claim, arguing that "we should assume *not* that Jesus ignored or opposed Jewish purity codes, but rather that he took them for granted as fundamental to the worship of the God who had revealed them, uniquely, to Israel." I think that this is an important point, but I don't entirely agree with Fredriksen, either. She is doubtless correct to insist that Jesus, as a Jew, could not disregard, much less simply "ignore," purity as a religious issue in Roman Palestine. I don't know that any ancient Palestinian Jew could talk about ethics and social stratification outside the framework of purity codes. But Fredriksen reacts to Crossan's position by swinging to the opposite end of the spectrum, concluding that Jesus in fact observed Jewish purity standards fairly closely— at least, as closely as any of his Jewish contemporaries, which is essentially to say that his purity practices were in no way remarkable.[11] I personally think that Jesus was deeply concerned about purity issues and about the psychosocial impact of these issues, but that he resolved the problem by emphasizing the moral dimension of purity to such an extent that it eclipsed the ritual/bodily dimension almost entirely. Hence, as you saw from my table of sage riddles in chapter 4, I think that the correct answer to the riddle at Mark 7:14–15 is found in Mark 7:19–20: what goes into the body winds up in the toilet, but what comes out of the heart reveals the inner person. Thus, for Jesus, if the heart is pure, the body is pure, and the dirty food is purified through contact with the clean person's body, rather than the other way around.

Because Jesus approached purity issues in this way—that is, from the perspective that dirty things cannot make a clean person unclean, but rather that contact with a clean person purifies what is polluted—and because he was apparently extremely confident of the purity of his own heart, Jesus could eat with sinners, touch lepers, and lodge in the homes of tax collectors under the assumption that inner goodness made him immune to physical defilement. Borrowing Crossan's terminology, I would say that Jesus' view of purity allowed him to engage in bodily practices (eating, touching, healing, traveling) that gave marginalized people unlimited access to him. These bodily practices, and the open fellowship that they created, were doubtless just as ambiguous to Jesus' contemporaries as many of his more radical reversal riddles. Further, I think that Crossan is entirely correct to suggest that Jesus also encouraged his disciples to engage in open fellowship, confident that their inner purity would spill out onto those gathered for meals in the peasant homes that they visited. Thus, the sources accurately portray Jesus and his disciples eating with sinners, touching lepers, casting demons out of crazy people, and lodging in unclean houses, all the while proclaiming repentance to everyone within earshot.

So what does all this talk about Jesus' view of purity have to do with the question of "brokerage"? One could fairly characterize the Kingdom of God as "brokerless" in the sense that Jesus' unusual outlook on purity allowed him to participate in meals and meetings that defied normal social standards of rank, shame, and patronage. Crossan is surely correct to suggest that Jesus did not just tear down one social hierarchy to build another, with all the poor people now sitting at the head of the table. But the Kingdom is more than a meal—it is, rather, a knowledge community—and "repentance" is more than dropping your social guard. As with any other community of knowledge, entering the Kingdom of God means acquiring information about a set of things, developing a conceptual framework for thinking about those things, and adopting a new set of traditions. This reading of the Kingdom forces me to reconsider the notion of "brokerage," and I would like to highlight the implications of my argument by posing, and then attempting to answer, a question: *what happened at Jesus' open table?* Did everyone just eat and drink a lot and then crawl back home after the party, full of food, empty of demons, and refreshed by the egalitarian spirit of the gathering? Or was there another step into a fuller comprehension of God's Kingdom?

Let me imitate Crossan's modus operandi by focusing these questions with an example from the sources, the familiar story of the call of Matthew/Levi (Matt. 9:9–13). My point here does not depend on the specific historicity of this event, although I would argue that it must accurately represent a large number of situations from Jesus' career and that I personally see no reason to doubt that it happened.

The Call of Levi
Matthew 9:9–13

[9]And going on from there, Jesus saw a man sitting in the toll booth named Matthew. And he said to him, "Follow me." And he rose and followed him.

[10]And it came about that, as he was reclining in the house, Behold!—many tax collectors and sinners were coming and dining with Jesus and his disciples. [11]And seeing this, the Pharisees said to his disciples, "Why does your teacher eat with the tax–collectors and sinners?"

[12]But hearing this, he [Jesus] said, "The strong have no need for a doctor; rather, the sick need him. [13]But go and learn what this means: 'I desire mercy and not sacrifice' [Hos. 6:6]. For I did not come to call righteous people, but rather sinners."

As the story opens, Jesus is wandering around Galilee—the exact location is uncertain and apparently irrelevant (see 9:1)—when he happens to find Matthew collecting taxes in a toll booth somewhere along the road. The text says almost nothing about what passed between them, save that Jesus invited Matthew to follow him and that Matthew responded by inviting Jesus back to his house for a meal. In the next scene we see Jesus and the disciples sitting down to dinner with a veritable rogue's gallery of local sinners, thus bringing the Kingdom of God to Matthew's home in the form of an open table. The local Pharisees are, of course, surprised by this, and they ask the disciples why their rabbi is eating with such people; Crossan would say, and I would agree, that Jesus' actions were in fact calculated to evoke this sort of response. Jesus rebuffs his opponents by stating that doctors are for the sick, a fairly unambiguous proverb that justifies (in his mind, at least) his efforts to reach across social barriers and bring the proclamation of the Kingdom to all people. Just as a physician must expose himself to the sick in order to bring healing, so must Jesus expose himself to the outcast in order to bring them back under God's sovereign rule. In many respects, then, Matthew 9:9–13 summarizes Jesus' vision of the Kingdom as Crossan understands it: itinerant ministry; open table fellowship; explicit and intentional violation of social norms regarding purity and shame; all this set in conscious and specific opposition to the recognized religious brokers of the day (the Pharisees).

But what did Jesus say to Matthew and his guests after the disgruntled Pharisees left the party? The text does not say, but let me suggest the following hypothetical exchange:

> Jesus: (watching the Pharisees exit) "Levi, let me tell you something. The Pharisees have taken the keys of knowledge and have hidden them. They have not entered, nor have they allowed those who want to enter to do so."

> Matthew: "Yes, I see what you mean, rabbi."

> Jesus: "You know, Levi, that in the Kingdom of God, the greatest person will be a servant."

> Matthew: "Oh, like at this banquet, rabbi? Something like that? You mean how women like that there, God wants them to repent so he can forgive them, but the Pharisees just want her to serve them?"

> Sinner 1: "Pompous bastards."

> Jesus: "Levi, what do you think? A man had two children. He went to one of them and said, 'Go work in the vineyard today.' And his son said, 'Sure, Dad, I'll go,' but he didn't. Then the man went to his other son and said the same thing—these were grown men we're talking about here, OK?—and he said to his father, 'I don't want to.' But later on, he felt ashamed of himself and decided to go. Now, which of those two sons did the will of their father?"

> Matthew: "Well, um, let's see. You say the first son said he didn't want to go, but then he went ahead and went anyway? But then the other one said he would go, but then later on he backed out?"

> Jesus: "Something like that."

Matthew: "OK. Well, gosh, you know really, if you think about it, I guess you'd have to say that the one who actually went and worked 'did the will of his father.' If you want to put it that way, I guess the second one would be what you want, technically speaking. But really, I guess you'd have to say, you know—really, I guess neither of them did the right thing, because that guy who went shouldn't have mouthed off to his old man that way, and then the other guy lied to his Dad."

Jesus: "Levi."

Matthew: "Yes, rabbi?"

Jesus: "You know, there once was this guy who had a hundred sheep, see? And one of his sheep wandered off one night. He's counting them, and he's like, 'Oh, man, I've lost a sheep here.' You know what he did?"

Matthew: "What, rabbi?"

Jesus: "He goes off into the wilderness—he leaves all the rest of his sheep out there in the open field, OK?—and he goes out in the desert and searches for that one lost sheep until he finds it. And Levi."

Matthew: "Yes, rabbi? Do you want more wine, rabbi?"

Jesus: "Yes, more wine, please. You know what that guy did when he found that sheep? He put that sheep up on his shoulders, and he carried that sheep back to his house—right inside the house, man—and then he called his friends and neighbors together and they had a big party."

Matthew: "Oh, I see. Wait, I get it. Kind of like what we're doing here, right?"

Jesus: "Whoever has ears to hear, let him hear."

Matthew: "So then, did they eat the sheep?"

Jesus: "What?"

Matthew: "That sheep, did they eat that sheep at the party? What did they do with it?"

Jesus: "Which sheep?"

Matthew: "That one he found out in the desert."

Peter: "He thinks you mean that they ate the sheep that the guy found at the party. That's what you were thinking, right?"

Jesus: "No. They did not eat the sheep at the party. No. Where's that wine? OK, it's like this, see? You're a tax collector, right? So tell me this, now. From whom do the kings of the earth receive customs and taxes? From their sons, or from strangers?"

Peter (to
Matthew under
his breath):   "Tell him, 'from strangers.'"

Jesus: "I heard that! Don't you listen to that! Let him think about it for a minute, you hear? Now Levi, where do kings get taxes: from their sons, or from strangers? Simple question."

Matthew: "Uh, from strangers?"

Jesus: "Exactly!"

Matthew: "So, rabbi?"

Jesus: "What?"

Matthew: "What does that mean, then?"

Jesus: "What does what mean?"

Matthew: "That about taxes and strangers? Are you saying that we shouldn't make the king's family pay the tolls? Only other people?"

Jesus: "No, no, it has nothing to do with that."

Matthew: "Because actually, I don't know whether you're familiar with this or not, we generally wouldn't ask anyone from the king's household to pay tolls, anyway. It's not really good for the company. You know how it is with all that."

Jesus: "Levi?"

Matthew: "Yes, rabbi?"

Jesus: "Just shut your mouth for a second and listen, OK?"

Matthew: "Sorry, rabbi."

Jesus: "All right. Maybe we can get to it this way. There was this man who had two sons, see? And his younger son said, 'Father, give me the part of the estate that falls to me.' So the man divides his property between them. Now, right after that . . ."

Matthew: "I'm sorry. Rabbi?"

Jesus: "What?"

Matthew: "Wait, I just want to be sure I heard that right. You're saying that this guy asked his father to give him his inheritance? While his father was still alive, right?"

Sinner 2:   "I'll tell you what my old man would've said if I'd asked him to give me my part of 'the estate.' He'd a looked at me and said, 'Boy, what the . . .'"

Jesus: "Will you just let me finish the story?"

Whether such an exchange ever actually occurred at Matthew's house—and even if it didn't, I think that Jesus must have been involved in discussions like this on an almost daily basis—it highlights the essence of my question. What would Jesus' riddles and parables about the Kingdom look like if we extracted them from all subsequent Christian interpretation of the Gospels over the past two millennia—where Jesus is always the focus and every detail of every teaching situation is treated as a framing device for the words in red—and contextualized these ambiguous statements the way that the sources themselves do, in open banquets and mass healing sessions, places where Jesus must have repeated such sayings often? What kind of response would Jesus' riddles and parables generate in those types of settings? Would every tax collector, sinner, leper, and prostitute suddenly come to a profound insight? Would the simple fact that Jesus ate with someone empower her to understand statements that completely subverted the conceptual foundations of Palestinian Judaism? Would a person like Matthew suddenly conclude that he himself was no longer a "sinner," but now rather a full citizen of God's Kingdom, just because Jesus broke bread with him, over against his own lifetime of beliefs, experiences, and cultural conditioning? My answer to these questions would be no; those who ate with Jesus would not automatically come to such an understanding. How, then, did they come to grips with his ambiguous, paradoxical teachings, and how did they learn to think the way that he did, so that they could take that same ambiguous message of the Kingdom to others? I would suggest two possible answers, both of which reveal the necessity of some model of intellectual brokerage.

First, many people probably came into Jesus' community of knowledge, and thus into his sapiential Kingdom of God, simply by asking him to give them the answers to his riddles and parables. In the scenario envisioned in my fictional dialogue above, it would not be long before Matthew or Peter would say, "Could we go back to that one, and could you explain exactly what you were talking about?" Of course, I can't prove they did this on that occasion, but I would point out that Mark, Matthew, Luke, John, and *Thomas* all suggest that this was how Jesus' closest disciples normally entered his knowledge group (Mark 4:10–12; Matt. 13:10–12, 36; Luke 8:9–10; John 16:23–30; *Thomas* 13; 113). I am not arguing here that Mark's explanation of the parable of the Sower does or does not accurately reflect Jesus' own understanding of that story. I am arguing that Mark's explanation of how the disciples came to a basic understanding of this and similar ambiguous statements about the Kingdom—by asking Jesus to explain it to them in private—is entirely reasonable. This is not to say that Jesus' followers would always necessarily understand his answers any better than his questions, only that they would have depended on him to help them understand how to think according to the Kingdom perspective. They would, in other words, appeal to Jesus as an intellectual broker and a gatekeeper of his community of knowledge.

But, second, what about those people who did not enjoy a private audience with Jesus? Most particularly, what about those people on the other end of the mission statements at Luke 9:2–6 and 10:4–9, 16–17—people who heard the message of repentance, witnessed the Kingdom power of healing and exorcism, and ate at an open table with *the disciples* rather than with Jesus himself? How did these people learn how to unlock the riddles and parables so as to enter into a fuller understanding of Jesus' sapiential Kingdom? They would, of course, learn these things from the disciples themselves, who would presumably, like Jesus, explain the message of repentance in more detail during their egalitarian gatherings and healing services. In this respect, the disciples would serve as brokers of the Kingdom to other people, initiating those who heard the call into a community of knowledge and thus empowering these individuals to think and live as though God were on the throne instead of Caesar.

Whether you agree with me that people entered Jesus' community of knowledge and learned to think the way he thought in either or both of these ways, my basic point here is that entrance into any community of knowledge requires some level of intellectual brokerage. Returning to the purity question, I would argue that Jesus' vision of the Kingdom essentially eliminated bodily boundaries—boundaries of purity, gender, and class—but replaced those bodily barriers with intellectual barriers that were sky high and well-nigh impenetrable without the aid of a broker. In my mind, this hypothesis best explains why *all* of the Gospels suggest that even Jesus' closest disciples had to wait for his answers. Jesus postured himself as a broker of the Kingdom, and seems to have taught his disciples how to broker it to others as well.[12] For things to be otherwise, Jesus would have needed to talk about the Kingdom of God much more clearly than he did—that is, without using riddles and parables.

But even if we accept that some level of intellectual brokerage was necessary for people to enter the Kingdom—to develop a way of thinking that would empower them to understand Jesus' ambiguous discourse and to apply his outlook to their own situations—what does Jesus' riddling tell us about relationships *within* the Kingdom? Did Jesus view all members of the Kingdom as brokers to outsiders, but as equal to one another? In Crossan's view, Jesus' movement was characterized by "an absolute equality of people that denies the validity of any discrimination between them and negates the necessity of a hierarchy among them."[13] I would agree with this conclusion in the sense that those who sat at Jesus' table or preached the Kingdom from house to house did not depend on someone else's intercession for special access to God. I would also point out, however, that not all of Jesus' followers would

---

Thatcher's Keys to the Kingdom

1. The Kingdom of God is a community of knowledge, that group of people who could understand Jesus' riddles and apply his way of thinking to their own lives.

2. Jesus built his image of the Kingdom by using riddles and parables to subvert and realign normal ways of thinking and acting.

    ◗ Jesus played with taboos to reverse normal ways of thinking.

    ◗ Jesus played with paradoxes to question the very possibility of "categories" and "hierarchies."

    ◗ Jesus' bodily practices enacted the conceptual reversals encoded in his riddles and parables.

3. Jesus saw himself and his disciples as intellectual brokers of the Kingdom.

    ◗ Outsiders would need help from Jesus or a disciple to get inside.

    ◗ Insiders would be distinguished by their varying levels of under-standing.

---

possess the same level of comprehension; some would be better able to think like Jesus and would possess a larger store of group traditions (i.e., stock answers to his ambiguous questions) than others. Returning to the example above, Peter might be equal to Matthew in status for fellowship while also functioning as Levi's intellectual mentor in matters of the Kingdom, helping him to develop the mental skills necessary to unlock the hard sayings of Jesus. I do not mean to suggest that members of the Jesus movement underwent an annual review of understanding such as that envisioned in the Qumran community's "Manual of Discipline" (1QS 5.20–24), but I do see certain parallels.

Essentially, then, I think that Jesus the Riddler saw himself as an intellectual broker of the Kingdom of God and that he expected and empowered his followers to catch his unique vision and become intellectual brokers to others. They might do this on the road or, depending on their personal circumstances, in day-to-day dialogue with the people in their familial and patronage groups.

In the process, the secret wisdom of the Kingdom—secret to the world, but common knowledge among all followers of Jesus—would guard their minds against the crushing weight of the ancient Mediterranean social system, even if that system continued to restrain their bodies. In these situations, the power of the riddle to subvert all social realities would reach its highest potential in the form of an invisible empire of wit.

Notes

Preface: The Quest for Jesus the Riddler; or What This Book Will and Won't (Try to) Prove

1. The "Riddle of the Sphinx," apparently solved by Oedipus. The answer is "a human being," who crawls on all fours in infancy, walks upright in adulthood, and hobbles on a cane in old age. Different versions of this riddle are attested in ancient sources: compare, for example, Athenaeus, *Deipnosophistae* 10.456, with the version in *The Greek Anthology* 14.64.

2. Judges 14:14. The answer, derived from Samson's immediately preceding experience, is "a swarm of bees making honey in the carcass of a lion."

3. Cited in Mark Bryant, *Riddles Ancient and Modern* (New York: Peter Bedrick, 1983), 191. The answer is "a cider apple."

4. J. R. R. Tolkien, *The Hobbit; or, There and Back Again* (Boston: Houghton Mifflin, 1966), 88. The answer is "time."

5. Both quotes Thomas A. Burns, "Riddling: Occasion to Act," *Journal of American Folklore* 89 (1976): 144–45.

6. W. J. Pepicello and Thomas A. Green, *The Language of Riddles: New Perspectives* (Columbus: Ohio State University Press, 1984), 155.

7. Robert W. Funk, Roy W. Hoover, and the Jesus Seminar, *The Five Gospels: The Search for the Authentic Words of Jesus* (New York: Polebridge, 1993), 105, 237–38, all emphasis added.

8. Robert W. Funk with Mahlon H. Smith, *The Gospel of Mark Red Letter Edition* (Sonoma, CA: Polebridge, 1991), 188.

9. Robert W. Funk and the Jesus Seminar, *The Acts of Jesus: The Search for the Authentic Deeds of Jesus* (Sonoma, CA: Polebridge, 1998), 129, 237–38.

10. See Edgar Slotkin's "Response to Professors Fontaine and Camp," in *Text and Tradition: The Hebrew Bible and Folklore*, ed. Susan Niditch, Society of Biblical Literature Semeia Studies (Atlanta: Scholars Press, 1990).

11. Viv Edwards and Thomas J. Sienkewicz, *Oral Cultures Past and Present: Rappin' and Homer* (Cambridge, MA: Basil Blackwell, 1991), 172–80.

12. See the list and summary in Tom Thatcher, "The Riddles of Jesus in the Johannine Dialogues," in *Jesus in Johannine Tradition*, ed. Robert T. Fortna and Tom Thatcher (Louisville, KY: Westminster John Knox, 2001), 268–72.

13. Herbert Leroy, *Rätsel und Missverständnis: Ein Beitrag zur Formgeschichte des Johannesevangeliums*, Bonner Biblische Beiträge (Bonn: Peter Hanstein, 1968); David Rhoads and Donald Michie, *Mark as Story: An Introduction to the Narrative of a Gospel* (Philadelphia: Fortress, 1982), 55–58; Robert M. Fowler, *Let the Reader Understand: Reader-Response Criticism and the Gospel of Mark* (Minneapolis: Fortress, 1991), 195–209; N. T. Wright, *Jesus and the Victory of God* (Minneapolis: Fortress, 1996); Tom Thatcher, *The Riddles of Jesus in John: A Study in Tradition and Folklore*, Society of Biblical Literature Monograph Series (Atlanta: Society of Biblical Literature, 2000); Narry Santos, *The Slave of All: The Paradox of Authority and Servanthood in the Gospel of Mark*, Journal for the Study of the New Testament Supplement Series (Sheffield: Sheffield Academic Press, 2003).

14. See Wright 1996, 510, 573–74, 644–45.

15. For this very reason, although riddles have been a distinct topic of academic inquiry since the seventeenth century, Archer Taylor could still complain in the mid-1940s that the full range of "the stylistic varieties of true riddles are virtually unknown" ("The Riddle," *California Folklore Quarterly* [*Western Folklore*] 2 [1943]: 139).

16. Funk, Hoover, and the Jesus Seminar, 1993, 31–32.

17. See the discussion in chapters 7 and 8 of Thatcher 2000, 231–94.

18. Archer Taylor, *The Literary Riddle before 1600* (1948; reprint, Westport, CT: Greenwood Press, 1976), 31–37. See also Raymond Theodore Ohl, *The Enigmas of Symphosius* (Philadelphia: University of Pennsylvania Press, 1928), 9–13.

19. On Jewish riddles, see Josephus, *Antiquities* 8.143–149 (par. 1 Kings 5, 9); Claudia V. Camp and Carole R. Fontaine, "The Words of the Wise and Their Riddles," in *Text and Tradition: The Hebrew Bible and Folklore*; James L. Crenshaw, *Samson: A Secret Betrayed, A Vow Ignored* (Atlanta: John Knox, 1978), 99–111; V. Hamp, "חידה *chîdhâh*," in *Theological Dictionary of the Old Testament*, ed. G. Johannes Botterweck and Helmer Ringgren, trans. David E. Green (Grand Rapids: Eerdmans, 1980), 4.320–23; Galit Hasan-Rock, "Riddle and Proverb: Their Relationship Exemplified by an Aramaic Proverb," *Proverbium* 24 (1974): 936–40; Joseph Jacobs, "Riddle," in *The Jewish Encyclopedia*, ed. Isidore Singer (New York: Funk & Wagnalls, 1905), 10.408–9; Solomon Schrecter, "The Riddles of Solomon in Rabbinic Literature," *Folklore* 1 (1890): 349–58; John M. Thompson, *The Form and Function of Proverbs in Ancient Israel* (The Hague: Mouton, 1974), 74–75, 92–93; Harry Torcyzner, "The Riddle in the Bible," *Hebrew Union College Annual* 1 (1924): 125–50. On Greco-Roman riddles, see Aristotle, *The Poetics* 22.1–7; Athenaeus of Naucratis (170–230 CE), *The Deipnosophists* 10.448–59; *The Greek Anthology* Book 14; Friedrich Hauck, "παροιμία," in *Theological Dictionary of the New Testament*, ed. Gerhard Friedrich, trans. Geoffrey W. Bromiley (Grand Rapids: Eerdmans, 1967), 5.854–55; Konrad Ohlert, *Rätsel und Rätselspiele der alten Griechen*, 2nd ed., 1912 (reprint, New York: Olms, 1979). The studies by J. B. Friedreich, *Geschichte des Rätsels* (Dresden: Rudolf Kuntze, 1860), Mathilde Hain, *Rätsel* (Stuttgart: J. B. Metzler, 1966), and Mark Bryant (1983) survey both Jewish and Greco-Roman riddles, as well as modern European riddles. As a complement to Taylor's *Literary Riddle*, see Michele DeFilippis, *The Literary Riddle in Italy to the End of the Sixteenth Century* (Berkeley: University of California Press, 1948).

Chapter 1: So What Is a "Riddle"?

1. For a more detailed discussion of riddles and recent riddle research, see Tom Thatcher, *The Riddles of Jesus in John: A Study in Tradition and Folklore*, Society of Biblical Literature Monograph Series (Atlanta: Society of Biblical Literature, 2000), 109–81.

2. The basic distinction here between riddles and "normal/conventional" language is borrowed from W. J. Pepicello and Thomas A. Green, *The Language of Riddles: New Perspectives* (Columbus: Ohio State University Press, 1984), 125–29. See also their "Wit in Riddling: A Linguistic Perspective," *Genre* 11 (1978): 3; "The Folk Riddle: A Redefinition of Terms," *Western Folklore* 38 (1979): 7.

3. See Pepicello and Green 1984, 13, 97–100, 124–29.

4. Ibid., 111.

5. My definition does not recognize "intentional vagueness." In popular usage, elusive statements that seek to avoid a direct answer are frequently described as "vague." Following the discussion here, such statements would actually be "ambiguous" because they admit of several possible meanings and thereby attempt to lead the audience away from the truth. For my purposes, "vagueness" is an accident, a failed attempt to communicate either clearly or ambiguously.

6. The definition of "ambiguity" offered here is in my view compatible with, yet more precise than, those definitions that emphasize the possibility of multiple interpretations. For example, Hartmann and Stork define a statement as "ambiguous when more than one interpretation can be assigned to it," and the *Oxford Dictionary* says that language is ambiguous when it admits "more than one interpretation, or explanation . . . or [is] of several possible meanings" (R. R. K. Hartmann and F. C. Stork, *Dictionary of Language and Linguistics* [New York: John Wiley & Sons, 1972], 11; *The Oxford English Dictionary*, 2nd ed. [Oxford: Clarendon Press, 1989], 386). Technically, even a "clear" statement may admit of "more than one interpretation," because every hearer/reader will interpret the text and the referent from the perspective of her own personal ideological horizon. An "ambiguous" statement, however, can be interpreted in more than one way by *each individual* hearer/reader. Hence, while a "clear" statement might mean three things to three different people, an "ambiguous" statement might mean three different things to one person. In my view, my definition is consistent with, if perhaps narrower than, that of Robert Fowler: "Verbal ambiguity occurs when an utterance can be taken by the hearer in two or more discrete ways or when the hearer has an indefinite range of possibilities from which to choose" (*Let the Reader Understand: Reader-Response Criticism and the Gospel of Mark* [Minneapolis: Fortress, 1991], 197).

7. Pepicello and Green 1984, 13; 1978, 5.

8. Jack Glazier and Phyllis Gorfain Glazier, "Ambiguity and Exchange: The Double Dimension of Mbeere Riddles," *Journal of American Folklore* 89 (1976): 211.

9. Both riddles cited from Mark Bryant, *Riddles Ancient and Modern* (New York: Peter Bedrick, 1983), 191, 163.

10. Cited from Bryant 1983, 122.

11. Elli Köngäs Maranda, "Riddles and Riddling: An Introduction," *Journal of American Folklore* 89 (1976): 131; also Glazier and Glazier 1976, 212–17.

12. In this sense, riddles overlap with what Santos calls "both-and" paradoxes, paradoxical statements that bring together two apparently antithetical concepts where "one side of the paradox shows one truth that upsets its hearers, and the

other side shows the truth that balances it. The second truth does not restrict the first, but only places it in the proper perspective" (Narry Santos, *The Slave of All: The Paradox of Authority and Servanthood in the Gospel of Mark,* Journal for the Study of the New Testament Supplement Series [Sheffield: Sheffield Academic Press, 2003], 8). As I will argue in chapter 10, Jesus' riddles often utilize paradox, but generally require the audience to provide the answer that "places it in the proper perspective" themselves.

13. Roger D. Abrahams, "Introductory Remarks to a Rhetorical Theory of Folklore," *Journal of American Folklore* 81 (1968): 149.
14. See especially Abrahams 1968, and also his *Between the Living and the Dead: Riddles Which Tell Stories,* Folklore Fellows Communications Series (Helsinki: Suomalainen Tiedeakatemia, 1980), 13–17. Also Elli Köngäs Maranda, "The Logic of Riddles," in *Structural Analysis of Oral Tradition,* ed. Pierre Maranda and Elli Köngäs Maranda (Philadelphia: University of Pennsylvania Press, 1971); "Theory and Practice of Riddle Analysis," *Journal of American Folklore* 84 (1971); "A Tree Grows: Transformations of a Riddle Metaphor," in *Structural Models in Folklore and Transformational Essays,* ed. Elli Köngäs Maranda and Pierre Maranda (The Hague: Mouton, 1971).
15. Köngäs Maranda, "Theory and Practice," 54.
16. Ibid.
17. Ian Hamnet, "Ambiguity, Classification, and Change: The Function of Riddles," *Man* n.s. 2 (1967): 382.
18. Joseph A. Fitzmeyer, *The Gospel according to Luke,* Anchor Bible (Garden City, NY: Doubleday, 1985), 2.1062–63.
19. I. Howard Marshall, *The Gospel of Luke: A Commentary on the Greek Text,* New International Greek Testament Commentary (Grand Rapids: Eerdmans, 1978), 592.

Chapter 2: "Everybody Knows That One"

1. Mark Bryant, *Riddles Ancient and Modern* (New York: Peter Bedrick Books, 1983).
2. First riddle, Elli Köngäs Maranda, "The Logic of Riddles," in *Structural Analysis of Oral Tradition,* ed. Pierre Maranda and Elli Köngäs Maranda (Philadelphia: University of Pennsylvania Press, 1971), 198–99; second riddle, Elli Köngäs Maranda, "A Tree Grows: Transformations of a Riddle Metaphor," in *Structural Models in Folklore and Transformational Essays,* ed. Elli Köngäs Maranda and Pierre Maranda (The Hague: Mouton, 1971), 119–21.
3. Quote Archer Taylor, "The Varieties of Riddles," in *Philologica: The Malone Anniversary Studies,* ed. Thomas A. Kirby and Henry Bosley Woolf (Baltimore: Johns Hopkins Press, 1949), 3; see also Taylor's "The Riddle," *California Folklore Quarterly* [*Western Folklore*] 2 (1943): 145; W. J. Pepicello and Thomas A. Green, "The Folk Riddle: A Redefinition of Terms," *Western Folklore* 38 (1979): 17–19; "Wit in Riddling: A Linguistic Perspective," *Genre* 11 (1978): 1, 5; survey and discussion in Tom Thatcher, *The Riddles of Jesus in John: A Study in Tradition and Folklore,* Society of Biblical Literature Monograph Series (Atlanta: Society of Biblical Literature, 2000), 147–51, 164.
4. Compare Taylor 1943, 146–47, with his later "Riddles in Dialogue," *Proceedings of the American Philosophical Society* 97 (1953): 62–65.
5. Roger D. Abrahams and Alan Dundes, "Riddles," in *Folklore and Folklife: An Introduction,* ed. Richard Dorson (Chicago: University of Chicago Press, 1972), 137.

6. Köngäs Maranda, "Logic," 195–96.
7. Edgar Slotkin, "Response to Professors Fontaine and Camp," in *Text and Tradition: The Hebrew Bible and Folklore*, ed. Susan Niditch, Society of Biblical Literature Semeia Studies (Atlanta: Scholars Press, 1990), 154.
8. Ibid., 154–55.
9. Ibid., 154. See also Jack Glazier and Phyllis Gorfain Glazier, who comment on one Mbeere riddle, "Once again we may be struck by the arbitrariness of the correct answer. The acceptable reply is dictated by the rules of riddling, not by a rule which admits any logical response" ("Ambiguity and Exchange: The Double Dimension of Mbeere Riddles," *Journal of American Folklore* 89 [1976]: 216).
10. Herbert Leroy, in a detailed form-critical study of misunderstanding in the Gospel of John, refers to that group of people who possess the lexical or factual information needed to answer a riddle as "die Sprachgemeinschaft der Sondersprache" (*Rätsel und Missverständnis: Ein Beitrag zur Formgeschichte des Johannesevangeliums*, Bonner Biblische Beiträge [Bonn: Peter Hanstein, 1968], 44).
11. Elli Köngäs Maranda, "Theory and Practice of Riddle Analysis," *Journal of American Folklore* 84 (1971): 53.
12. Thomas A. Burns, "Riddling: Occasion to Act," *Journal of American Folklore* 89 (1976): 143–45. See also the convenient summary in Bryant, 17–21.
13. See discussion in Köngäs Maranda, "Logic," 195–96. Many scholars consider monk's questions to be "false riddles" because they do not meet the criterion of solvability.
14. Köngäs Maranda, "Tree Grows," 119; "Riddles and Riddling: An Introduction," *Journal of American Folklore* 89 (1976): 131.
15. James L. Crenshaw, *Samson: A Secret Betrayed, A Vow Ignored* (Atlanta: John Knox, 1978), 100. See also Leroy, who emphasizes that the ability to answer riddles establishes one's worthiness to hold membership in a group (1968, 45–47).

Chapter 3: Riddling Sessions

1. For the complete text of this ancient riddle, which gets more graphic as it goes along, see *The Greek Anthology* 14.55, trans. W. R. Paton, Loeb Classical Library (Cambridge, MA: Harvard University Press, 1960).
2. J. R. R. Tolkien, *The Hobbit; or, There and Back Again* (Boston: Houghton Mifflin, 1966), 83–91.
3. Roger D. Abrahams, "The Complex Relations of Simple Forms," in *Folklore Genres*, ed. Dan Ben-Amos (Austin: University of Texas Press, 1976), 202, emphasis added. In play, one can experience "motives we don't normally allow ourselves under the circumstances of real life" (203).
4. Tolkien 1966, 90. The narrator's comment here is undermined by the fact that Gollum then attempts to eat Bilbo, a circumstance Tolkien justifies by recourse to the criterion of solvability: "And after all that last question [What have I got in my pocket?] had not been a genuine riddle according to the ancient laws."
5. Athenaeus, *The Deipnosophists* 10.457–59.
6. Answer: "Ohio." This is an example of an "orthographic riddle," an ambiguous question "whose referents are words and letters as orthographic rather than linguistic entities" and whose clues often describe the sound or shape of the letters of the answer (Roger D. Abrahams and Alan Dundes, "Riddles," in

Folklore and Folklife: An Introduction, ed. Richard Dorson [Chicago: University of Chicago Press, 1972], 135). Riddles of this type obviously require literacy as a special knowledge prerequisite.

7. Elli Köngäs Maranda, "Theory and Practice of Riddle Analysis," *Journal of American Folklore* 84 (1971): 58.

8. John R. Donahue and Daniel J. Harrington, *The Gospel of Mark,* Sacra Pagina (Collegeville, MN: Liturgical Press, 2002), 139.

9. Ben Witherington III, *The Gospel of Mark: A Socio-Rhetorical Commentary* (Grand Rapids: Eerdmans, 2001), 165–66.

10. John Dominic Crossan, *The Historical Jesus: The Life of a Mediterranean Jewish Peasant* (San Francisco: HarperSanFrancisco, 1991), 349. Crossan interprets "Whoever has ears" to mean that Jesus' vision and social program will be obvious to anyone who bothers to look at what he's doing and listen to what he's saying.

11. Elizabeth Struthers Malbon, *Hearing Mark: A Listener's Guide* (Harrisburg, PA: Trinity Press International, 2002), 30–31.

12. Obviously, several of the sayings units on this table are parables. I will discuss in a later chapter how parables can function as riddles.

13. William Lane, *The Gospel according to Mark: The English Text with Introduction, Exposition and Notes,* New International Commentary on the New Testament (Grand Rapids: Eerdmans, 1974), 277; see also Donahue and Harrington 2002, who interpret the "test" against the backdrop of signs of true prophets, 248–50; Robert H. Gundry, *Mark: A Commentary on His Apology for the Cross* (Grand Rapids: Eerdmans, 1993), 401–2. Some scholars interpret the requested "sign" as a "spectacular and portentous heavenly miracle of an apocalyptic kind," one that could not be faked or accomplished by demonic power (Hugh Anderson, *The Gospel of Mark,* New Century Bible [Greenwood, SC: Attic Press, 1976], 199; see also James A. Brooks, *Mark,* New American Commentary [Nashville: Broadman, 1991], 127).

14. Note Gundry's comments on ἀφείς, which here "stresses his [Jesus'] judgementally quick departure from the sign-seeking generation of Pharisees" (1993, 407).

15. Compare, for example, France, who thinks that "this generation" includes the disciples, with Gundry, who argues that it does not (Robert T. France, *The Gospel of Mark: A Commentary on the Greek Text,* New International Greek Testament Commentary [Grand Rapids: Eerdmans, 2002], 312–13; Gundry 1993, 406).

16. Lane 1974, 282.

17. I lean toward the NASB translation here, which suggests that the disciples were discussing the fact "that" they had no bread; the NIV takes ὅτι to mean "because" and makes v. 16 the disciples' explanation of Jesus' comment in v. 15—"he's mad *because* we don't have any bread." See Larry Hurtado, *Mark,* New International Bible Commentary (Peabody, MA: Hendrickson, 1989), 126.

18. Lane 1974, 281.

19. Gundry 1993, 408.

20. Donald H. Juel, *Mark,* Augsburg Commentary on the New Testament (Minneapolis: Augsburg Fortress, 1990), 115.

21. Mary Ann Tolbert, *Sowing the Gospel: Mark's World in Literary-Historical Perspective* (Minneapolis: Fortress, 1989), 102–3.

Notes

159

22. France, Gundry, and Hare prefer the title "The Parable of the Seeds" because the focus is on the harvest yield (France 2002, 188; Gundry 1993, 191–93; Douglas R. A. Hare, *Mark*, Westminster Bible Companion [Louisville, KY: Westminster John Knox, 1996], 53–54). John Painter, however, says that this designation is more appropriate to Luke's presentation, and refers to Mark's version as "The Parable of the Soils" (*Mark's Gospel: Worlds in Conflict*, New Testament Readings [New York: Routledge, 1997], 76–78). Donald Juel takes a compromise position and labels the story "The Sower and the Soils" because it focuses on the results of Jesus' preaching and the need to respond to that message (1990, 68–70); this is apparently also the view of Craig Blomberg, *Interpreting the Parables* (Downers Grove, IL: InterVarsity, 1990), 226–29, and Hurtado (1989, 71–75).
23. France 2002, 193.
24. Ibid., 208–10. See also Hare 1996, 57.
25. Painter 1997, 83.
26. Gundry 1993, 211. Thus, at vv. 11 and 13, αὐτός ("them") refers to the disciples, whereas at vv. 2 and 21 αὐτός refers to the "great crowds."
27. Both riddles and proverbs play on traditional knowledge, and in many cultures they share similar forms and functions. For these reasons, a proverb can function as a riddle, or vice versa, depending on the context of the remark and the speaker's intention (see, for example, Mehmet Ilhan Başgöz, "Riddle-Proverbs and the Related Forms in Turkish Folklore," *Proverbium* 18 [1972]: 655–68; Galit Hasan-Rock, "Riddle and Proverb: Their Relationship Exemplified by an Aramaic Proverb," *Proverbium* 24 [1974]: 936–40; Matt Kuusi, "Southwest African Riddle-Proverbs," *Proverbium* 12 [1969]: 305–12; Archer Taylor, "Problems in the Study of Riddles," *Southern Folklore Quarterly* 2 [1938]: 1–9).
28. See, for example, W. D. Davies and Dale C. Allison Jr., *A Critical and Exegetical Commentary on the Gospel according to Saint Matthew*, International Critical Commentary (Edinburgh: T. & T. Clark, 1997), 3.214; Robert H. Gundry, *Matthew: A Commentary on His Handbook for a Mixed Church under Persecution*, 2nd ed. (Grand Rapids: Eerdmans, 1994), 442. Of course, if Matthew's version is based on independent tradition (= not derived from Mark), "What do you think?" could simply be a characteristic feature of that tradition.
29. See Davies and Allison 1997, 2.738.
30. As Blomberg notes, the Greek construction here implies an affirmative answer (*Matthew*, New American Commentary [Nashville: Broadman, 1992], 269–70); hence the Scholars Version, "Your teacher pays his temple tax, doesn't he?" (cf. NASB and NIV). Of course, the tax collectors' optimism does not necessarily mean that Jesus supported, or regularly paid, the tax.
31. Donald Senior, *Matthew*, Abingdon New Testament Commentaries (Nashville: Abingdon, 1998), 202–3.
32. See discussion in Davies and Allison 1997, 2.744.
33. Even if one wished to translate ἀλλότριοι as "subjects" or some equally neutral term, I would still argue that the point of the riddle lies in the opposition between this group and "sons": the fact that you must pay means that the king—whether God or Caesar—is treating you as a person outside his household. The tax is thus a mark of status, specifically a mark of lower status that functions to demonstrate that the "king" is above you and treats you as such.

Chapter 4: Finding Riddles in Written Texts

1. Bennett Cerf, *Pop-Up Riddles* (New York: Random House, 1967).
2. Note that other possible criteria have been excluded, due to the limited scope of my discussion. Specifically, I have included only criteria that are relevant to "sage riddles"—riddles that demonstrate Jesus' wit and wisdom as a teacher while making no explicitly christological claims.
3. Jesus proceeds to give an extended answer at John 10:7–18 that clarifies the issue for John's reader but leaves "the Jews" just as confused as they were before (vv. 19–21).
4. Of course, one could argue that the authors/narrators of the sources may have misunderstood the intentions of the historical Jesus from time to time, portraying as riddles some sayings that Jesus thought were unambiguous or reducing the ambiguity of sayings that were originally offered as challenges. I concede this possibility here for sake of argument, and would therefore stress that criterion #1 cannot be used to demonstrate that the historical Jesus and/or his associates understood a particular statement to be intentionally ambiguous, only that the author of the source in question understood that statement to be ambiguous.
5. The Fourth Gospel, which includes a large number of riddles and riddling sessions, sometimes implies that Jesus wishes that "the Jews" could understand him a little better than they do. In John's view, however, the problem does not lie in Jesus' communication skills, but rather in the fact that "the Jews" are children of the devil who cannot comprehend Christ because they are "from below" while he is "from above" (8:23, 44). "The Jews" therefore could not answer Jesus' riddles, even if he wanted them to answer. Their confusion is simply a measure of their ontological status, not a measure of Jesus' skill as a riddler.
6. Robert J. Miller, ed., *The Complete Gospels: Annotated Scholars Version*, rev. ed. (Sonoma, CA: Polebridge, 1994).
7. Of course, it may be that in these cases the authors of the sources simply assume that their readers are already familiar with the "correct" answers: i.e., Mark may rely on the implied reader's foreknowledge of his community's traditional way of explaining something that Jesus said. This approach would, however, obviously leave such statements ambiguous for prospective readers outside those communities.

Chapter 5: The Art of the Absurd

1. Herman C. Waetjen, *A Reordering of Power: A Socio-Political Reading of Mark's Gospel* (Minneapolis: Fortress, 1989), 104–5. David Rhoads and Donald Michie make the same point about the distinction between "insiders" and "outsiders" but argue that all of Mark's parables should, in fact, be viewed as riddles (*Mark as Story: An Introduction to the Narrative of a Gospel* [Philadelphia: Fortress, 1982], 55–58).
2. See Luke 7:41–42 (the Two Debtors, which functions in Luke's context as an alternative riddle); 12:35–38 (the Returning Master; note Peter's request for clarification at v. 41); 15:4–6 (the Lost Sheep; Jesus provides the answer at v. 7); 15:8–9 (the Lost Coin; Jesus provides the answer at v. 10).
3. Rhoads and Michie 1982, 55.
4. Including those parables that use some variant of the phrase "Whoever has ears" to signal that an answer is expected (see *Thomas* 8:1–4; 21:1–4, 10; 63:1–4;

65:1–8; 96:1–3). The possible exception appears at 64:12, if the reference to "buyers and merchants" is intended as a definitive solution to the parable of the Banquet. In my view, if Thomas did see v. 12 as the answer, he missed the point of the story entirely, because the parable does not seem to focus on the motivations of the merchants who did not attend the feast, but rather on the open fellowship of those who ultimately sat at the table.

5. Luke Timothy Johnson, *The Gospel of Luke*, Sacra Pagina (Collegeville, MN: Michael Glazier, 1991), 173. I personally assume, by the way, that the bandits in the story are also Jewish, making this a case of Jew-on-Jew violence. My reading further highlights the compassion of the Samaritan by contrasting his kind acts with the violent act of these renegade Jews.

6. Mary Ann Tolbert also emphasizes the parable's integration into its present narrative setting, but claims that Luke's contextualization "confuses the [reader's?] attempt to follow the narrative's logical movement and clarify its elements" (*Perspectives on the Parables: An Approach to Multiple Interpretations* [Philadelphia: Fortress, 1979], 59–60). I agree that the question, "Which of these three seems to have been a neighbor of the one who fell victim to the bandits?" (Luke 10:37), is a bit jarring on the heels of the parable, because it changes the terms of the argument: the "neighbor" is now no longer an object of love, but rather the one who shows love. But I would personally see this as a very mild "confusion" compared to the shock that the story itself would generate. I would also argue that the shift in the terms of the question is completely consistent with the dynamics of a riddling session, yet another strategy that Jesus could have used to make this already difficult parable almost impossible to unlock. Tolbert's observations demonstrate that the parable is ambiguous in relation to its current context; she concludes from this that Luke has made it hard to determine what the historical Jesus did with the story. I agree that the parable is ambiguous in relation to its current context; I conclude from this that Luke's presentation likely reflects the way that Jesus himself would have used this parable as a riddle.

7. Johnson 1991, 175.

8. John Dominic Crossan, *The Dark Interval: Towards a Theology of Story*, rev. ed. (Sonoma, CA: Polebridge, 1988), 85–88, first quote 85; "Parable and Example in Jesus' Teaching," *New Testament Studies* 18 (1971–72), second quote 291, third quote 295.

9. Broadly speaking, by calling the parables "metaphors" I am following in the tradition of C. H. Dodd: "At its simplest the parable is a metaphor or simile drawn from nature or common life, arresting the hearer by its vividness or strangeness, and leaving the mind in sufficient doubt about its precise application to tease it into active thought" (*The Parables of the Kingdom*, 3rd ed. [London: Nisbet, 1936], 16). But in my view, the essential points of the discussion to follow would remain relevant whether one prefers to call parables "metaphors," "analogies," "symbols," or anything else. John Sider, for example, treats parables as "analogies" with "proportional comparison," though he still finds it convenient to analyze them in terms of the interplay between "tenor" and "vehicle" (*Interpreting the Parables: A Hermeneutical Guide to Their Meaning* [Grand Rapids: Zondervan, 1995]). And of course, a number of prominent theorists—including Norman Perrin and Brandon Scott—have produced very fruitful results by treating the parables as "symbols," which they distinguish from "metaphors" for a number of reasons (I will interact with their

approaches in a later note). I am not seeking to contradict the work of these scholars, nor do I wish to be dogmatic. It is sufficient for my purposes to call Jesus' parables "metaphors" because I am more concerned with their rhetorical strategy than with a precise definition of the genre. As Tolbert has observed, "metaphor does not provide an exact picture of a parable, but it can be viewed as an analogue to a parable: it [metaphor] functions on its semantic level in a way that corresponds to what we can observe concerning the functioning of a parable at the level of story" (1979, 44).

10. The concept of linguistic "emptiness," as I develop it here, will doubtless smell familiar to anyone who is even slightly acquainted with poststructural models of interpretation. For people who are interested in such approaches, I would stress only that what I am calling an "empty metaphor" is a rhetorical strategy, not a way or a product of reading. The empty metaphor is, in other words, a rhetorical device that speakers (such as Jesus) and authors (such as Mark and Thomas) would have utilized intentionally in order to produce a particular effect on their audiences. Of course, they would not have called this device an "empty metaphor."

11. My emphasis on Richards does not reflect a disregard for any other theories of metaphor and symbol that might be, or have been, utilized in discussions of Jesus' parables. For example, Perrin's landmark research leaned heavily on Philip Wheelwright and Paul Ricoeur, and Scott's excellent study refers to Richards but also interacts with Ricoeur, Eco, and Lakoff and Johnson (Norman Perrin, *Jesus and the Language of the Kingdom: Symbol and Metaphor in New Testament Interpretation* [Philadelphia: Fortress, 1976], see 29–32, 60–63; Bernard Brandon Scott, *Hear Then the Parable: A Commentary on the Parables of Jesus* [Minneapolis: Fortress, 1990], see 45–51, 56–62). I like Richards because his approach seems to fit well with the data at hand; I focus on Richards exclusively, even though his approach has many obvious points of contact with other theorists, simply for convenience and to limit the scope of the discussion here. I should also note that Richards' theory applies to all types of signs; I have focused on "words" here only for sake of clarity.

12. I. A. Richards and C. K. Ogden, *The Meaning of Meaning*, 8th ed. (New York: Harcourt Brace, 1956), 50–57. I should note that Richards, when compared to other language theorists, is somewhat reductionistic in the sense that he tends to emphasize personal experience over broad cultural influences; one might say that, for him, psychology (sometimes even neuropsychology) takes precedence over sociology. Thus, for Richards language "means" what it means to each individual "organism" against the backdrop of her personal life experiences, which may be unique. Of course, each person's life is contextualized within a broader set of common cultural influences, making it possible for different people to agree on common meanings of signs.

13. Ibid., 21. I am indebted to Stephen Depoe for bringing the "semantic triangle," and Richards' work in general, to my attention.

14. Ibid., 11.

15. Technically, metaphors make their comparisons directly, using (or implying) the verbs "is/was" or "are/were." When the comparison is indirect, including terms like "like" or "as," the figure is called a "simile." I mention this only because many of Jesus' parables are technically similes rather than metaphors, in the sense they include the words "like" or "as" (ὡς)—"The Kingdom of God is like . . ." Although some scholars have highlighted the differences between

similes and metaphors, for purposes of my discussion it will not be necessary to distinguish them (see especially Robert W. Funk, *Language, Hermeneutic, and the Word of God: The Problem of Language in the New Testament and Contemporary Theology* [New York: Harper & Row, 1966], 136–37, and subsequent research that has engaged his conclusions).

16. I. A. Richards, *The Philosophy of Rhetoric* (New York: Oxford University Press, 1964), 97.

17. This is not to say that the vehicle simply describes the tenor. Richards stresses that the metaphor makes "two thoughts of different things active together . . . whose meaning is the result of their interaction." Thus, "vehicle and tenor in cooperation give a meaning of more varied powers than can be ascribed to either" alone (Richards 1964, 93, 100). The "meaning" of a metaphor lies in the interaction between the psychological contexts of its two elements, which combine to produce a third and distinct conceptual entity.

18. Ibid., 94, emphasis original.

19. For purposes of this discussion, which is concerned with the rhetorical strategy of parables rather than their surface form, it is not necessary to distinguish between different types of parable: "figurative sayings," "similitudes," "example stories," "true parables," "allegories," etc. As C. H. Dodd noted seventy years ago, "it cannot be pretended that the line can be drawn with any precision between these . . . classes of parable" because "one class melts into another" (1936, 18; see also Klyne R. Snodgrass, "Parable," in *The Dictionary of Jesus and the Gospels*, ed. Joel B. Green, Scot McKnight, and I. Howard Marshall [Downers Grove, IL: Inter-Varsity, 1992], 593–94). In my view, all classes of parables—if it is relevant to distinguish them—function rhetorically in the way that I describe here. I therefore subscribe to Funk's assertion that "whether there is involved a simple metaphor, an elaborated or picture metaphor (similitude), or a metaphor expanded into a story (parable proper) is not immediately differentiating. . . . What is more significant is the nature of the metaphor or simile itself" (1966, 136).

20. Mark's version has been cited here, but many scholars feel that *Thomas* 20:2–3 is closer to Jesus' own words (see Robert W. Funk, Roy W. Hoover, and the Jesus Seminar, *The Five Gospels: The Search for the Authentic Words of Jesus* [New York: Polebridge, 1993], 484–85).

21. Scott 1990, 50–51.

22. Thus Jeremias, who argues that both the Mustard Seed and the Leaven "compare the Kingdom of God with the final stage of the process there described— with the tall shrub giving shelter to the birds, and with the mass of dough wholly permeated by the leaven" (*Rediscovering the Parables*, trans. Frank Clarke [New York: Charles Scribner's Sons, 1966], 117). Many commentators have followed Jeremias in stressing that these parables are concerned with the *results* of growth, not the process of growth. Larry Hurtado, for example, concludes that "the lesson [of the Mustard Seed] is not that the kingdom of God comes by quiet, prolonged growth, but rather that, though many might think the manifestation of the kingdom in Jesus' ministry insignificant, they would be proven wrong in the day of its full appearance" (*Mark*, New International Bible Commentary [Peabody, MA: Hendrickson, 1989], 77).

23. John R. Donahue and Daniel J. Harrington, *The Gospel of Mark*, Sacra Pagina (Collegeville, MN: Liturgical Press, 2002), 151. They note, by the way, that "the term 'parable' is used [at Mark 4:30] in the Jewish wider senses of 'illustration' or even 'riddle.'"

24. Robert T. France, *The Gospel of Mark: A Commentary on the Greek Text*, New International Greek Testament Commentary (Grand Rapids: Eerdmans, 2002), 217.

25. Dodd 1936, 20. It should be noted that Dodd stresses the "remarkable realism" of the parables in order to emphasize the differences between parables and "allegories." A parable, in Dodd's view, "presents one single point of comparison," meaning that its individual details simply enhance the reality of the scene rather than pointing to secondary meanings. At the same time, Dodd acknowledges that parables often play on the unusual: "if they [a character's actions] are surprising, the point of the parable is that such actions *are* surprising" (18–21).

26. Jeremias 1966, 21.

27. Scott 1990, 381–83.

28. See Crossan 1988, 76–77; Dodd 1936, 190; Donahue and Harrington 2002, 152; France 2002, 216–17; Scott 1990, 383–86.

29. Scott 1990, 386.

30. John Dominic Crossan, *The Historical Jesus: The Life of a Mediterranean Jewish Peasant* (San Francisco: HarperSanFrancisco, 1991), 278–79. Crossan points out that the mustard seed remains a subversive metaphor whether one prefers to think of cultivated mustard plants or wild mustard that grows as a weed in cultivated fields. In either scenario, mustard "tends to take over where it is not wanted" (278).

31. Crossan 1988, 77.

32. Some may insist that what I here call an "empty metaphor" should instead be labeled a "symbol." As Funk notes, "symbolism is metaphor with the primary term suppressed"; i.e., symbolic language refers to the vehicle and assumes that the audience will supply the tenor (1966, 136–37). Scott builds on this premise to specify that a metaphor uses the "structural network" of the vehicle—the range of ideas and mythemes that the vehicle potentially evokes—to describe a stated tenor, while a symbol "cannot be coded with specificity" because "its content is nebula," meaning that the audience is left to construct the precise referent and its value (Scott 1990, 56–61). I acknowledge the relevance of this distinction, and hence would not object if one preferred to substitute the term "symbol" for "empty metaphor." In my view, the difference in terminology would not substantially impact my argument, and I will therefore fall back on Funk's disclaimer: "Illuminating as it would be to follow up what has been written on simile, metaphor, and symbol . . . it is more germane [here] . . . to focus on the difference between metaphorical and discursive language" (1966, 137).

33. Of course, some of Jesus' contemporaries may have had a preformed set of ideas about "the Kingdom of God." This set of ideas would, however, represent the psychological context of the term "Kingdom," not a referent for the term—thoughts about the thing that Jesus was talking about, not the thing itself. And in cases where this psychological context was very different from the set of ideas evoked by a parable's analogy, it would become even more difficult for the audience to identify possible referents. In other words, as the discrepancy between the psychological context of the parable and one's preformed ideas about the Kingdom increased, it would become even harder to be sure that one really understood what entity Jesus was talking about when he said, "Kingdom of God."

34. I obviously assume here, as all the sources indicate, that Jesus did not offer a specific "answer" to this parable for the crowd. Matthew and Luke imply that

he never answered it at all, or at least do not suggest that he did. Mark suggests that Jesus elaborated its true meaning for the disciples in private (4:34), although notably he does not share this private interpretation with the reader.

35. By saying that the word "Kingdom" is ambiguous, I do not thereby suggest that Jesus himself had no idea what he was talking about or that he had nothing particular in mind. The term would be "ambiguous" from the perspective of the audience, particularly members of Jesus' audience who had not yet learned to think in the way that he did—i.e., people who were not members of his community of knowledge.

36. I would argue that this is the case whether or not we care to accept all, some, or none of the answers and interpretations that the sources occasionally provide. For example, even if Mark's lengthy allegorical explanation of the Sower at 4:13–20 "is generally recognized to be not from Jesus himself, but from the early church" (Donahue and Harrington 2002, 146), Mark is certainly correct to suggest that the parable itself was perplexing even to Jesus' disciples. As Oesterley noted quite some time ago, this story is so incredibly ambiguous that it "must have sounded pointless to those who heard it without any explanation" (W. O. E. Oesterley, *The Gospel Parables in Light of Their Jewish Background* [London: SPCK, 1936], 32). Similarly, even if Luke has created an artificial application of the Good Samaritan by contextualizing the parable as Jesus' definition of the word "neighbor" (10:25–37)—and I personally do not see why we must conclude that he has—he is still certainly correct to suggest that this parable inherently attempts to redefine key terms.

Chapter 6: It's Good to Be the Riddler, unless You're Playing with Jesus

1. J. R. R. Tolkien, *The Hobbit; or, There and Back Again* (Boston: Houghton Mifflin, 1966), 89–90.

2. Claudia Camp and Carol Fontaine have attempted to show that Samson's riddle could be answered through normal channels of logic: the Philistines just need to reflect on the linguistic ambiguities of the question and apply "a complex of culturally known associations" between love/marriage, lions, and honey. Samson's riddle is thus a well-crafted text, "answerable, if exceedingly difficult" ("The Words of the Wise and Their Riddles," in *Text and Tradition: The Hebrew Bible and Folklore*, ed. Susan Niditch, Society of Biblical Literature Semeia Studies [Atlanta: Scholars Press, 1990], 138–48). Though this reading is very clever, in my view it ultimately reflects a greater concern for the criterion of solvability than for the actual dynamics of Judges 14. The author of Judges makes no apology for the fact that Samson's puzzle is inherently unfair, and in fact seems to see this whole episode as just another excuse for God to punish the Philistines (14:4, 19).

3. Obviously, I would disagree with those who suggest that Jesus is somehow surprised at the disciples' incomprehension because he expects them to figure out the parables on their own. Waetjen, for example, interprets Jesus' statement that the Kingdom "has been given" to the disciples to mean that "they should have no difficulty grasping his similitudes"; the fact that they can't grasp them suggests that "it may be necessary for them to scrutinize their discipleship" (Herman C. Waetjen, *A Reordering of Power: A Socio-Political Reading of Mark's Gospel* [Minneapolis: Fortress, 1989], 104–5). It may well be that they need to scrutinize their discipleship, but in my view the Kingdom is not given to them in the form of the parables, but rather in the form of the answers

(without which the parables remain hopelessly ambiguous). Mark seems to think that those answers must come from Jesus himself.

4. John R. Donahue and Daniel J. Harrington, *The Gospel of Mark*, Sacra Pagina (Collegeville, MN: Liturgical Press, 2002), 344; also Robert T. France, who notes that the term is used "normally of animals for food" (*The Gospel of Mark: A Commentary on the Greek Text*, New International Greek Testament Commentary [Grand Rapids: Eerdmans, 2002)], 467).

5. This is, at least, Luke's interpretation of the situation (Luke 20:20). France concurs that the question about the poll tax was "an essentially political one, aimed to elicit Jesus' stance with regard to 'Zealot' ideology" (2002, 465).

6. N. T. Wright, *Jesus and the Victory of God* (Minneapolis: Fortress, 1996), 503.

7. See discussion in France 2002, 465; also, and in more detail, F. F. Bruce, "Render to Caesar," in *Jesus and the Politics of His Day*, ed. Ernst Bammel and C. F. D. Moule (Cambridge: Cambridge University Press, 1984), 252–54. If the "Herodians" were clients of Antipas, they would also presumably be exempt.

8. Note that in Luke the Sanhedrin will soon attempt to secure Jesus' death by telling Pilate that Jesus urges people not to pay taxes (Luke 23:2).

9. Many scholars see Jesus' request for a denarius as one aspect of his strategy to undermine the Pharisees. N. T. Wright, for example, argues that Jesus thereby forces the Pharisees to implicate themselves: the coin was inherently blasphemous because it bore an image of the emperor and an inscription that exalted him as a deity; "Jesus' questioners were thus themselves already heavily compromised by possessing such an object" (1996, 503; see also France 2002, 465–66; James R. Edwards, *The Gospel according to Mark*, Pillar New Testament Commentary [Grand Rapids: Eerdmans, 2002], 363). To this I would say two things: first, Wright's reading would support my analysis by further emphasizing Jesus' intellectual superiority over his opponents, who foolishly play into his scheme by providing the requested coin; second, despite its advantages to my argument, Wright's reading seems to me to be a stretch. It isn't clear from the text who brought the coin—it could have been one of the disciples, or just someone standing in the crowd that day (Mark 12:16); Mark doesn't seem to implicate anyone for possessing such a coin; and finally, as Robert Gundry notes, "people use a coin for its value in exchange whether or not they acknowledge the sovereignty of the ruler whose image and superscription is stamped on the coin" (*Mark: A Commentary on His Apology for the Cross* [Grand Rapids: Eerdmans, 1993], 694).

10. Wright 1996, 503–6.

11. The Egerton Gospel includes the tax riddle (although not attributing it to the Pharisees, despite the fact that the interlocutors' flattery echoes the words of Nicodemus at John 3:2) and insists that Jesus saw through the trap, but does not include any form of his answer. Instead, Jesus becomes angry and quotes Isaiah 29:13 (à la Mark 7:6–7; "this people honors me with their lips, but their hearts are far from me") in disgust.

12. France 2002, 470.

13. See Gundry 1993, 702; Donahue and Harrington 2002, 352.

14. Morna Hooker rejects this reading because the verb "I am" does not appear in Mark 12:26 or the Hebrew text of Exodus 3:6. Jesus' argument, in her view, "depends on the belief that God would not have described himself as the God of dead heroes"; Hooker therefore lays emphasis on the maxim, "He is not God of the dead, but rather of the living" (*The Gospel according to Saint Mark*, Black's

New Testament Commentary [Peabody, MA: Hendrickson, 1991], 285). I may be missing something, but it seems to me more likely that the verb εἰμί (present tense, "I am") is simply implied in this context. In any case, I don't think that this issue would substantially impact my argument.

15. C. S. Mann, *Mark: A New Translation with Introduction and Commentary*, Anchor Bible (Garden City, NY: Doubleday, 1986), 476.

16. Hooker 1991, 285.

17. Quote Mann 1986, 476.

Chapter 7: "Your Answer or Your Life"

1. See discussion in W. J. Pepicello, "Linguistic Strategies in Riddling," *Western Folklore* 39 (1980): 1; W. J. Pepicello and Thomas A. Green, "Wit in Riddling: A Linguistic Perspective," *Genre* 11 (1978): 5; "The Folk Riddle: A Redefinition of Terms," *Western Folklore* 38 (1979): 14–15; *The Language of Riddles: New Perspectives* (Columbus: Ohio State University Press, 1984), 22. I should note that Pepicello and Green treat "wit" as a dimension of the riddle text itself, consistent with their view that the "riddle," as a unit of language, includes the question, the answer, and the necessary links of logic between these two structural elements.

2. Some folklorists might argue that the verbal traps that appear in the sources for Jesus are not true "neck riddles" because they do not play on personal information known only to the riddler. I concede this point, but would also note that, despite their form, many of these traps *function* as neck riddles in their current narrative contexts: Jesus, or one of his opponents, must ask or answer a difficult ambiguous question in order to avoid shame and loss of status. On the basis of this observation, I would argue that the evidence from the Gospels may, in fact, call for a broader understanding of the formal features of the genre "neck riddle." For further discussion of neck riddles, see Roger D. Abrahams, *Between the Living and the Dead: Riddles Which Tell Stories*, Folklore Fellows Communications (Helsinki: Suomalainen Tiedeakatemia, 1980), 9; Roger D. Abrahams and Alan Dundes, "Riddles," in *Folklore and Folklife: An Introduction*, ed. Richard Dorson (Chicago: University of Chicago Press, 1972), 133; James L. Crenshaw, *Samson: A Secret Betrayed, A Vow Ignored* (Atlanta: John Knox, 1978), 113–14; Pepicello and Green 1979, 17–19; Charles T. Scott, *Persian and Arabic Riddles: A Language-Centered Approach to Genre Definition* (Bloomington: Indiana University Press, 1965), 69–71; Archer Taylor, "The Varieties of Riddles," in *Philologica: The Malone Anniversary Studies*, ed. Thomas A. Kirby and Henry Bosley Woolf (Baltimore: Johns Hopkins Press, 1949), 6.

3. Abrahams and Dundes 1972, 140.

4. See summaries and discussion in Raymond Brown, *The Gospel according to John: A New Translation with Introduction and Commentary*, Anchor Bible (New York: Doubleday, 1966), 1.333–34; D. A. Carson, *The Gospel according to John* (Grand Rapids: Eerdmans, 1991), 335–36. Both of these scholars conclude that the content of Jesus' writing must not have been of particular significance, as evidenced by the fact that John does not reveal it.

5. Reflecting this consensus, *The Complete Gospels* prints the pericope separate from the rest of the Gospel of John, in a chapter entitled "Orphan Sayings and Stories," ed. Robert J. Miller (Sonoma, CA: Polebridge, 1994), 453.

6. In my view, it is easier to see this woman as a prostitute than to explain how she was "caught in the act" while her lover escaped (see Brown 1966, 1.333;

Carson 1991, 334). Of course, the accusers call her an "adulteress" rather than a "prostitute," but this is likely the case because the Law clearly prescribes the death penalty for adultery while it is somewhat vague on prostitution (compare Lev. 20:10, Num. 5:11–31, and Deut. 22:22–24 with Lev. 19:29 and Deut. 23:17–18). Prostitution could easily be construed as a form of "adultery" if the woman were married and/or caught soliciting a married man, and such a scenario would be more than adequate for the purpose of trapping Jesus in a legal dispute.

7. Carson 1991, 335. In my view, Carson's generous description here is more applicable to the Synoptic Jesus than the Johannine Jesus—perhaps yet another reason to view this passage as an interpolation?—yet his comments are consistent with the dynamics of the riddling session in this immediate context. Carson also points out that such a ruling might portray Jesus as "infringing the exclusive rights of the Roman prefect, who alone at this period had the authority to impose capital sentences."

8. See discussion in Taylor 1949, 8; "The Riddle," *California Folklore Quarterly* [*Western Folklore*] 2 (1943): 145–46. I should note that Taylor does not consider alternatives to be "true riddles" because many of them do not meet the criterion of solvability. He comes to this conclusion apparently on the basis of the fact that, in many cases, neither of the alternatives supplied by the question is desirable, and in his view all "true riddles" must provide clues to a satisfactory answer.

9. I say this in full awareness of Paula Fredriksen's argument that the sheer size of the temple complex would make it unlikely that any significant number of people witnessed Jesus' actions. Specifically, in her view only "those in his retinue and those standing immediately around him" would have seen these things (*Jesus of Nazareth, King of the Jews: A Jewish Life and the Emergence of Christianity* [New York: Alfred A. Knopf, 2000], 231–32). While I find many aspects of Fredriksen's argument compelling, it appears to me that she here assumes (a) that few or none of "those in his retinue" told others what Jesus had done; (b) that few or none of "those standing immediately around him" told others what Jesus had done; (c) that the vendors and moneychangers did not report what Jesus had done to the authorities, either Roman or Jewish or both; (d) that Jesus himself said nothing about the incident later on so as to draw attention to what he had done. She assumes, in other words, that word of this incident would not spread like wildfire through the grapevine, and that Jesus himself would not publicly discuss what he had done and draw people's attention to his actions. While I don't have time to discuss the issue here, I personally do not find Fredriksen's approach to be satisfactory on this particular point and can easily envision that the temple authorities would learn what Jesus had done and, subsequently, seek to challenge his credentials so as to discredit his comments. Essentially, then, I have no difficulty accepting the basic logic of Mark's proposed sequence of events.

10. Robert T. France, *The Gospel of Mark: A Commentary on the Greek Text*, New International Greek Testament Commentary (Grand Rapids: Eerdmans, 2002), 452.

11. It is perhaps relevant to note that Mark does not debate this point, and in fact seems to grant it. Whether or not Jesus possessed official rabbinic credentials, and what such credentials would have looked like in the Late Second Temple period, are beyond the scope of this study. In my view, my reading of Mark 11:27–33 would stand whether Jesus was an "ordained" rabbi or not: the chief

priests have not authorized him to teach, and he proceeds to demonstrate his credentials through a display of wit.

12. First quote Robert H. Gundry, *Mark: A Commentary on His Apology for the Cross* (Grand Rapids: Eerdmans, 1993), 657; second quote France 2002, 452.

13. France 2002, 454; see also William Lane, *The Gospel according to Mark: The English Text with Introduction, Exposition and Notes*, New International Commentary on the New Testament (Grand Rapids: Eerdmans, 1974), 413. Gundry argues this point quite emphatically and specifically refutes other possible references (1993, 666).

14. Philip Carrington, *According to Mark: A Running Commentary on the Oldest Gospel* (Cambridge: Cambridge University Press, 1960), 245. Carrington's reference to the "splitting" of the narrative seems to refer to Mark's assimilation of an older story. At the same time, Carrington stresses that 11:27 did not necessarily occur the day after the temple incident even in that primitive tradition; Mark is thus not inconsistent with Luke's suggestion that this exchange may have taken place during "a considerably later appearance" of Jesus in the temple (1960, 245).

15. Gundry believes that Jesus continued to prevent traffic through the temple courts after the initial incident, and so would presumably prefer the paraphrase, "By what authority *are you doing what you are doing* in the temple?" (1993, 657).

16. N. T. Wright, *Jesus and the Victory of God* (Minneapolis: Fortress, 1996), 495–97. Similarly, Carrington refers to Jesus' counterquestion as "an affirmation of solidarity between John's mission and his; it was one movement, and it was of divine authority; or what was of divine authority in John's mission passed into his" (1960, 246). Of course, if Jesus really is making a messianic claim here, one might wonder why he does not say as much directly, or at least why Mark does not alert the reader to the true significance of Jesus' question about the Baptist. Indeed, France seems quite surprised that Jesus did not seize this moment as a prime opportunity to reveal his true identity to the world, and explains Mark's reticence to pursue this point in some detail. First, in terms of plot, Mark is not quite ready to give away the messianic secret, which he wishes to reserve for the climactic confession before the Sanhedrin at 14:62. Second, and at a more practical level, France agrees with Wright that "there is little doubt that an open declaration of Jesus' messianic claim at this point would have offered . . . ammunition which his opponents will need to denounce him to the Roman authorities" (France 2002, 452–53; similarly Wright 1996, 495–97).

17. Larry Hurtado, *Mark*, New International Bible Commentary (Peabody, MA: Hendrickson, 1989), 189.

18. Ben Witherington III, *The Gospel of Mark: A Socio-Rhetorical Commentary* (Grand Rapids: Eerdmans, 2001), 321.

19. First and third quotes Douglas R. A. Hare, *Mark*, Westminster Bible Companion (Louisville, KY: Westminster John Knox, 1996), 148; second and fourth quotes France 2002, 453.

20. See the summary discussion in Robert W. Funk, Roy W. Hoover, and the Jesus Seminar, *The Five Gospels: The Search for the Authentic Words of Jesus* (New York: Polebridge, 1993), 100; Robert W. Funk and the Jesus Seminar, *The Acts of Jesus: The Search for the Authentic Deeds of Jesus* (Sonoma, CA: Polebridge, 1998), 124.

21. Hare 1996, 148.
22. See Gundry 1993, 666.
23. See discussion in David Rhoads and Donald Michie, *Mark as Story: An Introduction to the Narrrative of a Gospel* (Philadelphia: Fortress, 1982), 117–22, quote 117; Elizabeth Struthers Malbon, *In the Company of Jesus: Characters in Mark's Gospel* (Louisville, KY: Westminster John Knox, 2000), 149–52, 164–65. Of course, one might argue that the chief priests and elders only really begin to factor as significant opponents to Jesus in this episode, making it unlikely that they were even aware of Jesus' earlier activity, much less specifically opposed to it. Yet I am persuaded by Malbon that Mark's portrait of the Jewish leaders is essentially unified, with the shift of emphasis from opposition by Pharisees to opposition by chief priests reflecting the natural movement of the narrative from Galilee to Jerusalem (2000, 152–56, 164–65). Note in this connection Fredriksen's observation that "the sorts of encounters that Mark [11–12] relates between Jesus and the chief priests, the scribes, the Sadducees and Pharisees, may have happened whenever Jesus was there" in Jerusalem; nothing about the content of these encounters explicitly ties them to the last week of Jesus' life (2000, 240).
24. John R. Donahue and Daniel J. Harrington, *The Gospel of Mark*, Sacra Pagina (Collegeville, MN: Liturgical Press, 2002), 334; see also Hare 1996, 148.
25. Gundry 1993, 667, 669.
26. Craig Blomberg's comments on Matt. 17:24 could suggest that the tax collectors' original query to Peter was also a "catch riddle" of sorts. Their question is phrased "as if they expect an affirmative answer"—i.e., they seem to assume that Jesus does pay the tax—but this does not necessarily mean that the inquiry is friendly. "[F]ormally ordained rabbis" were exempt from the tax; the collectors might, then, be trying to corner Peter into an admission that his master does not possess official credentials (*Matthew*, New American Commentary [Nashville: Broadman, 1992], 269–70). Translated into the terms of my discussion, the tax collectors' question can be interpreted as an alternative riddle that seeks to discredit Peter by challenging Jesus' authority: "If your teacher doesn't pay the tax, does he claim to be a rabbi? So where are his credentials?"; "If your teacher does pay the tax, is that an admission that he really doesn't have proper credentials?" Either choice would be embarrassing to both Jesus and Peter. Such a reading would, of course, forward my overall argument, but I nevertheless tend to think that the tax collectors' inquiry is not, at least in Matthew's view, hostile. I can easily imagine that questions of that kind were often directed to Jesus' disciples—both the disciples of the historical Jesus and later Matthean Christians—and that the tone of such encounters was sometimes hostile. But whether or not this was the case, Matthew seems, to me at least, to be disinterested in the motives of the tax collectors on this particular occasion. Their question simply provides a basic narrative framework for Jesus' demonstration of wit by raising the issue of the tax, thus creating a context for the exchange between Jesus and Peter.
27. Blomberg 1992, 270.
28. Leon Morris, *The Gospel according to Matthew* (Grand Rapids: Eerdmans, 1992), 454. Morris reads the statement christologically to mean that Jesus, as God's Son, was not obligated to pay a tax in support of his own Father's house; see also Daniel J. Harrington, *The Gospel of Matthew*, Sacra Pagina (Collegeville, MN: Michael Glazier, 1991), 261.
29. First quote Rudolf Schnackenburg, *The Gospel of Matthew*, trans. Robert R.

Barr (Grand Rapids: Eerdmans, 2002), 169–70; second quote Robert H. Gundry, *Matthew: A Commentary on His Handbook for a Mixed Church under Persecution*, 2nd ed. (Grand Rapids: Eerdmans, 1994), 356–57. See also Donald Senior, *Matthew*, Abingdon New Testament Commentaries (Nashville: Abingdon, 1998), 203–4, and Augustine Stock, who views this episode as evidence that the Matthean Christians "were living in close proximity to a vigorous Jewish community" (*The Method and Message of Matthew* [Collegeville, MN: Michael Glazier, 1994], 282).

30. See discussion in Funk 1993, 212–13.
31. The symbolic and political implications of the imperial tax for post–70 CE Christians are explored in detail by Warren Carter, who notes that the tax "had punitive and propaganda value" as a reminder of "Roman political, military, economic, and religious sovereignty and superiority sanctioned by Jupiter" (*Matthew and the Margins: A Sociopolitical and Religious Reading*, The Bible and Liberation Series [Maryknoll, NY: Orbis, 2000], 356–60, quote 357). In such a context, Jesus' riddle would interpret payment of the tax as an acknowledgment of the validity of these imperial claims.
32. Horbury argues that the "sons" must be "Israel in general" because "the unadorned description of other Jews [Jews other than Jesus and his disciples] as foreigners . . . does not occur elsewhere in Jesus' teaching" (William Horbury, "The Temple Tax," in *Jesus and the Politics of His Day*, ed. Ernst Bammel and C. F. D. Moule (Cambridge: Cambridge University Press, 1984), 283. This may be true, but I would point out that Jesus himself is not designating anyone as a "foreigner." He says, rather, that the temple and/or Roman authorities are treating a certain group of people as foreigners by levying taxes, and he seems to oppose this move.

Chapter 8: The Messianic Ambiguity

1. The *Gospel of Thomas* never calls Jesus "rabbi" and only once refers to him as "teacher" (13:4), yet I am hesitant to conclude that this evidence casts doubt on the historical value of either or both of these terms. First, the vast majority of the sayings in *Thomas* have minimal narrative frameworks, leaving the characters in *Thomas* with few opportunities to use "rabbi," "teacher," or any other title for Jesus. Second, the circumstances of the one occurrence of "teacher" in *Thomas* would tend to suggest that the author accepts the historical validity of the title: the disciple Thomas himself is the one who refers to Jesus as "teacher," and here uses the word "teacher" as a normal form of address, over against the titles "just angel" and "wise philosopher" in the immediately preceding verses (14:2–3); Jesus rebukes Thomas for calling him "teacher," but immediately proceeds to teach him three secret sayings (14:6). If anything, the evidence suggests that the author of the *Gospel of Thomas* knew that Jesus' disciples sometimes called him "teacher" but did not go out of his way to use that designation, or any other designation, for Jesus.
2. Jesus is called "rabbi" or "teacher" by disciples at Mark 4:38; 9:5, 38; 10:35; 11:21; 13:1; 14:45; Matt. 26:25, 49; John 4:31; 9:2; 11:8, 28; 20:16; *Thomas* 13:4; by opponents or those who don't know him well at Mark 5:35; 9:17; 10:17–20, 51; 12:14, 19, 32; Matt. 8:19; 9:11; 12:38; 17:24; Luke 7:40; 10:25; 11:45; 12:13; 19:39; John 1:38, 49; 3:2; 6:25; 8:4.
3. Against this backdrop, I would interpret Matthew 23:8–9 to mean that Jesus preferred not to be called "rabbi," because he felt that the term had been abused by the Jewish authorities. I would then interpret *Thomas* 13:5 against

John 7:37–39 (i.e., "bubbling spring that I have tended" = "river of living water from my belly") to mean that Thomas has no need for a teacher because God has become his teacher.

4. John Dominic Crossan, *The Historical Jesus: The Life of a Mediterranean Jewish Peasant* (San Francisco: HarperSanFrancisco, 1991), 304–10.

5. It is relevant to note that a christological reading of Luke 13:32 does not resolve the inherent ambiguities of this riddle. Even if we suspect that "third day" somehow alludes to the resurrection, we still must ask, (a) What does that have to do with Jesus' healings and exorcisms? and (b) Why does the Lukan Jesus say that his work will be "finished" at the resurrection, whereas the Johannine Jesus says that he is "finished" as he dies on the cross (John 19:30)?

Chapter 9: An Unbrokered Kingdom of Nobodies

1. At first glance, it may appear that Crossan's database is quite different from the one utilized in this study. Appendix 5.B of *The Historical Jesus: The Life of a Mediterranean Jewish Peasant* (San Francisco: HarperSanFrancisco, 1991) lists the twelve complexes of sayings that inform Crossan's discussion of the Kingdom (where available, I give the respective references in the canonical Gospels, noting that Crossan often prefers the version in *Thomas*): Mark 10:13–16; Mark 4:30–32; Luke 6:20; Luke 17:23//*Thomas* 3:1; *Thomas* 22:3–4; Luke 11:2–4; Luke 7:28; Matt. 13:24–30; Matt. 13:45–46; Luke 13:20–21; Matt. 13:44; Mark 10:23–27. Notably, only four of these twelve complexes—Mark 10:13–16, Mark 4:30–32, Luke 6:20, Mark 10:23–27—are represented on my database of sage riddles in chapter 4. This apparent discrepancy, however, mainly reflects the differences in our respective criteria for building a database. My database is based on the function of sayings (i.e., it includes only sayings that function as riddles), while Crossan's database is based on the content of the sayings and multiple attestation (i.e., it includes only complexes that specifically mention "the Kingdom" and appear in more than one independent source). I would also note that four other complexes on Crossan's list are parables—Matt. 13:24–30, Matt. 13:45–46, Luke 13:20–21, Matt. 13:44—and I have argued in chapter 5 that parables are closely akin to riddles and that it is reasonable to think of all parables as riddles in the sense that they inherently generate ambiguity. Finally, the condensed version of Crossan's study, *Jesus: A Revolutionary Biography* (San Francisco: HarperSanFrancisco, 1994), includes three chapters (3, 4, and 5) that directly address Jesus' understanding of the Kingdom. In those chapters, Crossan discusses nine complexes of sayings as evidence for Jesus' view of the Kingdom: Luke 14:26; Mark 3:31–35; Luke 11:27–28; Luke 12:51–53; Luke 6:20; Mark 10:13–16; Mark 4:30–32; Luke 14:15–24; Luke 10:2–11. Six of these nine appear in my database of sage riddles, and two others—Luke 11:27–28 and Luke 14:15–24—could easily be added to my table if we were to relax my literary criteria only slightly. I might also mention that the rhetorical impact of two events that are key to Crossan's argument—Mark 1:40–44 and Mark 1:16–38—would generate the type of ambiguity that riddles exploit. Hence, I think it fair to assert that Crossan's list of Kingdom sayings is similar to the one used in this study, even though our respective databases are built on very different sets of criteria.

2. First quote Crossan 1994, 55; second quote Crossan 1991, 266.

3. Crossan 1994, 55.

4. Ibid., 101.

5. Crossan 1991, 291; see also Crossan 1994, 55.
6. Crossan 1991, 292, 287; see also Crossan 1994, 55–56.
7. Crossan 1994, 56; see also Crossan 1991, 292.
8. Crossan 1991, 292; see also Crossan 1994, 56.
9. Crossan 1994, 56. Note that the verbs in the quote are past tense in Crossan's original ("wrote and proclaimed").
10. Ibid., 56–58, quote 58.
11. Ibid., 58. In Crossan's view, Jesus' sapiential/peasant outlook on the Kingdom is epitomized by the Lord's Prayer (Matt. 6:9–15//Luke 11:2–4). While the available versions of the prayer do not go back to Jesus, they "must be a very early summary of themes and emphases from Jesus' own lifetime" (Crossan 1991, 294).
12. Crossan 1994, 58.
13. Crossan 1991, 300. Jesus' attack on the ancient family structure also emerges in texts like *Thomas* 99//Mark 3:31–35 and the "Blessed is the womb" saying at *Thomas* 79//Luke 11:27–28. In these instances, "Jesus declares his followers to be a replacement family" (Crossan 1991, 299). Similarly, Crossan observes that the complex of sayings around Jesus' teaching on divorce is "strikingly anomalous" because Jesus' emphasis on the rights of both sexes explicitly flies in the face of "the androcentric tradition of Jewish Palestine" (1991, 301–2). Ultimately, the most significant cluster of antifamily statements relates to Jesus' analogy between the Kingdom and children (see Mark 10:13–16; *Thomas* 22:1–2; et al.). In Jesus' culture, "to be a child was to be a nobody, with the possibility of becoming a somebody absolutely dependent on parental discretion and parental standing in the community." The point of the analogy is thus that "a kingdom of children is a kingdom of nobodies" (Crossan 1991, 269; see also 1994, 62–64).
14. Crossan 1994, 60. It should be noted that Crossan translates οἱ πτωχοί at Luke 6:20 as "the destitute" rather than "the poor," so that Jesus' blessing does not fall on the typical poor peasant but rather on the homeless beggar who is completely marginalized. The saying is a comment on the systemic injustice of imperialism: "blessed" here means "innocent," in the sense that the destitute do not profit from, and are therefore not accountable for, "the system's own evil operations" (1991, 270–73; 1994, 60–62).
15. Crossan 1991, 349.
16. Crossan wishes to "emphasize as strongly as possible that Jesus was not just a teacher or a preacher in purely intellectual terms, not just part of the history of ideas. He not only discussed the Kingdom of God; he enacted it, and said others could do so as well" (1994, 93).
17. Crossan 1994, 77; emphasis original. Following Mary Douglas, Crossan asserts that "the physical body is a microcosm of the social body so that there is a dialectic between the personal and the social, the individual and the corporate, with regard to taboos and boundaries, with regard to the acceptable, the permissible, and the tolerable" (1991, 313).
18. First quote Crossan 1991, 262; second quote Crossan 1994, 68–69.
19. Crossan 1994, 68–69; see also Crossan 1991, 262. In Crossan's view, the Banquet may be used as an interpretive key "to ground all of those aphorisms, dialogues, and parables about the Kingdom of God" (1994, 66).
20. Crossan 1991, 320–21; Crossan 1994, 91.
21. Crossan 1991, 336–37; Crossan 1994, 80–81. Crossan notes that it might be relevant to make a threefold distinction in discussions of bodily infirmity:

"disease" = bodily irregularities; "sickness" = the assignment of social values to disease (the sociological dimension); "illness" = the impact of disease and sickness on individual consciousness (the psychological dimension; Crossan 1991, 337). For sake of convenience, he finds it sufficient to combine "sickness" and "illness" into one larger psychosocial package.

22. Crossan 1994, 82–83. Obviously, the business of touching a leper raises questions about Jesus' interaction with ancient Jewish purity codes, but Crossan explains this dynamic of the episode in psychosocial terms as well. People in colonial cultures, such as the Jews of Roman Palestine, tend to emphasize bodily purity regulations as an expression of the need to maintain sharp ideological boundaries between themselves and the oppressor. The leper, whose body is inflicted with unusual orifices that allow impure elements to enter, is dangerous as a source of "symbolic contamination" because his condition threatens "in microcosm the very identity, integrity, and security of society at large" (Crossan 1994, 78–79).

    Crossan's reading of Jesus' exorcisms also highlights the psychosocial dimension of disease, treating demon possession as a form of colonial illness. The frequency of possession in the sources may be explained by "the almost schizoid position of a colonial people": the oppressed must submit to rule in order to survive, yet in so doing they "conspire in their own destruction"; if they rebel, they admit that the hated imperial power is greater than themselves and, therefore, to some extent desirable (Crossan 1991, 317–18). "An occupied country has, as it were, a multiple-personality disorder," at once both envying and despising the oppressor (Crossan 1994, 89). This confusion of identity could manifest itself in the bodies of oppressed individuals as demon possession. As a result, when Jesus "healed" people of demonic oppression, he was also making a pointed statement about the injustice of colonialism; indeed, "colonial exorcisms" are themselves acts of "individuated symbolic revolution" (Crossan 1991, 318). Crossan illustrates this point through a political analysis of the story of the Gerasene demoniac at Mark 5:1–17, noting especially that (a) the name "Legion" could refer to Roman military power, (b) the "swine" into which the demons are cast are utterly unclean, and (c) every Jewish revolutionary must have fantasized about seeing the legions of Rome pushed into the Sea of Galilee. Detecting these overtones, the Gerasenes ask Jesus to leave the region because they are afraid to endorse the political implications of his actions (Crossan 1991, 314–15; Crossan 1994, 90–91).

23. Crossan 1994, 99; see also Crossan 1991, 348–49.

24. Crossan assumes, in my view correctly, that the mission statements are reflective of Jesus' own agenda, in the sense that his instructions to the disciples reflect what he himself was already doing. "I presume, in other words, that dress and itinerancy, miracle and table, healing and commensality, characterized Jesus just as much as his missionaries and that they characterized them not just once but all the time" (Crossan 1991, 349). The latter portion of this quotation reveals a second key assumption: "The missionaries were not some specific and closed group sent out on one particular mission at one particular time. They were predominantly *healed healers*, part of whose continuing healing was precisely their empowerment to heal others" (Crossan 1994, 109–11; see also Crossan 1991, 334).

25. Crossan 1991, 339–44, quote 344; see also Crossan 1994, 112–13. In a similar vein, Crossan emphasizes both the similarities and differences between Jesus' dress code and that of the Cynic philosophers. The disciples' mandatory uni-

form would resemble the Cynic costume, and both Jesus and the Cynics postured this unique attire as a rhetorical gesture, a denial of current social and
political norms and obligations. But Jesus' command that the disciples must
not carry a bag or bread strategically contradicts the Cynic custom: Cynics carried a purse and food as symbols of self-sufficiency; the disciples, by contrast,
must specifically lodge in houses and share food, symbolizing their union with
those to whom they carried the message. "They [the disciples] could not and
should not dress to declare itinerant self-sufficiency but rather communal
dependency" (Crossan 1994, 115–19, quote 119; see also Crossan 1991, 338–39).
26. Crossan 1991, 345.
27. Ibid., 304.
28. Crossan 1994, 71.
29. Crossan 1991, 298, emphasis added.
30. Crossan 1994, 96–97.
31. I stress the word "illustrative" here. Crossan is uncertain of the historicity of
this sequence, both because it appears to be a typical scenario and because it
does not enjoy multiple attestation (see 1991, 346–47; 1994, 101).
32. Crossan 1991, 346.
33. Crossan 1994, 101; see also 1991, 346–47. In the same way, Crossan explains
Mark 6:4 (and John 7:3–5?) to mean that Jesus' family accepted his power and
basic message but did not agree with his itinerant mode of delivery. They
expected, instead, that Jesus would settle down in one place and become a
patron, with his mother and brothers as brokers and those whom he healed as
clients (Crossan 1994, 99–100).

Chapter 10: The Empire of Wit; or Maybe Peter Really Did Have the "Keys to the Kingdom"

1. John Dominic Crossan, *The Historical Jesus: The Life of a Mediterranean Jewish Peasant* (San Francisco: HarperSanFrancisco, 1991), 304.
2. John Dominic Crossan, *Jesus: A Revolutionary Biography* (San Francisco: HarperSanFrancisco, 1994), 113.
3. See Paula Fredriksen, who emphasizes the judgment theme in the teachings of both John and Jesus and sees both calling for some sort of moral reform (*Jesus of Nazareth, King of the Jews: A Jewish Life and the Emergence of Christianity* [New York: Alfred Knopf, 2000], 191–97).
4. Elli Köngäs Maranda, "Riddles and Riddling: An Introduction," *Journal of American Folklore* 89 (1976): 131.
5. Robert T. France, *The Gospel of Mark: A Commentary on the Greek Text*, New International Greek Testament Commentary (Grand Rapids: Eerdmans, 2002), 405.
6. In the same Lukan context, one would also have to think that only people with deep emotional problems would be "happy" when suffering persecution, ostra-cization, and insults (6:22). We may need to go beyond Crossan in referring to a "Kingdom of nobodies and undesirables [and masochists]" (see 1991, 298).
7. In France's view, the "slave of all" saying epitomizes "the alternative value scale of the kingdom of God," here in specific contrast to the leadership style of the Gentile rulers mentioned in v. 42 (2002, 419). I would add only that Jesus achieves this radical reversal not just by challenging the political status quo, but by saying something that seems inherently paradoxical. Taken literally, the saying assumes that there will be servants in the Kingdom, but in any conceiv-able social setting a "slave" cannot be "first"—how would we know who should

serve and who should be served? And as Donahue and Harrington note, the ambiguity of this saying is further enhanced by the phrase "slave *of all*" (πάντων διάκονος), which is "deliberately paradoxical" in the sense that "a slave usually belongs to one owner and does the bidding of that one owner," not the bidding of "all" people (*The Gospel of Mark*, Sacra Pagina [Collegeville, MN: Liturgical Press, 2002], 313).

8. John Dominic Crossan, "Parable and Example in Jesus' Teaching," *New Testament Studies* 18 (1971–72): 295.

9. Crossan 1991, 280–82. The parable of the Leaven plays on the fact that yeast was a symbol of the profane and the immoral in Jesus' culture; the impurity is magnified here because a "woman" hides the yeast in the dough.

10. Ibid., 263.

11. Fredriksen 2000, 197–207, quote 203; note that her discussion includes a reading of Mark 1:40–44 that counters Crossan's interpretation.

12. In this connection, I find it interesting that the Gospel of John, which makes the most explicit claim of all the sources to a direct connection with the historical Jesus (19:35; 21:24), develops a pneumatology in which the Spirit functions as an intellectual broker by "guiding" the disciples into a deeper understanding of Jesus' teaching (14:26; 16:13). If Jesus spoke about the Holy Spirit, and especially if he thought of wit as a divine endowment, the Fourth Gospel's presentation may accurately reflect his beliefs on that issue.

13. Crossan 1994, 71.

Works Cited

Abrahams, Roger D. *Between the Living and the Dead: Riddles Which Tell Stories.* Folklore Fellows Communications. Helsinki: Suomalainen Tiedeakatemia, Scientiarum Fenniga, 1980.

———. "The Complex Relations of Simple Forms." Pages 193–214 in *Folklore Genres.* Ed. Dan Ben-Amos. Austin: University of Texas Press, 1976.

———. "Introductory Remarks to a Rhetorical Theory of Folklore." *Journal of American Folklore* 81 (1968): 143–58.

Abrahams, Roger D., and Alan Dundes. "Riddles." Pages 129–43 in *Folklore and Folklife: An Introduction.* Ed. Richard Dorson. Chicago: University of Chicago Press, 1972.

Anderson, Hugh. *The Gospel of Mark.* New Century Bible. Greenwood, SC: Attic Press, 1976.

Aristotle. *The Poetics.* Trans. W. Hamilton Fyfe. Loeb Classical Library. Cambridge, MA: Harvard University Press, 1982.

Athenaeus of Naucratis. *The Deipnosophists.* Trans. Charles Burton Gulick. Loeb Classical Library. Cambridge, MA: Harvard University Press, 1927.

Başgöz, Mehmet İlhan. "Riddle-Proverbs and the Related Forms in Turkish Folklore." *Proverbium* 18 (1972): 655–68.

Blomberg, Craig. *Interpreting the Parables.* Downers Grove, IL: InterVarsity, 1990.

———. *Matthew.* New American Commentary. Nashville: Broadman, 1992.

Brooks, James A. *Mark.* New American Commentary. Nashville: Broadman, 1991.

Brown, Raymond. *The Gospel according to John: A New Translation with Introduction and Commentary.* Anchor Bible. New York: Doubleday, 1966, 1970. This two-volume resource is abbreviated throughout as "Brown 1966," the publication date of the first volume.

Bruce, F. F. "Render to Caesar." Pages 249–63 in *Jesus and the Politics of His Day.* Ed. Ernst Bammel and C. F. D. Moule. Cambridge: Cambridge University Press, 1984.

Bryant, Mark. *Riddles Ancient and Modern.* New York: Peter Bedrick, 1983.

Burns, Thomas A. "Riddling: Occasion to Act." *Journal of American Folklore* 89 (1976): 139–65.

Camp, Claudia V., and Carole R. Fontaine. "The Words of the Wise and Their Riddles." Pages 127–51 in *Text and Tradition: The Hebrew Bible and Folklore*. Ed. Susan Niditch. Society of Biblical Literature Semeia Studies. Atlanta: Scholars Press, 1990.

Carrington, Philip. *According to Mark: A Running Commentary on the Oldest Gospel*. Cambridge: Cambridge University Press, 1960.

Carson, D. A. *The Gospel according to John*. Grand Rapids: Eerdmans, 1991.

Carter, Warren. *Matthew and the Margins: A Sociopolitical and Religious Reading*. The Bible and Liberation Series. Maryknoll, NY: Orbis, 2000.

Cerf, Bennett. *Pop-Up Riddles*. New York: Random House, 1967.

Charlesworth, James H. *The Old Testament Pseudepigrapha*. Garden City, NY: Doubleday, 1983.

Crenshaw, James L. *Samson: A Secret Betrayed, A Vow Ignored*. Atlanta: John Knox, 1978.

Crossan, John Dominic. *The Dark Interval: Towards a Theology of Story*. Rev. ed. Sonoma, CA: Polebridge, 1988.

———. *The Historical Jesus: The Life of a Mediterranean Jewish Peasant*. San Francisco: HarperSanFrancisco, 1991.

———. *Jesus: A Revolutionary Biography*. San Francisco: HarperSanFrancisco, 1994.

———. "Parable and Example in Jesus' Teaching." *New Testament Studies* 18 (1971–72): 285–307.

Davies, W. D., and Dale C. Allison Jr. *A Critical and Exegetical Commentary on the Gospel according to Saint Matthew*. International Critical Commentary. Edinburgh: T. & T. Clark, 1997.

DeFilippis, Michele. *The Literary Riddle in Italy to the End of the Sixteenth Century*. Berkeley: University of California Press, 1948.

Dodd, C. H. *The Parables of the Kingdom*. 3rd ed. London: Nisbet, 1936.

Donahue, John R., and Daniel J. Harrington. *The Gospel of Mark*. Sacra Pagina. Collegeville, MN: Liturgical Press, 2002.

Edwards, James R. *The Gospel according to Mark*. Pillar New Testament Commentary. Grand Rapids: Eerdmans, 2002.

Edwards, Viv, and Thomas J. Sienkewicz. *Oral Cultures Past and Present: Rappin' and Homer*. Cambridge, MA: Basil Blackwell, 1991.

Fitzmeyer, Joseph A. *The Gospel according to Luke*. Anchor Bible. Garden City, NY: Doubleday, 1985.

Fowler, Robert M. *Let the Reader Understand: Reader-Response Criticism and the Gospel of Mark*. Minneapolis: Fortress, 1991.

France, Robert T. *The Gospel of Mark: A Commentary on the Greek Text*. New International Greek Testament Commentary. Grand Rapids: Eerdmans, 2002.

Fredriksen, Paula. *Jesus of Nazareth, King of the Jews: A Jewish Life and the Emergence of Christianity*. New York: Alfred A. Knopf, 2000.

Friedreich, J. B. *Geschichte des Rätsels*. Dresden: Rudolf Kuntze, 1860.

Funk, Robert W. *Language, Hermeneutic, and the Word of God: The Problem of Language in the New Testament and Contemporary Theology*. New York: Harper & Row, 1966.

Funk, Robert W., Roy W. Hoover, and the Jesus Seminar. *The Five Gospels: The Search for the Authentic Words of Jesus*. New York: Polebridge, 1993.

Funk, Robert W., and the Jesus Seminar. *The Acts of Jesus: The Search for the Authentic Deeds of Jesus*. Sonoma, CA: Polebridge, 1998.

Funk, Robert W., with Mahlon H. Smith. *The Gospel of Mark Red Letter Edition*. Sonoma, CA: Polebridge, 1991.

Glazier, Jack, and Phyllis Gorfain Glazier. "Ambiguity and Exchange: The Double Dimension of Mbeere Riddles." *Journal of American Folklore* 89 (1976): 189–238.

The Greek Anthology. Trans. W. R. Paton. Loeb Classical Library. Cambridge, MA: Harvard University Press, 1960.

Gundry, Robert H. *Mark: A Commentary on His Apology for the Cross*. Grand Rapids: Eerdmans, 1993.

———. *Matthew: A Commentary on His Handbook for a Mixed Church under Persecution*. 2nd ed. Grand Rapids: Eerdmans, 1994.

Hain, Mathilde. *Rätsel*. Stuttgart: J. B. Metzler, 1966.

Hamnet, Ian. "Ambiguity, Classification, and Change: The Function of Riddles." *Man* n.s. 2 (1967): 379–92.

Hamp, V. "חידה *chîdhāh*." Pages 4.320–23 in *Theological Dictionary of the Old Testament*. Ed. G. Johannes Botterweck and Helmer Ringgren. Trans. David E. Green. Grand Rapids: Eerdmans, 1980.

Hare, Douglas R. A. *Mark*. Westminster Bible Companion. Louisville, KY: Westminster John Knox, 1996.

Harrington, Daniel J. *The Gospel of Matthew*. Sacra Pagina. Collegeville, MN: Michael Glazier, 1991.

Hartmann, R. R. K., and F. C. Stork. *Dictionary of Language and Linguistics*. New York: John Wiley & Sons, 1972.

Hasan-Rock, Galit. "Riddle and Proverb: Their Relationship Exemplified by an Aramaic Proverb." *Proverbium* 24 (1974): 936–40.

Hauck, Friedrich. "παροιμία." Pages 5.854–55 in *Theological Dictionary of the New Testament*. Ed. Gerhard Friedrich. Trans. Geoffrey W. Bromiley. Grand Rapids: Eerdmans, 1967.

Hooker, Morna D. *The Gospel according to Saint Mark*. Black's New Testament Commentary. Peabody, MA: Hendrickson, 1991.

Horbury, William. "The Temple Tax." Pages 265–86 in *Jesus and the Politics of His Day*. Ed. Ernst Bammel and C. F. D. Moule. Cambridge: Cambridge University Press, 1984.

Hurtado, Larry. *Mark*. New International Bible Commentary. Peabody, MA: Hendrickson, 1989.

Jacobs, Joseph. "Riddle." Pages 10.408–9 in *The Jewish Encyclopedia*. Ed. Isidore Singer. New York: Funk & Wagnalls, 1905.

Jeremias, Joachim. *Rediscovering the Parables*. Trans. Frank Clarke. New York: Charles Scribner's Sons, 1966.

Johnson, Luke Timothy. *The Gospel of Luke*. Sacra Pagina. Collegeville, MN: Michael Glazier, 1991.

Josephus. *Antiquities of the Jews*. Trans. H. St. J. Thackeray. Loeb Classical Library. Cambridge, MA: Harvard University Press, 1966.

Juel, Donald H. *Mark*. Augsburg Commentary on the New Testament. Minneapolis: Augsburg Fortress, 1990.

Köngäs Maranda, Elli. "The Logic of Riddles." Pages 189–232 in *Structural Analysis of Oral Tradition*. Ed. Pierre Maranda and Elli Köngäs Maranda. Philadelphia: University of Pennsylvania Press, 1971.

———. "Riddles and Riddling: An Introduction." *Journal of American Folklore* 89 (1976): 127–37.

———. "Theory and Practice of Riddle Analysis." *Journal of American Folklore* 84 (1971): 51–61.

———. "A Tree Grows: Transformations of a Riddle Metaphor." Pages 116–45 in *Structural Models in Folklore and Transformational Essays*. Ed. Elli Köngäs Maranda and Pierre Maranda. The Hague: Mouton, 1971.

Kuusi, Matt. "Southwest African Riddle-Proverbs." *Proverbium* 12 (1969): 305–12.

Lane, William. *The Gospel according to Mark: The English Text with Introduction, Exposition and Notes*. New International Commentary on the New Testament. Grand Rapids: Eerdmans, 1974.

Leroy, Herbert. *Rätsel und Missverständnis: Ein Beitrag zur Formgeschichte des Johannesevangeliums*. Bonner Biblische Beiträge. Bonn: Peter Hanstein, 1968.

Malbon, Elizabeth Struthers. *Hearing Mark: A Listener's Guide*. Harrisburg, PA: Trinity Press International, 2002.

————. *In the Company of Jesus: Characters in Mark's Gospel*. Louisville, KY: Westminster John Knox, 2000.

Mann, C. S. *Mark: A New Translation with Introduction and Commentary*. Anchor Bible. Garden City, NY: Doubleday, 1986.

Marshall, I. Howard. *The Gospel of Luke: A Commentary on the Greek Text*. New International Greek Testament Commentary. Grand Rapids: Eerdmans, 1978.

Miller, Robert J., ed. *The Complete Gospels. Annotated Scholars Version*. Rev. ed. Sonoma, CA: Polebridge, 1994.

Morris, Leon. *The Gospel according to Matthew*. Grand Rapids: Eerdmans, 1992.

Oesterley, W. O. E. *The Gospel Parables in Light of Their Jewish Background*. London: SPCK, 1936.

Ohl, Raymond Theodore. *The Enigmas of Symphosius*. Philadelphia: University of Pennsylvania Press, 1928.

Ohlert, Konrad. *Rätsel und Rätselspiele der alten Griechen*. 2nd ed. 1912. Reprint. New York: Olms, 1979.

The Oxford English Dictionary. 2nd ed. Oxford: Clarendon Press, 1989.

Painter, John. *Mark's Gospel: Worlds in Conflict*. New Testament Readings. New York: Routledge, 1997.

Pepicello, W. J. "Linguistic Strategies in Riddling." *Western Folklore* 39 (1980): 1–16.

Pepicello, W. J., and Thomas A. Green. "The Folk Riddle: A Redefinition of Terms." *Western Folklore* 38 (1979): 3–20.

————. *The Language of Riddles: New Perspectives*. Columbus: Ohio State University Press, 1984.

————. "Wit in Riddling: A Linguistic Perspective." *Genre* 11 (1978): 1–13.

Perrin, Norman. *Jesus and the Language of the Kingdom: Symbol and Metaphor in New Testament Interpretation*. Philadelphia: Fortress, 1976.

Rhoads, David, and Donald Michie. *Mark as Story: An Introduction to the Narrative of a Gospel*. Philadelphia: Fortress, 1982.

Richards, I. A. *The Philosophy of Rhetoric*. New York: Oxford University Press, 1964.

Richards, I. A., and C. K. Ogden. *The Meaning of Meaning*. 8th ed. New York: Harcourt Brace, 1956.

Santos, Narry. *The Slave of All: The Paradox of Authority and Servanthood in the Gospel of Mark*. Journal for the Study of the New Testament Supplement Series. Sheffield: Sheffield Academic Press, 2003.

Schnackenburg, Rudolf. *The Gospel of Matthew*. Trans. Robert R. Barr. Grand Rapids: Eerdmans, 2002.

Schrecter, Solomon. "The Riddles of Solomon in Rabbinic Literature." *Folklore* 1 (1890): 349–58.

Scott, Bernard Brandon. *Hear Then the Parable: A Commentary on the Parables of Jesus*. Minneapolis: Fortress, 1990.

Scott, Charles T. *Persian and Arabic Riddles: A Language-Centered Approach to Genre Definition*. Bloomington: Indiana University Press, 1965.

Senior, Donald. *Matthew*. Abingdon New Testament Commentaries. Nashville: Abingdon, 1998.

Sider, John. *Interpreting the Parables: A Hermeneutical Guide to Their Meaning*. Grand Rapids: Zondervan, 1995.

Slotkin, Edgar. "Response to Professors Fontaine and Camp." Pages 153–59 in *Text and Tradition: The Hebrew Bible and Folklore*. Ed. Susan Niditch. Society of Biblical Literature Semeia Studies. Atlanta: Scholars Press, 1990.

Snodgrass, Klyne R. "Parable." Pages 591–601 in *The Dictionary of Jesus and the Gospels*. Ed. Joel B. Green, Scot McKnight, and I. Howard Marshall. Downers Grove, IL: InterVarsity, 1992.

Stock, Augustine. *The Method and Message of Matthew*. Collegeville, MN: Michael Glazier, 1994.

Taylor, Archer. *The Literary Riddle before 1600*. 1948. Reprint. Westport, CT: Greenwood Press, 1976.

———. "Problems in the Study of Riddles." *Southern Folklore Quarterly* 2 (1938): 1–9.

———. "The Riddle." *California Folklore Quarterly* [*Western Folklore*] 2 (1943): 129–47.

———. "Riddles in Dialogue." *Proceedings of the American Philosophical Society* 97 (1953): 61–68.

———. "The Varieties of Riddles." Pages 1–8 in *Philologica: The Malone Anniversary Studies*. Ed. Thomas A. Kirby and Henry Bosley Woolf. Baltimore: Johns Hopkins Press, 1949.

Thatcher, Tom. *The Riddles of Jesus in John: A Study in Tradition and Folklore*. Society of Biblical Literature Monograph Series. Atlanta: Society of Biblical Literature, 2000.

———. "The Riddles of Jesus in the Johannine Dialogues." Pages 263–80 in *Jesus in Johannine Tradition*. Ed. Robert T. Fortna and Tom Thatcher. Louisville, KY: Westminster John Knox, 2001.

Thompson, John M. *The Form and Function of Proverbs in Ancient Israel*. The Hague: Mouton, 1974.

Tolbert, Mary Ann. *Perspectives on the Parables: An Approach to Multiple Interpretations*. Philadelphia: Fortress, 1979.

———. *Sowing the Gospel: Mark's World in Literary-Historical Perspective*. Minneapolis: Fortress, 1989.

Tolkien, J. R. R. *The Hobbit; or, There and Back Again*. Boston: Houghton Mifflin, 1966.

Torcyzner, Harry. "The Riddle in the Bible." *Hebrew Union College Annual* 1 (1924): 125–50.

Waetjen, Herman C. *A Reordering of Power: A Socio-Political Reading of Mark's Gospel*. Minneapolis: Fortress, 1989.

Wise, Michael, Martin Abegg Jr., and Edward Cook. *The Dead Sea Scrolls: A New Translation*. San Francisco: HarperSanFrancisco, 1996.

Witherington III, Ben. *The Gospel of Mark: A Socio-Rhetorical Commentary*. Grand Rapids: Eerdmans, 2001.

Wright, N. T. *Jesus and the Victory of God*. Minneapolis: Fortress, 1996.

Author/Subject Index